Austria's Eastern Question

☙ AUSTRIA'S

EASTERN QUESTION
1700-1790

Karl A. Roider, Jr.

PRINCETON UNIVERSITY PRESS

Published by Princeton University Press, 41 William Street,
Princeton, New Jersey
In the United Kingdom: Princeton University Press, Guildford, Surrey

Publication of this book has been aided by a grant from the
Paul Mellon Fund of Princeton University Press

This book has been composed in Linotron Garamond
Designed by Barbara Werden

Printed in the United States of America by Princeton
University Press, Princeton, New Jersey

For my parents

Contents

Maps

Acknowledgments

As is true of most authors of scholarly works, I owe a great deal of thanks to many people for assisting me with advice, funding, and guidance in my research and writing. I would like to thank particularly the staffs of the Austrian National Library, the Kriegsarchiv, and the Haus- Hof- und Staatsarchiv—of the latter notably Dr. Anna Benna—for their aid in procuring for me the important materials to conduct this study. I also owe a debt to Jane Kleiner and Olar Bell of the interlibrary loan office at the Middleton Library on the LSU campus for finding those obscure books available in the United States but only after extensive searching.

For offering guidance and advice in writing the manuscript, I would like to acknowledge Professors Charles Ingrao of Purdue University, William Slottman of the University of California at Berkeley, and Gary Crump of Louisiana State University, the last especially for his peerless knowledge of precise grammar and word usage.

I owe substantial thanks to the National Endowment for the Humanities for a year in Vienna as a Younger Humanist Fellow and to the LSU Graduate Council for financial aid in sending me back to the Austrian capital to clear up some questions in my research. I would also like to thank Miss Miriam Brokaw, Associate Director and Editor of the Princeton University Press, and her staff for their consideration and kindness.

Finally, I am grateful to my wife and children for their encouragement and patience.

A Note on Form

For the spelling of most place names I have relied on the forms used by the National Geographic Society in their various publications. Because some of these names are not always familiar to students of eighteenth-century history, I have included in parentheses spellings often found in the secondary literature. A few names have become so common in the scholarly world that I have used the traditional spelling rather than the modern offering of the National Geographic Society. Some examples include Belgrade, Carlowitz, Passarowitz, and Sistova. For personal names, I have used the English form for rulers and the forms used at the time for most others. Throughout I have avoided the use of the term "Empire" as an equivalent for the Habsburg Monarchy; "Empire" here refers to the Holy Roman Empire.

Monetary values and their equivalents are a hazardous business in eighteenth-century studies, especially when covering a topic over a period of ninety years. Instead of trying to find a common value for all of the currencies, I have used instead the amounts contained in the original documents and offered equivalents only when I thought they would especially clarify a point for the reader. For tables showing general equivalents, see Robert and Elborg Forster, eds., *European Society in the Eighteenth Century* (New York, 1969), p. 410; and Lavender Cassels, *The Struggle for the Ottoman Empire, 1717-1740* (London, 1966), p. 208.

Austria's Eastern Question

 INTRODUCTION

The struggle between the Habsburg Monarchy and the Ottoman Empire is one of the great dramas in the diplomatic and military history of the early modern period. After the battle of Mohács in 1526, which brought the houses of Habsburg and Osman into direct conflict, these two mighty states engaged in repeated wars to determine which one would ultimately dominate southeastern Europe. The rivalry was far more than a struggle of great political powers; it became in the popular mind a contest between Christianity and Islam, between gods and prophets. The ability of the Habsburgs to halt and eventually to roll back the advance of the Moslem Turks won for them the title of defenders of Christendom. Without Habsburg troops forming battle lines and manning fortresses only a few miles east of Vienna, many villagers and townspeople of central Europe were convinced that hordes of unbelievers would overrun their homes and property, leaving death and destruction in their wake.

Such an image was popular in early modern Europe, and it has remained so among historians. As early as 1498, as Hans Sturmberger has pointed out, Emperor Maximilian I listed fear of the advancing Turks as a major reason for reforming his administration. From that point onward, although Habsburg policy was not always trusted by all Christians or by all the political figures of central Europe, the duty of the Habsburgs to defend Christianity was increasingly emphasized in public ordinances and official statements. In the early eighteenth century, when Charles VI called upon his lands to recognize the Pragmatic Sanction, he stressed that its acceptance was essential because "Against the ever present Turkish might one can do nothing else than maintain a powerful central control over the patriarchal kingdoms and lands."[1] In 1732 the Reichstag of the Holy Roman Empire accepted

3

the Pragmatic Sanction, in part because Austria represented the "bastion of Christianity" against the Turks. In his study of the last years of the Empire, Karl Otmar von Aretin noted that, after the Peace of Westphalia in 1648, the "true purpose" of the House of Habsburg in the eyes of the German princes was to protect them and their lands from the Turks.[2]

That "true purpose" underwent its severest test in 1683. The advance on Vienna by Grand Vizier Kara Mustapha and his mighty army, the ensuing siege, the salvation of the city, and the flight of the Turkish army constituted a high point in the history of the Monarchy.[3] The strategically significant consequence of the victory, however, was the subsequent expulsion of the Turks from Hungary. So often before, Habsburg victories had been wasted by an inability or unwillingness to exploit them, but in 1683 the opportunity was seized. The war with the Turks continued until 1699 when the Treaty of Carlowitz (Karlowitz, Sremski Karlovci) confirmed the Habsburg triumph. Turkish Hungary and Transylvania, with the exception of the small region in the south known as the Banat of Timişoara (Temesvar), came under the scepter of the Habsburgs. More importantly, the treaty initiated significant changes in the atmosphere of Austro-Turkish relations. For two centuries the Habsburgs and their subjects had stood in fear of the Turks; henceforth the Turks expressed a growing dread of the Habsburgs.

By the opening of the eighteenth century, the Austrians for the first time in almost two hundred years could feel some confidence in their military superiority over their dangerous foe. Although relations remained somewhat strained, the Austrians could find consolation in the great victories achieved between 1683 and 1699, victories that would surely make the Sublime Porte reluctant to take up arms soon without good cause or serious provocation. Within fifteen years of the Treaty of Carlowitz, the Austrians came to believe that the Ottoman state had in fact grown even weaker than they had imagined. In 1715 an Austrian envoy in Constantinople informed Vienna that Turkey had become so enfeebled that a

Habsburg army could march with ease to the Ottoman capital and, in the process, expel the Turks from Europe altogether. The Ottoman Empire seemed to possess but a shadow of its former power.

One would imagine that such an assessment would have brought comfort to the Austrian policy-makers who had lived so long with the fear of the Turks. Such was not the case. Even before assessments of Ottoman weakness became common, the Habsburg statesmen had become aware of a new and formidable participant in the struggle in southeastern Europe: Russia. Although not until 1677 had Russian and Ottoman regular troops clashed for the first time in over a century, not long afterward full-scale wars became common between them. The aggressiveness of Russia and the emergence of its able ruler, Peter the Great, in the late seventeenth century persuaded Vienna that the fortunes of southeastern Europe would not be decided by the Habsburg and Ottoman states alone. The participation of Russia could bode ill for the Habsburg Monarchy. In 1710 the Privy Conference, the body most concerned with high policy in Vienna at that time, expressed worry that, if the tsar's army should defeat the Turks in battle, it could march to the Danube River and possibly to Constantinople itself. Should that happen, the conference warned, Austria would face a far more formidable opponent in the Balkan Peninsula than the Ottoman Empire, an opponent that would pose a grave danger to the Monarchy itself.

These two issues, the growing weakness of the Ottoman Empire and the growing strength of Russia, constitute what historians and diplomats have called the Eastern Question. For most scholars of diplomatic history, the Eastern Question did not emerge until the latter half of the eighteenth century. Indeed, the major historian of Austro-Turkish relations, Adolf Beer, selected the Russo-Turkish Treaty of Kuchuk-Kainarji (Kücük Kaynarca) of 1774, in which Austria was not directly involved, as the beginning of a new era of Austrian concern with southeastern Europe.[4]

Yet a closer examination of Austrian policy reveals that in Vienna the Eastern Question became a serious issue as early as the second decade of the eighteenth century. From then on, the major dilemma facing Austrian policy-makers in southeastern Europe was precisely what to do about Ottoman decline and Russian expansion. Essentially, three alternatives emerged: the Monarchy could join the Russian state in expelling the Turks from Europe and then divide the Balkan lands between them; it could initiate its own effort to establish Habsburg rule over most or all of the old Ottoman possessions in Europe; or it could preserve the status quo by keeping Russia out of the Balkans—by force if necessary—and by bolstering the ever weaker and increasingly docile Ottoman state. During the eighteenth century, the policy-makers in Vienna considered all three alternatives at one time or another. The most preferred was maintaining the status quo, but the growing aggressiveness of Russia throughout the century made that policy difficult to follow. Moreover, no decision regarding the southeast could be divorced from Austrian concerns elsewhere. An aggressive Russia might be a threat to Austrian interests in the Balkans, but a boon to Austrian interests in western or northern Europe, especially after 1740 when its aggression might be deflected toward Prussia.

Throughout the century, survival of the Habsburg state depended on a foreign policy that avoided unnecessary dangers. Such a foreign policy, however, sometimes missed opportunities. And the eighteenth century offered the only opportunity for the Habsburgs to resolve the Eastern Question largely on their terms.

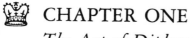

CHAPTER ONE
The Art of Diplomacy

On 7 December 1699 the Ottoman ambassador Ibrahim Pasha and the Austrian ambassador Count Wolfgang Öttingen, each accompanied by a substantial military escort, approached the Austro-Turkish border somewhere between the Turkish fortress of Belgrade and the Austrian fortress of Petrovaradin (Peterwardein). At the place of meeting stood three stakes, the center one marking the border itself, the other two ten paces on either side, one in Habsburg and one in Ottoman land. Some weeks before, each embassy had left its capital on the same day; each had journeyed to this spot where it was now to cross into the land of its former enemy.

On this day the Austrian commander of Petrovaradin, Guido Starhemberg, mounted on a handsome steed and bedecked in a gorgeous uniform bordered in gold, advanced toward the stake on the Austrian side. He was followed by 200 richly accoutred cavalrymen and two companies of infantry. Toward the stake on the Ottoman side proceeded the Turkish commander of Belgrade, as splendidly dressed as Starhemberg and leading an armed force of equal size and magnificence. Before each commander rode trumpeters and drummers and marched servants, lackeys, and pages dressed in costly liveries and leading richly mantled ponies. When both retinues were about sixty paces from the posts on their respective sides, the impressive escorts stopped. Both commanders and eight or ten fellow officers walked their horses at the same gait toward the center post. When the two had reached a spot three paces from the center post, they halted their mounts and began to converse. Because the wind was roaring so loudly in the trees, the translators had some difficulty making themselves heard; thus the Ottoman commander ordered one of his servants to bring two chairs covered with silver brocade for the generals to sit on.

Each officer then dismounted—being extremely careful that his foot did not touch the ground before that of his counterpart—and seated himself, again making certain that he sat at the same instant as his fellow. For an hour the two conversed and, to make the time pass more quickly and more cordially, Starhemberg ordered pastries and bottles of wine brought to him on silver serving dishes. To the Turk he offered the pastries but not, of course, the wine, since he knew that the man was forbidden by Moslem law to consume alcohol.

As the generals talked, the two ambassadors advanced with their retinues, moving increasingly slowly, looking one another directly in the eye, and making certain that neither approached more quickly or more slowly than the other. At the two outer poles the ambassadors dismounted, each again making certain that his foot did not touch the ground before that of the other. Each general then took the hand of his sovereign's ambassador and, as the Turkish and Austrian bands played different tunes concurrently, led him to the middle post and presented him to his opposite number. The two ambassadors then greeted one another, offered their hands, and exchanged a few friendly words. At that moment the soldiers on both sides let out a simultaneous cheer and fired their weapons in a deafening salvo, drowning for an instant the cacophony created by the two bands. Such a ceremony must have convinced each ambassador that he was entering a civilization decidedly different from his own.

An exchange of ambassadors between Vienna and Constantinople was a rare occurrence. They were dispatched only for special duties such as negotiating final drafts of peace treaties (Öttingen's assignment in 1699), delivering important messages, or sending congratulations to sovereigns upon their accession. They journeyed to the foreign capitals, stayed long enough to perform their assigned function and to engage in some social pleasantries, and then returned home.[1] The daily, monthly, and yearly business of the Austrian state at the Sublime Porte was performed by the permanent envoys, who were by no means so exalted as, but a good deal more important than, the ambassadors. In the early eighteenth century, they held the rather low rank of "resident," a title that had its origin in the early seventeenth century. When the first permanent envoy was assigned to Constantinople in 1612, he enjoyed the rank of "internuntius," a title just below that of ambassador. His successor, however, was simply called resident because he had "resided" with the internuntius until the latter had left for home.[2] Resident continued to be the most common title through the remainder of the seventeenth and during the first half of the eighteenth century, after which it gave way more and more to internuntius again.

No post in the Habsburg foreign service required a person with more skill and endurance than did the one in Constantinople, and none was less desirable. Besides the low rank, it posed language difficulties, cultural obstacles, and physical strains unlike those anywhere else. The post demanded a familiarity with the Ottoman language, that mixture of Persian and Turkish written in Arabic characters that was completely foreign to civilized society in the West. Throughout the sixteenth and into the seventeenth century the Habsburg monarchs, like other European rulers, had relied for their negotiations at the Porte primarily on translators either supplied by the Turks or hired in Constantinople. Because such people often proved untrustworthy, the Austrians began to train and employ *Sprachknaben*, boys who accompanied envoys to the Ottoman capital to learn not only the language but Ottoman customs as well. The exact origin of this practice is difficult to determine—the first *Sprachknabe* being perhaps Peter von Wollzogen, who accompanied the minister Joachim von Sinzendorf in 1578—but in 1640 Resident Johann Rudolf Schmid received funds to hire a couple of Croatian youths, to teach them Ottoman, and to retain them as translators.[3] For the next 100 years, one of the functions of the residents was to oversee the training of the *Sprachknaben* and to assign them to various duties as translators.[4] While their primary task was to serve in Constantinople, they also were employed at border towns, sent to the Barbary States when agreements with them were negotiated, used in Vienna when Turkish delegations arrived, and assigned to translate various works from Ottoman into Western languages.

In the eighteenth century, graduates of the school for *Sprachknaben* often became residents themselves, for, besides their skill in languages, no one in the Austrian service knew better than they the ins and outs of Ottoman affairs. The first envoy in the eighteenth century, Michael von Talman, began his career as a *Sprachknabe*, as did his son Leopold (period as envoy, 1729-1737), and the able Heinrich Christoph Penkler (1740-1755). In the eighteenth century the residents took translators with them to meetings with Ottoman officials only as a formality.

The school for *Sprachknaben* existed until 1753, when the training of boys for duty as translators was transferred to the newly established Oriental Academy in Vienna. The academy was conceived by the famous Wenzel Anton Kaunitz, chancellor to Maria Theresa and Joseph II and master of Austrian foreign policy from 1753 to 1790. Kaunitz recommended the establishment of the academy because the school for *Sprachknaben* had become too expensive to maintain. Besides the cost, he advised the empress, the school was not producing particularly competent graduates. "All of Pera had for a long time gossiped that the *k. k. Sprachknaben* were the most costly in numbers and in the ten, twelve, or sixteen years of schooling; however, in their ability, practice, learning, and general improvement they found little to praise."[5] On Kaunitz's recommendation, the Oriental Academy was established in Vienna and admitted its first students in 1753. From then on the academy enjoyed an illustrious history, counting among its few but select graduates Franz Amadeus Thugut, envoy to the Porte from 1769 to 1776 and principal adviser of the Habsburgs in foreign affairs from 1793 to 1801, and Joseph von Hammer-Purgstall, probably the most renowned scholar of Ottoman history and literature.

Aside from the obstacle of learning a difficult foreign language, the Austrian envoys at the Porte had to perform their functions in an alien cultural atmosphere as well. Unlike European courts, including Russia, where ambassadors had the opportunity to speak to foreign sovereigns regularly and often informally, in Constantinople the resident usually held audiences with the sultan but twice, to be introduced by the man he was replacing and a second time to introduce the man replacing him. In the early eighteenth century the resident had to wear a Turkish robe over his clothes when appearing before the sultan to spare him the sight of Christian attire, but this practice ended in 1719 when an Austrian ambassador appeared in European garb before the Ottoman sovereign.[6] The resident rarely saw the chief minister, the grand vizier, either; but he discussed matters often with the Ottoman foreign minister, the *reis effendi*, and even more frequently with the chief translator of the Porte, called by the Austrians the *pfortendollmetsch* and generally a Greek from the famous Phanar district in Constantinople. Dealing with the *pfortendollmetsch* was often a delicate business, because many enjoyed considerable influence and were often anti-Austrian.

Whereas an Austrian ambassador to a European court could always be assured of negotiating with men of similar education, social origin, and culture as himself, a resident often encountered Turkish officials with attributes unlike those in the West. Leopold von Talman reported on one occasion of the appointment of a grand vizier, " 'who can neither read nor write, which in this land is of little or no consequence because there have been many grand viziers who could do neither.' "[7] On another occasion in early 1772 Thugut had to cut short an all-night session with a *reis effendi* when the Turk, "one of the great lovers of opium," took a huge dose and passed out.[8]

Another obstacle faced by the Austrian envoys was the frequent turnover in Ottoman officials, who could lose their posts and sometimes their heads for any number of reasons including policies that failed, intrigue in the harem, personality clashes, displeasure among the religious authorities, whims of the sultans, or disapproval voiced by crowds in the streets.

While proceeding to Constantinople in 1740, an Austrian embassy heard that the current grand vizier had lost his post, an event that required a new letter of introduction with the proper greeting so that the new appointee would receive the Habsburg delegates. A member of the entourage remarked that the news caused little serious concern since "one knew that at this time grand viziers changed more often than the coiffures of the women at Versailles."[9]

A prominent feature of working in Constantinople was the prevalence of bribes and tips—the baksheesh for which the Ottoman Empire was so famous and whose legacy still exists in that part of the world. Bribery was common in all the courts of Europe as a means of securing favors and information, but it seemed especially rife in the Ottoman capital. Officials at all levels expected gifts or payments at every opportunity, and a resident was frequently at a disadvantage if he had nothing to offer or if what he offered was considered inadequate. Even when visiting an Ottoman official at the Porte or at his home, the resident had to distribute tips among the servants and lesser officials. During one period when negotiations required a large number of strenuous sessions, Thugut complained that his money was running short since every visit to the Ottoman foreign minister required him to distribute thirty piasters in tips and gratuities.[10]

If dealing with Ottoman officialdom was demanding, so was living among the Ottoman subjects. The residents, their families, and staffs were, after all, Christians and as such viewed with suspicion by the Moslems. From the time an envoy entered the Ottoman Empire, he was accompanied by guards to protect him from depredations of bandits and of Moslems who resented Christians in their midst. Upon arriving in Constantinople, the envoys were assigned guards and servants, plus an official who provided food, firewood, and clothing and who maintained the envoy's offices, which were also his living quarters. In Austro-Ottoman relations the host governments paid for the maintenance of the other's representatives; the Austrians usually came out ahead financially since the Porte sent no permanent envoys to Vienna but only special embassies that stayed short periods of time.[11]

The suburb of Pera, across the Golden Horn from the central part of Constantinople, was the location of the Austrian residence as well as many of the other European delegations, although it had not always been so. From 1700 to 1719 Austrian quarters were in the Christian district of Galata, and prior to that they were located in Stambul, the central district. In the summer the staff usually moved to villages outside of the city because of the prevalence of disease in Constantinople. In Pera social intercourse was usually confined to the personnel of the other European embassies. Although the Turks officially forbade European diplomats from speaking to one another except for a formal introduction when one envoy replaced another, even in the seventeenth century this restriction had lapsed, and by the early eighteenth century envoys were entertaining each other regularly.[12]

The embassy personnel rarely ventured into the Moslem areas of Constantinople except on official business. That great observer of Ottoman life in the early eighteenth century, Lady Mary Wortley Montague, noted that foreigners avoided the Moslem streets because "Christian men are loath to hazard the adventures they sometimes meet with among the levents [*sic*] or seamen (worse monsters than our watermen) and the women must cover their faces to go there, which they have a perfect aversion to do."[13] One envoy, Franz Anton Brognard, did experience an adventure in the Moslem districts which nearly cost him his life. In March 1769 he and some staff members went to a house in Stambul to observe the famous parade of the Holy Flag of the Prophet, which was part of the city's preparations for war with Russia. As they were observing the procession, a Moslem religious official recognized them in the windows and cried to the crowd that no Christian should look upon the Prophet's banner and live. The people attacked the house where Brognard and his staff were located; half of the Westerners fled back to Pera while the other half, including Brognard, found refuge in the house of an Armenian. Brognard and his companions spent the night there and, instead of returning to Pera, ventured back into the Moslem streets the following morning to see what was going on. They were recognized and assaulted again. This time, however, the mob was not content merely to attack the foreigners but broke into a number of Christian homes and shops, leaving 100 dead and many more injured. Brognard again fled to an Armenian residence and the following day was escorted to Pera under armed guard. Since the Porte was anxious to maintain good relations with Austria at the time, it apologized to him and gave him substantial presents to ease the impact of the disturbance.[14]

The Porte did not always treat foreign representatives so courteously as it did Brognard. Traditionally at the outbreak of an Ottoman-Christian war, the Porte either imprisoned the envoys of hostile states in the forbidding Fortress of the Seven Towers or forced them to travel with the Turkish army while sending their staffs to the galleys as slaves. In the eighteenth century, however, the Turks treated the Habsburg diplomats far better. At the opening of two of the three Austro-Turkish wars, the Porte allowed them to return to Austria peacefully. Nonetheless, neither the representatives nor Vienna could be sure that the Turks would be so beneficent, and, just prior to the outbreak of the last Austro-Turkish war in 1788, the internuntius became almost hysterical over the prospect of being confined in the Fortress.[15] His fears proved unwarranted, and shortly after delivering Austria's declaration of war, he was allowed to depart for home. The Russian representatives were not so lucky. At the outbreak of the Russo-Turkish wars, they were almost always conducted to the Fortress of the Seven Towers, and one of the Austrian residents' functions was to plead for their release.

Besides the cultural differences Turkey posed for an Austrian diplomat and his staff, there was also considerable physical strain. The Ottoman Empire was known as the land of the bubonic plague, and in 1710 Vienna established the *Pestkordon* along the Military Frontier to keep the plague out of

Habsburg lands. The Austrian envoys had to pass that cordon in the wrong direction, entering the areas where the plague abounded. They expressed constant concern about the plague and complained vigorously that the Turks did nothing to stop its spread. As mentioned above, the officials left the Ottoman capital for outlying villages every summer to avoid the plague, but even then personnel regularly caught the disease and died. Despite the unhealthy atmosphere, only one resident died while on duty in the eighteenth century, although two others requested to be relieved because they felt that they needed Western medical attention, one remarking succinctly that he required "a long period of rest and the advice of a good Christian doctor."[16]

Hostile crowds and disease were not the only dangers envoys faced. Constantinople was well-known for its frequent and destructive fires, and the Austrian residences did not always escape. In the seventeenth century one resident had to move twice in seven years because his house and offices burned. Fires endangering the Austrian buildings were not as frequent in the eighteenth century, but in 1762 the embassy and all of its possessions—including the archives—perished in an inferno that consumed sixty other structures in Pera.[17] Hammer remarked that the Habsburg acquisition of Venice in 1797 delighted the Austrian staff in Constantinople because it enabled them to move to the Venetian embassy, which was made of stone and thus less likely to burn.[18]

Although their working conditions were not always the best, the Austrian representatives were expected to carry out their duties like all other diplomats, and their duties were many and varied. Their principal functions were the same as those of ambassadors elsewhere: to represent Austrian interests at the Porte; to assess Ottoman policies and politics; and to gather as much information as possible about intrigues, meetings among important officials, ministers in and out of favor, and relations between the Porte and other foreign ambassadors.

The Austrian envoys did, however, have a few responsibilities not common to Habsburg ambassadors at other courts. For example, the residents and their staffs were responsible for freeing as many Austrian and German citizens who had been sold into slavery as possible. In 1700 Öttingen concluded a special convention with the Porte granting imperial representatives the right to purchase and to free slaves who had been captured in imperial lands or who had been prisoners of war. That right applied to slaves of both sexes and to any children born in slavery.[19] The manumissions generally took place as the diplomats were going to and from the Ottoman capital. When they passed through the countryside, members of their staffs were on the lookout for Western European slaves and, if they found some, bought and freed them immediately. The great embassies even had attached to them Catholic clergymen whose function was to find and to free slaves.[20]

While anxious to free Christians who entered Ottoman service against their wills, the envoys also watched the activities of those who had escaped from Habsburg lands and found refuge at the Porte. These included especially political renegades, who Vienna feared might be using Ottoman territory as headquarters for plotting conspiracies of various kinds, and Habsburg subjects who had fallen into substantial debt, so substantial that they believed Moslem territory a safer haven than other Christian lands. The residents obviously considered the political refugees more important than those fleeing their financial obligations and consequently spent more energy and money monitoring their activities.

Another function of the Austrian delegates was to appeal to the Porte on behalf of Roman Catholics in the Ottoman Empire and to insure the various Catholic privileges at the Christian Holy Places in Palestine.[21] Because of the limited number of Catholics living in Ottoman lands, the Austrians never exploited such rights to the same degree as the Russians were to do on behalf of the Orthodox after 1774 and in fact were rarely as vigorous in the defense of Roman Catholics as were the French.

Besides their duties at the Porte, the Austrian envoys often had to deal with problems other than those directly affecting the central Ottoman government. For example, they were responsible for the Austrian consuls throughout the Ottoman Empire, who after 1748 reported directly to Pera rather than to Vienna. This responsibility also required them to deal with commercial matters which, as the century progressed, became increasingly important. Indeed, the last Austrian envoy in the century, Peter Herbert-Rathkael, regarded the improvement of Habsburg commerce to be his foremost duty. In addition to overseeing consular activities throughout the Turkish state, the resident had to negotiate as well with the *hospodars* of Moldavia and Walachia, who in this century were invariably Greeks with close ties to the Greek community in Constantinople. The tenure of these men was often short and their loyalty to any patron—Moslem or Christian—suspect, so the envoys and Vienna were usually reluctant to grant them any lasting favors or serious commitments.

The resident generally did not become involved in troubles that occurred periodically on the Austro-Turkish border. In the event of encroachment by one side or the other, the resident either issued or received a protest and then arranged with the Porte for the commanders of nearby fortresses to resolve the differences. The officers generally found solutions so that the resident did not have to consider the matter again.[22] After the conclusion of treaties, the actual delimitation of the borders was assigned not to the residents but to commissions usually consisting of military officers, engineers, and *Sprachknaben*.[23]

Residents did discharge duties of a cultural nature, one of which was collecting books, manuscripts, and artifacts for the court library in Vienna. Ever since the embassy of the celebrated Ogier Ghiselen de Busbecq in the sixteenth century, Habsburg ministers had been expected to gather classical manuscripts that might appear on the market and, by the beginning of the eighteenth century, to purchase old and new Ottoman writings as well. After the first Ottoman press began publication in 1728, the residents had to procure copies of every work that appeared as part of an effort to buy for the court library all major works appearing in Europe.[24] A less demanding cultural task was the acquisition of animals for the zoo at Schönbrunn, an assignment the residents apparently did not pursue with much vigor.[25]

Notwithstanding all of these duties, serving Habsburg interests at the Porte remained the chief function of the permanent representative. Just as the post was a special one in the Austrian diplomatic corps, so the resident, in the first half of the century, did not report to the court chancellor in Vienna, the man officially in charge of diplomatic correspondence, but to the war ministry (Hofkriegsrat). The reason for this practice initially was the sultan's refusal to recognize any sovereign as his peer, which prevented Vienna from dealing with the Porte through normal diplomatic channels. In 1753, as part of Kaunitz's effort to centralize all the correspondence in his office, the resident was instructed to stop sending reports to the Hofkriegsrat and to forward them instead directly to the chancellor.[26]

Almost all of the business between Austria and Turkey was conducted by the Habsburg resident at the Porte, for the sultan's embassies to Vienna were largely ceremonial. Only on a few occasions, primarily when the Porte wished to assure the emperor that it desired continued peaceful relations between the two powers, did an Ottoman delegation have a particular charge to fulfill. The arrival of a Turkish embassy caused considerable excitement in Vienna because of the exotic appearance of the visitors, their raiment and baggage, and the camels that they usually brought with them. Just as the Christian envoys in Constantinople usually resided in Christian quarters like Pera, so the Ottomans were housed not in the all-Christian sections of Vienna but in the Leopoldstadt, the district across the Danube Canal and the residential area of the Jews.[27]

While enjoying the novel appearance of the Turks, the Viennese were not totally ignorant of Moslem customs. The women of the city especially enjoyed teasing the Ottoman males, knowing that their own women were kept hidden from the view of other men. In 1774 Emperor Joseph II described some scenes to his brother: "The Turkish embassy occupies the attention of the whole city. Everyone runs to see it, the women allowing themselves to be visually caressed by the valets and errand boys of the suite without becoming angry about it. For me as an observer of such things they are truly comic."[28] Not only did the women of the streets tease the Moslem servants; the court ladies did the same to the ambassador himself. After attending a reception for him, Joseph wrote that "the coquetry of the women and the desire that they have to be alluring is truly incredible."[29]

Whether in Constantinople or Vienna, the Habsburg government enjoyed one advantage over its Western European counterparts in dealing with the Turks. The fastest and most reliable postal route to the Ottoman capital from most of Europe passed through Vienna, thus making it possible for the Austrians to intercept and to decipher mail going to and from the foreign embassies in Constantinople. Although the origin of the deciphering bureau is unclear, people were employed to open, read, and copy letters throughout most of the eighteenth century. As most government officials involved in such operations today would testify, this service sometimes supplied a surfeit of information that was not always a blessing. In 1750 Kaunitz complained that "all the abundant communications of papers and especially of intercepts produces only confusion and worry. . . ."[30]

In the central government in Vienna conferences were occasionally held in the Hofkriegsrat and in the chancellery to discuss Turkish affairs and to recommend policy, but they had limited influence. In the eighteenth century the great men of Austrian affairs, in conjunction with their monarchs, usually formulated policy toward the Ottoman Empire. In the first third of the century the most influential figure was Prince Eugene of Savoy, the military genius who headed the Hofkriegsrat from 1703 to his death in 1736. For the remainder of the 1730s and through most of the 1740s the moving force was Johann Christoph Bartenstein, secretary of the Privy Conference, whom Maria Theresa praised as her most loyal supporter during the early and difficult years of her reign. From the 1750s to 1790 Ottoman affairs rested largely in the hands of the greatest Habsburg statesman of the century, Kaunitz. Because a few men dominated Austrian policy toward Turkey and because they all faced similar problems, each man often found himself assessing that policy in much the same terms and with much the same results as his predecessor.

CHAPTER TWO
Turkey in Austria's
"World War," 1700-1714

Viewed from the twentieth century—or from the nine-teenth—the Treaty of Carlowitz appears as the great turning point in Austro-Turkish relations. From that time on, the Turks no longer threatened Austria's existence but feared a possible Habsburg onslaught that would strip them of additional land and power. On the other hand, the Austrians, it is thought, looked upon the Ottoman Empire as seriously weakened and had only to choose the right moment to push the Turks farther into the Balkan Peninsula and possibly out of Europe altogether. Quite to the contrary, in the years immediately following the treaty, few in Vienna shared this confident opinion of Austrian superiority. The Ottoman sultan still appeared to be a formidable enemy who at any moment might dispatch his hordes to retake his lost lands and to inflict great blows upon his erstwhile conqueror.

As Turkey appeared still dangerous, after Carlowitz Russia seemed to be a minimal threat. Although Moscow had joined Austria, Poland, and Venice against the Ottoman Empire in the great war of 1683-1699, it had not coordinated its military efforts with its western allies. In 1687 and 1689 Russian forces had advanced to the Crimea, only to disintegrate owing to mismanagement and lack of supplies. In 1696, however, Peter the Great had scored a significant victory by taking the fortress of Azov, located where the Don River flows into the Sea of Azov. Peter's success sufficiently impressed Vienna to warrant the conclusion of the first formal Austro-Russian treaty of alliance in 1697, an accord directed particularly against the Ottoman Empire.

The alliance, however, was short-lived. After Azov, Peter,

21

instead of undertaking further operations against the Turks, preferred to keep his troops on the defensive while he embarked on his famous tour of Western Europe, learning what he could about everything he encountered. The lack of offensive spirit on the part of the Russians, the brilliant victory over the Turks by Prince Eugene at Zenta in 1697, and growing concern about the Spanish succession inspired Vienna to seek a separate peace with the Turks, despite a personal visit by the tsar to the Habsburg capital to plead with his ally not to do so. At that time not as respectful of the Russian tsar or the Russian alliance as they would later become, the Habsburg statesmen concluded the Treaty of Carlowitz anyway and allowed the Russian union to lapse. Cordial relations between Vienna and Moscow continued, however, and in 1701 the two powers exchanged permanent ambassadors for the first time.

For the first decade of the eighteenth century, Austrian concern in the East was directed not toward Russia but toward Turkey, for, as the century opened, the Habsburg Monarchy faced an abundance of dangers, any of which could be exploited by its recent foe. In 1701 occurred the outbreak of both the War of the Spanish Succession—which involved Austria in a titanic struggle with France—and the Great Northern War—which, while not involving Austria directly, could through alliances or spillovers draw the Monarchy into further conflict. If these two wars became one, as was certainly possible, Austria would face enemies to the south, west, and north. The east was no more peaceful, for in 1703 the peasants of northeastern Hungary rose in rebellion, attracted some discontented noblemen, accepted as their leader the popular aristocrat Francis Rákóczi, and soon spread their uprising throughout Hungary and Transylvania. The Habsburgs were now menaced from all directions.

Turkish interference in any of these troubles would cause the Habsburgs enormous grief, and the policy-makers in Vienna knew it. If the Ottomans elected to assist the Hungarian rebels (and Rákóczi pleaded for them to do so), they would reopen the struggle for Hungary and seriously hinder Vienna's war effort against France. If they chose to take part in the Great Northern War, that struggle could easily spill over into Hungary and Silesia and embroil the Monarchy in conflict there. Finally, if the Porte decided to assist its old friends the French by attacking Austria, Vienna would find itself fighting major wars on two fronts, which it probably could not sustain. Any of these possibilities would place the Monarchy in danger of serious and perhaps total defeat.[1]

In view of the danger, one would assume that from 1701 on Vienna labored mightily to keep the sultan at peace. At first, however, such was not the case. From 1701 to 1703 the government displayed an astonishing lack of concern about future Ottoman policy; during those years it did not even assign a permanent representative to the Porte to monitor Turkish affairs or to counter French machinations.[2] Scholars have explained this oversight in two ways. Either the Austrians assumed the influence of their Dutch and British allies sufficient to defeat French intrigue, or Emperor Leopold I and his advisers believed that, after Carlowitz, Vienna no longer need fear the Turks.[3] A more likely reason than either, however, is the general lethargy that infected Leopold and his aged counselors at the time. Awed by the ubiquitous threats to Austria, they trusted that God, rather than any human effort on their part, would protect them from the Turks. He had done so in the past, and surely He would do so in the future.[4]

In any case, a permanent representative was not assigned to the Porte until 1703.[5] The man chosen was Michael von Talman, a graduate of the school for *Sprachknaben* and one of the negotiators at Carlowitz. Talman might be described as a professional diplomat, for he possessed a thorough knowledge of the difficult Ottoman language and knew well the Ottoman practices in dealing with Christian powers. He would hold the post of resident through most of the War of the Spanish Succession and would work vigorously to keep the Turks from assaulting Habsburg borders. He complained regularly that he was hampered in his efforts by two shortcomings: inadequate funds, which meant that he could not compete with his colleagues in bribing Ottoman officials, and inadequate status, the title of resident placing him at a disadvantage especially when competing with the ambassador from France.[6] Talman might have stressed the latter deficiency because he coveted the greater income that he would have received as an official of higher rank. In any event, he seemed at times to exaggerate rumors of impending Ottoman hostility and his own successes at dealing with it, mixing with these reports appeals for promotion and increases in salary.

Talman assumed his post at a critical time for both Vienna and Constantinople. Although the threat of war between the Ottoman and Habsburg states arose regularly throughout the first decade of the century, it was never more serious than during the first two years of Talman's tenure. In July 1703 the janissaries and the people of the Ottoman capital expelled Sultan Mustafa II along with most of the high officials who had concluded the Treaty of Carlowitz. With these men dead or exiled, Talman and his British and Dutch colleagues feared that the new regime of Ahmed III would be anxious to placate the chronically rebellious people by going to war against Austria.

And no time seemed more propitious than the summer of 1703. The Hungarian rebels had achieved notable successes against the weak imperial forces in their homeland, and shortly thereafter Rákóczi's agents appeared in Constantinople to appeal for Turkish aid. That same year the Bavarians and the French invaded the Tyrol and, although eventually repulsed by the natives, for a time threatened to march to Vienna itself. In August the British representative at the Habsburg court summed up Austria's plight: "We want but one Disturbance more to be in as miserable a state as it is possible, I mean a Breach with the Ottoman Port, and of that there is too great an appearance."[7]

These serious dangers forced some important changes within

the Habsburg government. Leopold replaced some of his antiquated counselors with younger men, notably Prince Eugene of Savoy. Eugene, who became president of the Hofkriegsrat, not only assumed direction of the war ministry but, by virtue of his position, of Austria's relations with Turkey as well. The prince readily appreciated the implications of an Ottoman attack. "Should a Turkish war come," he advised the emperor, "Your Majesty can realize for himself into what danger and into what an unfortunate, almost irrevocable condition everything would fall."[8] To forestall such an eventuality, Eugene gave at this time what would become his customary advice: strengthen the army as much as possible. The key to the situation, he believed, was Hungary. "If the Hungarian rebellion is not quelled shortly the Porte will be compelled by its people to break the peace." Consequently, the emperor should bolster his forces in Hungary "so that at least one can crush the rebellion the sooner the better."[9] To that end Leopold authorized the formation of a force of 12,000 men, appointed as commander the veteran field marshal Sigbert Heister, and sent them off to do battle with the Hungarians.

As Vienna undertook these provisions to quell the trouble in the east and to discourage the Porte from mixing in Hungary, news arrived from Constantinople that an Ottoman embassy, led by Myri Alem Ibrahim, was setting out for Vienna to notify the Habsburg authorities formally of the accession of Ahmed III. When first hearing of the delegation, Eugene assumed that its purpose was to spy on Austrian military preparedness in the east. Consequently, he instructed the commander of Petrovaradin to delay the delegation and, if possible, to turn it back. He must do so, however, "with good manners and without causing dismay."[10] The commander stalled Ibrahim quite effectively for two months. In the meantime, reports arrived from Talman insisting that the embassy's mission was truly peaceful; trusting his resident's judgment, the prince allowed it to proceed to the Habsburg capital.[11]

Once in Vienna Ibrahim met not with the prince, who was with the army in the west, but with a number of counselors of the Hofkriegsrat, most notably Johann Tiell, the man left by Eugene in charge of negotiations and Turkish affairs in general.[12] Tiell found Ibrahim's expressions of Ottoman friendship quite sincere. According to the Turk there were only two outstanding problems: the sultan wished the razing of a few Habsburg outposts in the region of the Sava River and satisfaction for a raid by pirates from the Austrian coastal town of Senj (Zengg) who had entered the harbor of Durrës (Durazzo) and captured two French ships loaded with Turkish goods.[13]

Upon reading Tiell's reports, Eugene was delighted. The Turks seemed friendly and the problems minor indeed—hardly of the kind that would lead to Austro-Turkish hostilities. Despite the changes in the Ottoman government, the new sultan and his advisers evidently valued peace with Austria as much as the old ones. Vienna was free—at least for now—to prosecute the war in the west and the conflict in Hungary without fear of Ottoman intervention. The prince's pleasure was evident when he instructed Tiell to hound the beleagured treasury for presents to give to the Ottoman envoy to be sent to Talman for distribution at the Porte.[14] After Ibrahim set out for home in mid-September, the prince summed up his satisfaction and his new confidence that Vienna could preserve the good relations with the Ottoman Empire. "I am pleased that the preservation of peace on the part of the Porte appears so likely; in the meantime one must cultivate that feeling as much as possible as the *Herr Hofkriegsrat* knows so well since I have given all my advice and intentions toward that goal."[15]

Despite Vienna's joy at Ibrahim's expressions of good will, the motives behind them remained a mystery. Only in 1707 did the Austrians receive a plausible explanation for Turkey's reluctance to take advantage of the Monarchy's predicament. In that year an Austrian envoy, returning from Constantinople, stopped in Sofia as a guest of the local pasha. While there, he heard that in January 1704 the sultan's divan was ready to declare war. It did not do so only because of the arguments put forth by the grand vizier and the pasha of Sofia himself (who may have been exaggerating his own role to impress his guest). They convinced the divan that war was inadvisable because of the uncertain success of the Hungarian revolt, the doubtful results of French policy, and the likelihood that an Ottoman attack would prompt the emperor to make peace with Versailles and to turn his full force against the Turks. Should that come to pass, Turkey would suffer greater defeats than those of 1683-1699.[16]

Although Ibrahim's message seemed to insure Ottoman good will toward Austria, neither Talman nor the officials in Vienna could relax their vigilance. Each time a new grand vizier assumed power—and this happened often during the initial years of Ahmed's reign—the possibility arose that Turkish policy would change. In fact, the most difficult task facing Talman at the Porte was trying to judge when a grand vizier would fall from favor and what the policy of his successor would be.

Besides the worry over rising and falling grand viziers, Talman had to contend with French intrigue, and here the critical factor seemed to be money. From the Austrian and British reports emanating from the Ottoman capital, the French ambassador was dispensing enormous sums in an effort to bribe the Turks to declare war. On one occasion, Talman reported that, after handing out large numbers of gifts and cash awards to various officials, the Frenchman promised to dispense an additional 200,000 thalers as soon as a declaration of war on Austria was proclaimed.[17] To neutralize the French largesse, Talman himself frequently asked Vienna for funds and was frequently refused. Austria was suffering financial stringency because of the War of the Spanish Succession and thus could not spare large sums to its envoys abroad. Moreover, Emperor Joseph I, who replaced his father in 1705, apparently agreed with Prince Eugene that money was better spent on the military than on bribes for foreigners.[18] In any event, when Talman requested the sum of 3,000 thalers to give to an official who promised to remove the anti-Habsburg pasha of Timişoara and *hospodar* of Walachia, the Hofkriegsrat informed him that such money would not be granted "as long as one does not know if such changes would make things better or worse."[19]

Talman was not, however, entirely without support from home in his fight against French intrigue. In the summer of 1706 Vienna sent to Constantinople a special envoy, Christoph Ignatius Guarient (Quarient) to notify the Porte formally of the accession of Joseph I and to assist Talman informally in his efforts to counter the French. Although condemned by the British ambassador for his "pusillanimity, weaknesse, and covetousnesse," Guarient proved to be quite able. A notable success came when the French ambassador sought to stir up the volatile public of Constantinople by publishing a pamphlet containing an imaginary conversation between a Turk and a Persian extolling the advantage of an Ottoman attack on Austria and the possible dangers of avoiding one. Guarient responded with a publication of his own, in which the same two characters praised Turkey's remaining at peace. Whether either pamphlet had much appeal to the people is difficult to say, but the diplomatic community agreed that Guarient's effectively undercut that of the Frenchman.[20]

Such successes as Guarient's and Talman's were aided by their mediocre French antagonists, especially Charles de Ferriol, ambassador from 1700 to 1710. Arrogant, haughty, and hampered by an ability to alienate most of the people he was supposed to influence, Ferriol from his arrival at the Porte antagonized the Turks, usually by ridiculing or disdaining Ottoman practices.[21] Consequently, although he distributed vast sums to various officials, they generally despised him and frustrated his hopes. Ferriol's ineffectiveness finally became obvious to Versailles in 1710, when he was replaced by the scarcely more able Pierre des Alleurs.

While Talman and Guarient engaged in their diplomatic fencing with Ferriol, Austro-Turkish relations from 1703 to 1707 remained generally peaceful. In 1707, however, a new crisis threatened to plunge the two states into conflict. It began in April with the massacre of several Turkish merchants by Austrian troops at the Hungarian town of Kecskemét. The merchants were trying to sell goods to Hungarian rebels when a force of Serbian hussars under Austrian command appeared before the town. Fighting was imminent and, afraid of becoming involved, the Turks sent an envoy to the commander to inform him of their presence. The officer, a Colonel Kovay, instructed the merchants to gather themselves and their belongings in one place so that they would not be harmed. When the Serbs attacked, however, they did not distinguish between Hungarian and Turk; fifty-five of the merchants were killed and most of their valuables stolen.[22]

The Porte protested this violation of Ottoman neutrality and demanded immediate compensation not only for the lives and goods lost at Kecskemét but also for the wares taken by the Senj pirates at Durëss three years earlier. Acting upon orders from the Hofkriegsrat, Talman suggested to the Porte the creation of a border commission to resolve the issue (standard procedure in such affairs), but this time his offer was rejected. Talman reported that the attitude of the Porte was becoming increasingly menacing and could lead to hostilities.[23]

The news of a possible Ottoman attack caused considerable consternation in Vienna. In 1707 the War of the Spanish Succession was going well for the Austrians, and in Hungary, although the rebels had formally renounced Habsburg sovereignty, military successes had given the Austrian forces the upper hand, especially in Transylvania where Joseph most feared an Ottoman invasion.[24] A Turkish declaration of war at this juncture would undermine all of the successes and plunge the Monarchy again into a struggle for its existence. Although Joseph displayed considerable bravado under the circumstances, in fact he and his advisers were gravely worried that a Turkish war was in the offing.[25] Such a possibility prompted the emperor to reject an Anglo-Dutch request to dispatch an army under Prince Eugene to aid Joseph's brother Charles (later Emperor Charles VI) in securing the Spanish throne. He informed London and The Hague that he could not spare the prince "not only because of his position as president of the military council and supreme commander but also because of threatening movement on the part of the Turks and perhaps even of the Swedes."[26]

Such concern on Joseph's part proved unwarranted, for in early 1708 a curious dispatch from Talman announced that the threat of war had passed. He claimed that he had achieved this remarkable feat by a combination of bribery and guile. He had subdued the sultan's master of the hunt and the *kizlar aga* (principal eunuch of the sultan's harem and an influential adviser) both with gifts and by playing upon their superstitious Moslem piety. After reminding the two officials of what happened to Kara Mustapha when he had challenged the Holy Roman Empire in 1683, the resident directed their attention to an obscure prophecy in the Koran that foretold the coming of a blond-haired ruler who would take the Greek empire, including Constantinople, away from Islam. After citing the portentous passage, he pointedly showed the two men a portrait of the blond Joseph. As Talman hoped, the officials relayed the story to the sultan. Upon hearing that the Ottoman ruler, whom Talman described as "peace-loving and timid by nature," had asked to see the portrait, the Austrian knew that his stratagem was successful. Almost immediately the Porte notified Talman that it sought nothing but good relations with the Emperor. "The fortunate change," the resident wrote with all due flattery, "can be attributed only to the portrait of His Royal and Imperial Majesty."[27]

Whether Talman's ingenious device was the real reason for the changed Turkish posture mattered not in Vienna, where the government moved quickly to take advantage of the Ottomans' renewed passivity. Joseph appointed negotiators to reach a settlement concerning the incident at Kecskemét and advised Talman to arrange compensation for the matter at Durëss as a token of "our love and peace."[28] Shortly thereafter Turkish and Austrian plenipotentiaries began negotiations at the border to resolve the issues. In the summer of 1709 Eugene expressed his satisfaction regarding Turkish policy in general: "It is good that in Turkey all is quiet, and it is certain that we have a great obligation to these people for remaining so peaceful in the present circumstances which are so easy to exploit in every way."[29]

Regrettably for him and for Austria, the prince's satisfaction was short-lived. In July 1709 the battle of Poltava occurred; there the Russians crushed the Swedish forces of Charles XII, and the Swedish king fled with some officers to Ottoman territory to escape capture. In Turkey Charles hoped to enlist support for his cause in the form of an armed force of 50,000 men to accompany him through Poland to his possessions in northern Germany. Such a prospect would possibly bring about the very situation Austria had been struggling to avoid; it would entangle the war in the west (on his return Charles would have to violate territory of the Holy Roman Empire), the Hungarian rebellion (the rebels wished to ally with Charles), and the Great Northern War. If Charles got his way, the entire eastern and northern borders of the Habsburg lands would become a battleground.

To prevent such a possibility, the Austrian policy-makers began a flurry of diplomatic activity. They issued a joint statement with Britain and the Dutch Republic declaring their intention to remain neutral in the Great Northern War, but at the same time to guarantee the integrity of the Holy Roman Empire. While sounding rather innocuous on the surface, the document directly warned Charles and the Turks that any violation of imperial boundaries would bring down upon them the wrath of all three powers.[30] To back up the declaration, Prince Eugene set out to create a northern army corps made up of allied units that would protect the neutrality of the Empire and presumably oppose the passage of Charles and any Turkish army.[31]

Vienna also warned the Porte directly against supporting Charles with force. Fearing a French scheme to involve the Swedes and the Turks in the western conflict, the prince issued the strongest threat to the Turks of the war years. While repeating his government's peaceful intentions and offering the Swedish king free passage home "with all his retinue and all the honors due him," he instructed Talman to warn the Porte against any violation of Austria's borders. Should the Turks undertake any hostile act, Vienna would meet "force with force" regardless of the war in the west.[32] In August 1710 Eugene added weight to his warnings by asking the Dutch and British governments "to allow their ministers in Constantinople to protest strongly and to threaten to undertake action with their forces in the [Mediterranean] Sea should the Porte dare to attack one of the allies."[33]

Prince Eugene had no hesitation about supporting these warnings with arms. He repeatedly admonished his various underlings in the Hofkriegsrat to raise funds and to put the army in Hungary in good condition.[34] Moreover, he regarded the situation as sufficiently serious to contemplate taking personal command of the troops in the east. In August 1710 he wrote from his headquarters in Belgium that he would return to Vienna as quickly as possible to find out "where my person can best serve His Majesty's service," the implication being that he was prepared for duty in Hungary.[35]

In the midst of all this activity, Joseph I and his ministers debated whether to ask Russia to join an alliance against the Ottoman Empire. By this time the Austrian statesmen were no longer as willing to ignore the policies and attitudes of the tsar as they had been at the time of Carlowitz. As early as 1707, when Charles XII had established his hegemony in Poland and was threatening to occupy Habsburg territory unless the Austrians granted him certain concessions, Joseph I and his ministers had been reluctant to grant those concessions because they feared a hostile and perhaps violent reaction from the mercurial tsar.[36] Moreover, they knew that Peter was negotiating with the Hungarian rebels regarding the promotion of Rákóczi as the Russian candidate for the throne of Poland and suspected that these talks might lead to his backing the Hungarian rebellion. Before these concerns were realized, however, Charles XII invaded Russia, forcing Peter to attend to protecting his homeland and to leave Rákóczi in the lurch.[37] Nonetheless, the tsar's behavior caused great mistrust in Vienna—mistrust that did not disappear quickly.

The misgivings about Peter were openly discussed by Joseph and his ministers as they talked about offering the tsar an alliance in 1710. A union with Russia would of course commit Peter to join with the Habsburgs in a war against the Ottoman Empire should the Porte support Charles XII with arms, and undoubtedly Russian aid would be welcome should hostilities erupt. As this issue was examined, Joseph and his advisers raised the question that would repeatedly come up throughout the century and become on occasion the most important issue in Habsburg foreign policy. A Turkish victory over Russia could be detrimental to Austrian interests, but would a Russian victory over Turkey be any more desirable? Probably not, they agreed, because Russian penetration into the Balkans would surely follow. "If the tsar is victorious," the Privy Conference informed the emperor, "he could throw himself into Turkish territory as far as the Danube and possibly force his way to Constantinople, which perhaps would be no better a political result [than a Turko-Swedish occupation of Poland]."[38]

Just as the question raised by the Habsburg statesmen would be repeated over the century, so would their solution to the question: Austria could prevent or restrict Russian aggrandizement in the Balkans better by allying with the tsar rather than by opposing him or by remaining neutral. The way to limit Russian expansion in southeastern Europe, they and their successors would agree, was not to oppose it openly, but to exercise control over it through Austro-Russian agreements and alliances. While this policy would be followed by Vienna later on, it required able diplomatic minds to know when and how to use it.

Joseph did in fact offer Peter an alliance in 1710, but the tsar declined it. The rejection turned out to be a blessing in disguise since the Porte was planning to attack only Russia at that time and to leave Austria alone.[39] In any case, in the autumn of 1710, Vienna's concern about a conflict with Turkey waned rapidly when news reached Vienna of the fall of the grand vizier who wanted to support Charles XII. Fully aware that a change of grand viziers generally meant a change of policy, the prince remarked, "Now we can wait to see if his successor is better inclined toward us and if the Swedish and French machinations will be broken thereby."[40] Undoubtedly he felt confident that the danger had passed; to an official in Belgium he commented, "I hope that the changes at the Turkish court will change the policies of Sweden and France substantially; in the meantime, there is at least nothing to fear soon."[41]

The optimism regarding the Turks was soon justified, for in December Talman reported that, instead of threatening Austria, the Porte had declared war on Russia.[42] Not long thereafter came further news; the sultan was sending to Vienna another envoy, Seifullah Aga, to assure the Habsburg court that he had no hostile intentions toward the emperor. Joseph and his ministers were understandably delighted. Prince Eugene even delayed his departure for the western front so that he could greet the Turk personally and hear his presentation. He met with Seifullah Aga on three different days, listening to and appreciating the envoy's claims of friendship.[43] After replying that peace was also the goal of the emperor, the prince set off for the front assured that there would be no Austro-Turkish war.

Accompanying the news of the Ottoman war with Russia came another heartening development in Austria's relations with the Turks: the end of the Hungarian rebellion. Negotiations with the rebels finally resulted in the Peace of Szatmar in May 1711.[44] Nonetheless, it was evident well before the signing that the Hungarian uprising was for all intents and purposes over, and the Turks especially were aware of it. As early as January 1711 the British ambassador had reported from Constantinople:

> The Turks as well as others, look upon the War in Hungary to be as good as ended, and a great many Hungarians as well as French Officers are lately retired thence into the Turkish Territories, into Poland, and hither in two great companies abandoning the Cause as desperate and at its last gasp, and the Pashaws on the other Frontiers of Hungary now cultivate with more than ordinary application a good correspondence with the Governors of the Emperor's Places.[45]

Even before the peace was concluded, the emperor ordered Talman to ask the Turks to deny succor to unrepentant rebels, notably Rákóczi himself. Should they venture into Ottoman territory, Talman was to ask the Porte to arrest them and either to turn them over to Austrian authorities or to imprison them there.[46] The Turks may have helped the Austrians resolve the Hungarian dispute, since their declaration of war on Russia deprived the rebels of their last hope of aid.

With the Hungarian rebellion ended and the Turks at war with the Russians, Vienna no longer anticipated any trouble in the southeast. The crushing defeat of the Russians at the Prut (Pruth) River was greeted with equanimity, for Vienna had been as concerned about Russian as Turkish involvement in Hungary.[47] When the news of the Peace of Prut arrived, Eugene even authorized the removal of some battalions from Hungary for service in Italy.[48] Justifying his decision he wrote, "From the Ottoman Porte nothing more need be feared . . . ; in the future I do not believe that the Turks will undertake a break without reason especially since we are again masters of Hungary. Also they cannot know if and how long the war with France will last."[49]

Despite the prince's confidence, there was some speculation, especially in Italian quarters, that the Ottomans might be inspired by their success over the Russians to turn against Austria.[50] Talman himself suggested such a possibility but added that it would depend on whether or not Peter the Great would abide by the agreement he had signed at the Prut, and Talman thought it unlikely that he would. If he did not, "the Porte will be in no position to assume hostilities toward other neighboring powers."[51]

Yet the situation was not without uncertainty. As Talman guessed, Peter refused to fulfill the conditions of his first treaty, and the Turks declared war on Russia again in December 1711. A brief struggle led to a second treaty in April 1712, but Russian refusal to comply with this agreement led to a third Turkish declaration of war. This time Prince Eugene feared that the struggle might indeed be a prelude to an attack on Austria. In mid-December 1712 the prince called together the ministers concerned with Turkish affairs to discuss "alarming news" that the Turks might be turning on the Habsburgs.[52] The ministers elected to send protests of neutrality to the Porte, while concurrently transporting a portion of the imperial troops in Belgium to the Ottoman frontier and collecting stores and improving fortifications in Hungary.[53] Shortly thereafter the prince instructed Talman to assume a posture of "studied indifference" regarding the Russo-Turkish war and "to show no partiality in speaking, writing, or any other way . . . toward one side or the other."[54] When the news reached Vienna of the serious falling-out between Charles XII and his hosts in January 1713, however, Eugene knew that the Porte planned no action in Hungary.[55]

A breach between the king of Sweden and the Porte and the subsequent Treaty of Adrianople between Turkey and Russia ended Vienna's fears of an Ottoman attack. The only question remaining was what the Turks would do with their now un-wanted Swedish guest. The answer came in September 1714 when Charles announced his intention to leave for his home-land without fanfare and, more importantly, without an army. Vienna renewed the offer to allow him to travel peacefully through imperial territory, and Charles accepted, returning home in November 1714. Earlier in that same year Austria and France had concluded a peace ending the War of the Spanish Succession. By the time the Swedish king passed secretly through the Habsburg capital, the Monarchy was enjoying a measure of peace for the first time in thirteen years.

A Turkish assault upon Habsburg possessions at any time during the War of the Spanish Succession could have inflicted a serious blow upon the Monarchy. And Vienna realized it. Consequently, throughout the war the government's goals were to keep the Porte at peace, to prevent it from interfering in the rebellion in Hungary, from allying with France in a grand coalition against the Habsburg state, and from supporting Charles XII in his struggles against his enemies. The goals were achieved. Vienna's expressions of friendship, its timely warnings, and the diplomatic adroitness and well-placed bribes of Talman and his Dutch and British counterparts undoubtedly diverted Ottoman belligerency at critical moments. While domestic troubles and concerns also played a role in dissuading the Porte from mixing in Austria's troubles, the greatest contribution to Turkish passivity might have been the memory of the crushing defeats suffered at the hands of the Habsburgs between 1683 and 1699. "Tis very discernable and evident," wrote the British ambassador in 1711, "that they have an extraordinary regard for the Emperor and have so great an Esteem and respect for his Arms, that I believe it is certain, that they will carefully, and as much as is possible, avoid giving him any just complaint or Disgust."[56]

The Turks already feared that the balance of power in southeastern Europe had shifted decisively in favor of the Habsburgs, and Vienna suspected it as well. During the War of the Spanish Succession, the Monarchy had to avoid hostilities with the Turks to defend its interests elsewhere. After it ended, the Monarchy was far less reluctant to cross swords with its archenemy. If the war ending in 1699 still left doubt as to whether Austria had achieved military superiority over the Turks, the next war would leave none at all.

♛ CHAPTER THREE
Victory, 1716-1718

In December 1714, shortly after Charles XII departed for Sweden, the sultan declared war on the Republic of Venice. The attack came as no surprise. Since 1700 Western representatives at the Porte had reported that, of all the losses suffered at Carlowitz, the Turks resented most the surrender of the Morea to Venice. Each time the Ottomans spoke of war, Venice seemed their most likely target. The Venetians were aware of the danger themselves. During the War of the Spanish Succession, their delegate in Constantinople joined the French and the Hungarians in encouraging the grand viziers to invade Austria. While harboring no particular antagonism toward the Habsburgs, Venice was frantically anxious to divert Ottoman attention from the Morea.[1]

In 1714, however, the Venetian efforts to deter the Turks finally failed. The Porte charged that the island city had displayed a hostile attitude toward Turkey by giving aid to the Montenegrins (who had rebelled against Ottoman rule in 1711) and by seizing a Turkish ship carrying the harem of a high-ranking official. Declaring that no ruler could tolerate such abuses of his sovereignty, the sultan jailed the Venetian ambassador and ordered his army to prepare for war.[2] The following spring Turkish troops invaded the Morea.

The Venetians were sorely unprepared. The fleet, once the Republic's pride and defender of its greatness, lacked both adequate sailors and effective officers; in the Morea the troops were poorly equipped and the fortresses in disrepair. In fact, the Austrian envoy in Constantinople commented that the Turks attacked the Morea precisely because they anticipated little resistance. "The inhabitants are ready to rebel against Venice's harsh treatment, and the garrisons have largely deserted."[3]

38

Faced with the Ottoman invasion, the Republic turned to the only power likely to offer aid: Austria. Since 1684 Venice and the Monarchy had been part of the Holy League, a loose alliance to counter Ottoman aggression which also included Poland and the Papacy. As soon as the word of the Ottoman declaration of war reached Venice, the Senate appealed to the emperor to honor his commitment to the Holy League.[4]

Most evidence indicated that he would not respond favorably. In 1714 Vienna was not on particularly good terms with Venice. The city's vacillating but frequently hostile policy toward the Habsburgs in the War of the Spanish Succession had done its reputation in Vienna no good, and neither had its well-known efforts to encourage the Porte to invade Hungary. Moreover, the Senate's efforts to maintain the Adriatic as a Venetian trading preserve had antagonized Austria's growing commercial interests. In fact, the ambassador assigned to Venice at the conclusion of the War of the Spanish Succession received explicit instructions to protest "the self-appointed Venetian dominion over the Adriatic Sea."[5]

There were other reasons why Austria was unlikely to support its hot and cold ally. The War of the Spanish Succession had left the Habsburg treasury virtually empty. In 1715 the Generalkriegscommissariat composed a financial statement listing the monetary needs of the army in the event of war with the Turks. The total for one year's campaign came to 16,450,000 thalers, which excluded 7,400,000 of capital and interest on debts unpaid. Combining these two figures, the total amount needed would be 23,850,000 thalers. This same document estimated the income from the Habsburg lands for 1715 to be 12,875,000 thalers, leaving a potentially staggering deficit for one year of 10,975,000.[6] Whether the government could raise sufficient funds from other sources to offset this deficit was questionable, and many of Charles VI's ministers opposed going to war for that reason alone.[7]

Besides the dislike of Venice and the prospective financial burden, Charles himself hesitated to challenge the Turks. Selected as the candidate of the British, Dutch, and Austrians for the throne of Spain, he had lived there from 1703 to 1711 and during his stay had fallen in love with his adopted people, especially the Catalans, who had fought so bravely for his cause. He was deeply disappointed when, as emperor, he had to relinquish the country he adored to his French rival, Philip of Anjou, who became Philip V. Even though Philip possessed the country in fact, Charles could not bring himself to recognize that possession formally and, while concluding treaties to end the war with France, had refused to negotiate a peace with Madrid. Thus, when the Turko-Venetian struggle erupted, Austria and Spain were formally still at war with one another. Charles feared that Philip would take advantage of a Habsburg-Ottoman conflict to attack Austria again, particularly the former Spanish possessions in Italy awarded to the Monarchy at the conclusion of the War of the Spanish Succession.[8]

Besides potential trouble with Spain, Vienna faced other serious international troubles in late 1714, the most important being its lack of firm allies in western Europe. Britain and the Dutch Republic, the Monarchy's two associates in the last war, had fallen from Vienna's grace when they had concluded a separate peace with France at Utrecht in 1713. Moreover, France, although now at peace with the Habsburgs, was still ruled by Louis XIV, who in Vienna's eyes might renew the war with the emperor at the slightest opportunity. In the event of Austrian hostilities with Turkey, France and Spain could reach a new alliance, invade Italy, and begin the War of the Spanish Succession all over again, this time with the Habsburgs fighting alone.[9]

Trouble in the west was not Vienna's only fear. The Great Northern War was still in progress and still posed the danger of spreading southward and westward, eventually involving the Monarchy. In a meeting of the Privy Conference in May 1715, the members expressed the concern that France, Sweden, Poland, Prussia, and—informally—the Ottoman Empire might forge an alliance "that would shortly plunge the whole German Empire into flames." The only way to avoid such a catastrophe, the conference suggested, was for Vienna to restore the alliance with Britain, secure support among the small German states, and reach agreement with Russia. At the time, however, none of these goals had much likelihood of being realized.[10] Moreover, as long as the war in the north continued, Vienna could expect no help against the Turks from Poland, the fourth member of the Holy League.

The final reason for Austria refusing to fight was that the Ottoman Empire had apparently no wish for war with the Habsburgs. In early May 1715 a Turkish delegation led by the Mutiferrika Ibrahim Aga arrived in the Habsburg capital to explain the motives for the sultan's attack on the Morea and to voice his master's desire to remain friends with the emperor. Ibrahim, described by the Austrian resident as "an apparently good, reasonable, and direct Turk," met with Eugene to plead his case.[11] He argued that the Porte had no wish to void the Treaty of Carlowitz but only to combat the covetousness of Venice and to end its maladministration of the Morea. In response, the prince uttered a few veiled warnings about continued Ottoman aggression but made no specific threats or promises. Neither party spoke in any but general terms, and shortly thereafter the Ottoman envoy left for home. If the Austrians did not wish any involvement, they could have put their trust in the Mutiferrika's pledges of peace and let the matter go at that.[12]

Despite all these objections, Vienna did decide to go to war as the ally of Venice. Why did the Austrians make this choice when so many considerations argued for peace? To this question most scholars have replied that the Monarchy was swayed by the overpowering influence of Prince Eugene. Because he enjoyed great fame as the finest commander in Austria—some would say in Europe—and because he was president of the Hofkriegsrat and the most important member of the Privy Conference, Austria would not refuse to make war if he wanted it. And he did favor war. One author wrote of the prince that this struggle was "the first and only of his career in which he personally directed every diplomatic and military detail and in which he had a completely free hand in strategy and politics."[13]

Scholars have offered a variety of reasons for the prince's decision, the most common being his desire to win for Austria the Banat of Timişoara and the fortress of Belgrade. Some see in this wish merely an intention to round off Hungary and to make its defense easier, while others look upon it as something deeper than that, something stretching back to the cultural conflict between Islam and Christianity that had for centuries plagued the Balkans. The eminent nineteenth-century historian, Alfred von Arneth, wrote:

> The Prince regarded the European possessions of the Ottoman Empire as stolen, without the slightest claim to legality, conquered only by the most brutal force, and which centuries of possession in no way legalized. In expelling the Turks from these lands, in not allowing them to retain possession of them, he saw the essence of civilization. From this historical point of view, he regarded nothing with more pleasure than, as he once did at Zenta, taking from them new lands through new victories.[14]

Not everyone credits the motive of territorial gain. In the opinion of some, Eugene feared that Ottoman success in the Morea might inspire the Turks to turn elsewhere, first to Venetian Dalmatia and then possibly to Hungary. By striking first, the Austrians could nip these buds of Ottoman expansionism before they had a chance to flower.[15] Another scholar points out that, since the sultan had attacked one of the emperor's formal allies, Eugene would feel the Monarchy morally bound to come to that country's defense. Despite all of the arguments against the war, Vienna must help its ravaged ally. To refuse would discredit the emperor's word in all of Europe.[16] Still another argues that Eugene and his associate Gundaker Starhemberg, the head of the Hofkammer (finance ministry), might have pushed the war to give themselves control of the administrative reforms being instituted in 1714-1716.[17]

Max Braubach, the foremost biographer of the prince, has acknowledged all of these motives, arguing that none predominated but all contributed to the prince's decision to make war. The only one he has rejected outright is the idea of a crusade. Eugene did not think in terms of crusades—that was a concept left over from the last Turkish war—but in terms of *ratio status*, reasons of state. It was politically advantageous for the Monarchy to join its ally, to push the Turks back from Dalmatia, to secure the Banat and Belgrade, and to create a solid wall in southeastern Europe that would protect central Europe against encroachments from the east. Prince Eugene envisioned a militarily secure Habsburg state, and a victory over the Turks would, in his mind, greatly augment that security.[18] Braubach is undoubtedly correct in his assessment of the prince's motives. The establishment of Turkish power in Venetian lands along the Adriatic could indeed pose future problems for the Habsburgs, especially since it might prompt the Turks to make incursions into Austrian Croatia and possibly into Hungary itself. Also, the conquest of the major fortresses of Timişoara and Belgrade would certainly improve the Habsburg defense of Hungary along its southern boundary.

But one more consideration should be added. Although he never expressed it openly, the prince undoubtedly believed that he could defeat the Turks and that a Habsburg victory now would lay to rest any dreams the Turks might have of retaking Hungary or any portion of it in the future. He had crushed the Turks at Zenta in 1697 when he was a relative novice at command, and now in 1715 he was the premier general on the Continent, certainly more than a match for any officer among the Turks. Moreover, at this time Vienna received the first assessments from its observers at the Porte suggesting that the Ottoman army possessed but a shadow of its former greatness and that the time might be ripe for the conquest of all the Balkan lands. The most important reports

came from the resident, Anselm Fleischmann, who as early
as February 1715 wrote, "Now exists the opportunity not
only to defeat the Turks, who, in the opinion of knowledg-
able and experienced people, are in a very confused and wretched
state, but also, God willing, to throw them completely out
of Europe."[19] Even after their victories in the Morea he commented, "I can safely say that 30,000 well-led Germans would
be sufficient to defeat the Turkish-Tartar army, which is more
accustomed to flight than to victory."[20] A war with the Turks,
therefore, offered three attractions to the prince: acquisition
of strategically important lands, protection against potential
Ottoman incursions, and an opportunity to convince the Porte
and Europe once and for all that Austria was now the dominant power in southeastern Europe and that Turkish pre-
sumptuousness would be permitted no longer. *"Turca vincens
et felix superbus, victus humillimus."*[21]

Although in the end the prince favored—indeed encouraged—war with the Ottoman Empire, when the news reached
Vienna in early 1715 of the Ottoman invasion of the Morea,
he was at first by no means enthusiastic about assisting Venice. In fact, for much of 1715 he advised against Austrian
involvement. After listening to the Venetian appeals, he told
Charles VI that a Turkish war would be most unpleasant "in
light of the treasury drained by the lengthy French war, the
broken-down war machinery, and the inadequate standing
army." He recommended that Charles remain neutral and try
to mediate a settlement between Venice and the Porte. Since
the peace effort might not produce results, however, the emperor should prepare the army for war, which was the prince's
customary advice whenever danger threatened.[22]

Throughout the spring and summer of 1715 Eugene's enthusiasm for war remained cool because the international situation was still discouraging. Before Vienna could even consider actively assisting the Venetians, some way had to be
found to secure the Habsburg lands in Italy from a Spanish
or Franco-Spanish attack. During the summer the Austrian
ministers approached various courts about provisions they might

make to defend Austria's Italian territory. Because the Venetians were most anxious to secure Habsburg participation in the Turkish war, Vienna approached them first, but they expressed great reluctance to become involved in any Italian trouble for the quite justifiable reason that they needed every available man to fight the Turks.[23] The Austrians turned next to Pope Clement XI, who seemed to be taking his role as defender of the faith quite seriously by sending letter after letter to Charles pleading for him to take up arms against the *"perfida Maometta."*[24] Clement's enthusiasm to defeat Islam considerably waned, however, when he was asked to guarantee Habsburg lands in Italy against Spanish aggression and to provide a substantial monetary contribution to the Austrian war effort.[25] The ministers did not even consider approaching the Monarchy's two old allies, Britain and the Dutch Republic, because at the time Vienna was embroiled in acrimonious negotiations with the Dutch over the Barrier Treaty to protect the Austrian Netherlands and the British were still disliked for signing the separate treaty with France in 1713.[26] The final and most certain way of securing Italy from Spanish attack, direct negotiations with Madrid, was out of the question, for it would require recognition of Philip as king of Spain, a condition the emperor refused to consider.[27]

While the diplomatic situation remained uncertain, military conditions grew worse for Venice. By September the Ottomans had expelled the Venetians from the Morea, and Vienna now feared a Turkish invasion of Venetian Dalmatia that might spill over into Habsburg lands.[28] The policy-makers could do nothing to discourage it, however, as long as Habsburg Italy remained exposed; the only thing to do was to hope that the Porte would accept Austrian mediation and begin peace negotiations.

Then, in late 1715 the diplomatic situation changed abruptly. Instead of inhibiting the Austrians from entering the war, it now offered them the encouragement to do so. The central event was the death of Louis XIV. Behind all of Vienna's fears of trouble with Spain loomed the specter of the

great French king; as long as he lived, the Habsburg ministers could never be certain that he would remain at peace.[29]
His death on 1 September seemed to lift an enormous weight
from their shoulders. A court commentator and historian,
Johann Francis Dumont, wrote on the occasion, "One is able
to say that the House of Austria has not for a hundred years
been in a situation so free as now. It should act to preserve
this situation and, in order to do so, should only avoid bad
treaties."[30]

Partly as a result of the French king's passing, the conditions necessary for Austria's participation in the Turkish war
soon fell into place. A special envoy sent to Versailles to settle
outstanding differences with the new French government reported that the ministers there assured him that they had no
intention of taking advantage of any Habsburg involvement
in the East to adopt anti-Austrian policies in Spain or in
Italy.[31] Shortly thereafter came news that Clement XI had
received a letter from Philip V with a Spanish guarantee of
the integrity of the Habsburg possessions in Italy for the du-
ration of the Turkish war.[32] There even followed a Spanish
offer to assist Venice with ships and men, but the emperor,
suspecting some ulterior motive on Philip's part, persuaded
the pope to decline it.[33] Finally, in mid-November the talks
with the Dutch Republic concerning the Barrier Treaty reached
a successful conclusion, and negotiations began shortly thereafter for the re-creation of the Austro-British-Dutch alliance.

As part of the diplomatic preparations for the war, the
Privy Conference quite naturally broached the question of
seeking assistance from Russia. Although Peter the Great was
still involved in the Great Northern War, his serious losses
at the Prut a few years earlier might persuade him now to
join the Austrians in seeking revenge upon the Turks. Moreover, an Austro-Russian effort would force the Turks to divide their army in order to resist blows coming from both
north and west. Since they seemed barely able to withstand
the onslaught of Austria alone, a serious Ottoman defeat and

corresponding allied victory appeared absolutely certain should Austria and Russia join together.

Yet the Privy Conference rejected the idea of an alliance with Russia because, in words reminiscent of 1710, they still believed the tsar likely to seek advantages from the Turks that would ultimately jeopardize Habsburg security. Prince Eugene summed up the doubts of the conference for the emperor:

> It is easy to recognize that an alliance with the tsar would force the Turks to divide their forces and thereby make it easier and more advantageous for us to fight a Turkish war. But we also have to fear that the tsar would make this alliance very costly for us and could try to make many difficulties for Your Majesty. . . . We should not doubt that the tsar follows only his own interests and will involve himself in nothing else.[34]

The following year the question of an anti-Ottoman accord with Russia rose again, and the conference, in rejecting the idea, echoed the prince's earlier sentiments—and forecasted sentiments about Russia that would appear among later Habsburg statesmen: "As numerous examples show, he causes his allies great difficulties and dictates more rules than he provides help. . . . He will make many unpleasant claims, especially concerning Moldavia and Walachia, and finally in future Turkish peace negotiations cause many damaging obstructions with his excessive demands."[35] Finally in 1717, in response to a Russian inquiry, Charles himself wrote that an alliance with the tsar would mean for Austria "more evil than good."[36]

By 1715 Vienna's policy-makers had accepted the essentials of Austria's Eastern Question. In their eyes, the Ottoman Empire was growing steadily weaker, and soon it might be unable to defend itself against European aggressors. Whereas this growing feebleness would surely reduce the danger of Ottoman encroachment on the Monarchy's southeastern border, it would also invite the Russians to penetrate the sultan's

European possessions and possibly to replace Ottoman suze-
rainty there with their own. And recent events indicated that
the emerging Russia of Peter the Great would make a more
dangerous neighbor than a declining Turkey. The tsar's interference in the Holy Roman Empire, his murder of his son
Alexis who had sought refuge at the Habsburg court, his
flirtation with Rákóczi, and his influence in Poland—all made
his motives and desires suspect in Vienna. Indeed on one
occasion in 1718 Eugene became so infuriated with a Russian
diplomatic maneuver that he suggested to Pope Clement XI
that war with Russia was "inevitable."[37] This statement was
made in a fit of pique, for no mention of it appears again,
but it illustrates the concern in Vienna about Russian intrigue
and aggressiveness.

By late 1715 Austria was prepared to fight the Ottomans
with the aid of no major power, and it would be the only
eighteenth-century Austro-Turkish war in which Russia was
not involved. Still some minor diplomatic difficulties had to
be resolved, but the prince was sufficiently confident by the
end of the year to tell Count Johann Schulenburg, the celebrated officer who would later defend the island of Corfu for
Venice, that the emperor would declare war if the Turks did
not make peace before the next campaigning season. Although sworn to secrecy by the prince, Schulenburg advised
the Venetian Senate that it should anticipate only defensive
operations in 1716 "in order to gain time to allow the Austrian cabinet to organize its armies and [other means of] help."[38]

There remained the problem of financing the war, although
now that diplomatic conditions appeared so favorable, financial matters seemed considerably less obstructive. An anonymous document of 1715 revealed the kind of attitude toward
funding that eventually prevailed in Vienna once the decision
to make war was taken. A Turkish war, the author suggested,
would actually reduce, rather than increase, military costs
because the army would live off the Ottoman countryside.
"One believes that the intended war will not last long and
that much can be won so that the army can be boarded and

fed in other lands and therefore the imperial provinces can be relieved of a bit of the burden [of caring for them]."[39] This solution turned out to be unsatisfactory, as one might suspect, but it did persuade Vienna to fight now and to worry about paying later.[40]

Confident now of the diplomatic and financial situations, Prince Eugene was ready to act. On 13 April 1716—the same day that Venice accepted Austria's terms for an alliance, including a Venetian guarantee of all Habsburg possessions in Italy—he sent the grand vizier an ultimatum that declared peace possible "only if the Porte ceases all hostilities against the Republic of Venice, offers an indemnity and compensation for the damage done to this Republic, and agrees to restore the provisions of the Treaty of Carlowitz," including the return of the Morea.[41] The grand vizier responded that he would gladly renew the Treaty of Carlowitz with the emperor but could not do so with Venice after "Allah had granted such victories to Ottoman arms."[42] On 20 May the prince informed Charles that, since the Turks had failed to answer the ultimatum satisfactorily, there was nothing else to do "but form the army as soon as possible and, in the name of the Almighty, begin the campaign."[43]

Austria was thus ready to embark on its first Turkish war of the eighteenth century. Whereas Eugene, Charles VI, and the other statesmen in Vienna might have joined the conflict for reasons of state, the crusading impulse was by no means forgotten among the people. The priests exhorted the people to pray for the success of Christian arms, the songwriters composed hymns of inspiration and of forthcoming victories, and the pamphleteers recalled the successes and sacrifices of the great war of 1683-1699. The spirit of these outbursts of popular enthusiasm was decidedly different than it had been before, however, for popular imagination viewed this struggle as an *Angriffskrieg*, a struggle in which the Christians would take the fight to the Turks rather than await the Turkish onslaught against Christendom. Also, among the people there seemed little doubt that the Christians would triumph be-

cause, as many of the songs reminded them, not only was the
Virgin still at the side of her faithful, but they now had the
mighty Prince Eugene as well, a combination that could not
lose. If Vienna had no plans to free Constantinople from the
infidel, many of the common people did.[44]

Although Vienna declared war in May 1716, the prince
did not reach his headquarters until early July and decided at
once that the campaigning season was too advanced to march
directly on Belgrade, which was his major objective. Instead
he chose to seek the main Turkish field army, which was in
the vicinity of Petrovaradin. He hoped to destroy it so that
it could not interfere with his plans to besiege Belgrade the
following year. His success was astounding. He met the Ottomans just outside Petrovaradin and inflicted a crushing defeat upon them. The grand vizier died in the fighting, and
the whole Turkish camp fell into the hands of the imperial
forces.[45] After the victory, the prince marched on Timișoara,
the capital of the Banat and the only major fortress in Ottoman possession north of the Danube. Not as well-defended,
-supplied, or -garrisoned as Belgrade, the place capitulated
on 13 October.

Stunned by their defeat at Petrovaradin and doubtlessly
envisioning the loss of Belgrade, the Turks sought an end to
the fighting. In October they released Fleischmann, who had
been imprisoned earlier, and sent him to Vienna with the
offer of an armistice. The Habsburg government welcomed
the former resident as a hero but ignored his mission.[46] The
Porte next appealed to the British and the Dutch, who had
mediated the Treaty of Carlowitz. Accepting the appeal, London appointed as mediator Edward Wortley Montague, husband of the brilliant Lady Mary. He proved a poor choice;
ignorant of military realities, Montague offered to conclude a
treaty but only after the Austrians had returned Timișoara
and the entire Banat to the Turks. Hearing the offer, Eugene
wrote to Charles that the Englishman must have composed
this letter under duress "because affairs now are not such,
praise God, that these terms must be accepted."[47] Charles was

less charitable. Calling the proposals "laughable," he remarked, "It was silly of him [Montague] to compose them and to send a courier with them."[48] The Dutch seemed more aware of what the Austrians had in mind. Their ambassador in Vienna wrote that the Habsburg court would likely reject an armistice because it "wants to become master of Belgrade."[49]

In 1717 the prince made ready to achieve his goal. The details of his successful siege of Belgrade are recorded in many histories, so a brief outline will suffice here.[50] After encamping his main force before the fortress in July, the prince soon found himself and his men surrounded in turn by the fortress to their north and a huge Turkish relief army to their south and east. After waiting in vain a few days for the Ottomans to attack, he decided to take the initiative himself. In the early morning of 16 August, his troops marched through a dense fog toward the lines of the Turkish relief army. In the ensuing engagement, which showed Eugene at his tactical best, the Turks were routed. Two days later, the Turkish garrison inside Belgrade, realizing that all hope for succor had vanished, surrendered the fortress to the Austrians. Although the victory was celebrated with great enthusiasm then and for a long time thereafter, Prince Eugene was not without his critics. Many accused him of unnecessarily risking the entire army in an all-or-nothing battle which he won largely through incredibly good luck.[51] Such critics forgot, however, that fortune often smiles upon a commander who seizes an opportunity and pursues it relentlessly. By attacking the Turks when and where they did not expect it and by gaining control of the flow of battle after the fog lifted, Eugene achieved one of the greatest victories in Habsburg history. To his old comrade Marlborough he wrote too modestly on the day following the battle:

> The day of August 16 was the most dangerous I have seen in my life. Threatened from the rear by the 30,000-man garrison in Belgrade, from the front by a well-

entrenched army twice that large, and at the decisive
moment engulfed by a heavy, dense fog that made it
impossible to see the right point of attack, all demanded
an army commander with sharper eyes than mine.[52]

Of all the events in eighteenth-century Austro-Turkish affairs, the victory at Belgrade was perhaps the most important.
It seemed to prove the superiority of Austrian arms beyond
all doubt and would serve as an example to future Habsburg
military officers of the gains that one could make through
good preparation and decisiveness. It also inspired visions of
further Austrian conquests, of effecting what Fleischmann had
suggested at the beginning of the war, the expulsion of the
Ottoman Empire from Europe and its replacement by Habsburg hegemony. In fact, the Privy Conference suggested in
September that it would be advisable to extend imperial control down the Danube to include Vidin and Nikopol (Nico-
polis) in order to secure commerce in the area.[53] Charles passed
this suggestion to Eugene and added that perhaps Moldavia
and Walachia be joined to the Monarchy as tributary states.[54]
During the winter of 1717-1718 Talman, now serving as an
adviser in the Hofkriegsrat, offered to the prince a strategy
for a campaign in 1718, in the event the war continued: "If
your lordship can begin the campaign toward the end of next
May, the army should reach Sofia and Plovdiv (Philippopolis)
or on the Danube Nikopol or Ruse (Rustchuk) before meeting
a prepared Turkish army. The enemy's main force will not be
composed before the middle of July, as experience in all wars
with the Porte has shown us."[55] With successful implementation of the plan, Talman argued, Austria could occupy the
Balkan Peninsula as far as Macedonia.

There is no direct evidence whether or not Prince Eugene
seriously considered extending Habsburg boundaries deep into
the Balkans. On one occasion he did suggest that the emperor
might like the Aegean port of Thessaloniki (Salonica) and the
Adriatic port of Durrës "if the Almighty grants his good will
to the fortunate progress of Your Majesty's arms," but he

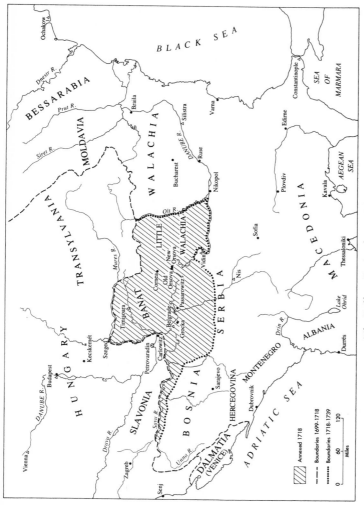

BLACK SEA

SEA OF MARMARA

AEGEAN SEA

ADRIATIC SEA

Ochakow

Dnestr R.

BESSARABIA

Prut R.

MOLDAVIA

Siret R.

TRANSYLVANIA

Braila

WALACHIA

Silistra

Varna

Constantinople

Edirne

DANUBE R.

Bucharest

Ruse

Nikopol

Plovdiv

Kavala

Oli R.

Mureş R.

LITTLE

New Orşova

WALACHIA

Vidin

Sofia

Thessaloniki

MACEDONIA

Cornea

Old Orşova

Lake Ohrid

Timişoara

BANAT

Belgrade

Passarowitz

Grocka

SERBIA

Niš

Kecskemét

Szeged

Petrovaradin

Carlowitz

ALBANIA

Durrës

Drin R.

HUNGARY

SLAVONIA

BOSNIA

Sarajevo

MONTENEGRO

HERCEGOVINA

Budapest

DANUBE R.

Sava R.

Drava R.

Dubrovnik

Vienna

Zagreb

Unna R.

DALMATIA (VENICE)

Senj

The Balkan Peninsula, 1700-1739

Annexed 1718

Boundaries 1699-1718

Boundaries 1718-1739

0   60   120

Miles

apparently had no real plans to advance that far.[56] In 1716
representatives from Macedonia and Montenegro appealed to
him to liberate their peoples, but he waved the pleas aside.[57]
After taking Belgrade he sent two expeditions into Bosnia,
but heavy Ottoman resistance forced both to withdraw.

Whatever dreams Vienna had of extending Habsburg influence into the Balkans, its attention was wrenched from Ottoman to western European affairs shortly after the victory at
Belgrade. At the end of August came news that the Spanish
fleet had landed 6,000 troops on the Habsburg island of Sardinia. All the careful diplomatic precautions—the Spanish
promise of neutrality, the rapprochement with France, the
alliance with Britain, the guarantees of Venice and the Papacy—in the end had failed to deter the Spanish king from
invading Habsburg Italy.[58]

The news of the invasion threw the Habsburg ministers
into a panic; they advised the emperor to conclude an immediate settlement with the sultan and to transfer the bulk
of the army to Italy.[59] But soon after, a letter arrived from
the prince's headquarters that restored a degree of calm. Eugene pointed out that the invading force was not large (an
army of 6,000 "seems great when it is aboard ship but on
land can do little") and, to do great damage, would have to
unite with troops from some Italian league "which 'til now
does not seem to exist."[60] Above all, he suggested, the emperor and his advisers at home should keep their heads and
await developments.

Developments were not long in coming, albeit from the
Turkish, not the Italian, theater. On 10 September Eugene
received a letter from Mustafa Pasha, the erstwhile commander of Belgrade, who suggested concluding peace on the
basis of *uti possidetis* (one keeps what one has occupied militarily at the time the treaty is signed) with the pasha serving
as mediator.[61] The prince was somewhat uncertain whether
this offer was genuine, but he recommended that, in view of
the danger in Italy, Vienna formulate some terms and try to
inaugurate peace talks. He advised the emperor to send Tal-

man to his headquarters with negotiating proposals and then suggested what he thought the proposals should be: *uti possidetis* should be the general principle, but Austria should also try to acquire all of Serbia and a few fortresses in Bosnia even though Habsburg forces did not occupy them.[62]

After Charles approved these terms, the prince received an official request from the grand vizier to discuss a treaty. To his dismay, the Ottoman proposal was quite different from that of Mustafa Pasha. Instead of a settlement based on *uti possidetis*, the grand vizier suggested an armistice with peace talks to come later. And, instead of appointing the former pasha of Belgrade plenipotentiary to talk directly with the Austrians, he again requested the mediation of the British. Prince Eugene liked neither condition, but, to make certain that talks at least began, he advised accepting British mediation while rejecting the armistice. He wished to give the Turks no opportunity to regroup their forces.[63] The emperor concurred, and preliminary talks began.

To Vienna's surprise, no progress was made toward a settlement for the next six months. The Turks did not appoint delegates until February 1718, and they did not agree to Passarowitz (Pozarevac) as a meeting place until late March.[64] Even when the various envoys arrived at the site, the Austrians found the Turks unwilling to begin talks. The reason for the delay lay in the internal affairs of the Porte, about which Vienna knew but could do nothing. From the first peace overtures in September, the Porte had been the scene of a struggle between one faction advocating the continuation of the war and another demanding peace. Not until mid-May was the struggle resolved in favor of the peace party; on the 20th of that month word came to Vienna that a new grand vizier, Damad Ibrahim, was anxious to reach a settlement.[65] This report was confirmed a few days later when instructions arrived at Passarowitz ordering the Turkish delegates to treat with the Austrians on the basis of *uti possidetis* and the Venetians on the basis of *justa satisfactionis* (just satisfaction, mean-

ing whatever the negotiators agreed was a fair settlement).[66]
Within a week the delegates sat down to work.

Despite the new Turkish willingness to negotiate, the talks
snagged almost immediately. The Ottomans absolutely refused to accept the Austrian demand for all of Serbia and the
Bosnian fortresses, which, they correctly argued, no Habsburg forces occupied. On 11 June Eugene received at his
headquarters in Belgrade a personal letter from the grand vizier stressing his desire for a settlement but only on the basis
of strict *uti possidetis*. If he wished to keep his post, he told
the prince, he could concede no territory not actually held by
Austrian troops.[67] By now eager to conclude a treaty owing
to the continued uncertainty in Italy, Eugene instructed the
two Austrian delegates (Talman and Count Damian Hugo
von Virmond) to abandon the claims to the lands not in
Habsburg hands. To pursue them "would place the advantages that we have in unnecessary danger and also inspire
rebuke from the emperor that we are unable to secure a successful peace."[68]

With their new orders, Talman and Virmond reached an
agreement with the Turks by the second week in July. There
remained the problem of Venice, of which Virmond wrote,
"The Porte and the Turkish nation have a special repugnance
about compensating this nation and reconciling their differences with it."[69] Nonetheless, because the Venetians had already consented to give up the Morea—on the grounds of *uti
possidetis*—a settlement with them was not long in coming.
On 21 July the treaty was signed and the war ended. Charles
reacted to the news: "Thank God that this peace is concluded.
Now our hands are free to pull the teeth of all those who
wish to chew on us."[70]

The first Austro-Turkish war of the eighteenth century had
ended, and the Habsburgs had emerged victorious. In fact, it
would be the only one of the three eighteenth-century wars
that Austria would clearly win. But it also raised some of the
fundamental questions that would carry over into the other
two wars and would be discussed during the periods of Aus-

tro-Turkish harmony as well. In this conflict the Ottoman military appeared to be merely a shell of its former self, unable to defend the sultan's lands against the armies that the Austrians could now muster. Since it was so weak, the Ottoman possessions in Europe seemed ripe for the taking if the Habsburgs could arrange the diplomatic conditions necessary to free themselves of trouble in the West. Indeed, the obvious way to prevent possible Russian aggrandizement in the sultan's European possessions would have been for the emperor to annex them himself. Viewing the situation in this way, scholars have usually interpreted subsequent Habsburg policy toward Turkey as designed to reap the easy harvest and have expressed surprise—and at times chagrin—that it was not successful. They have neglected to ask other questions: Did Austria want to annex those lands? Did it really wish to push the Turks out of the Balkans and establish Habsburg hegemony there? Clearly the Austrian statesmen were thinking about such a possibility. At the same time, however, they had their doubts whether such conquests would be worth the effort, and these doubts would be expressed by Habsburg ministers and rulers under different circumstances and at different times throughout the remainder of the century. In mid-1718 Prince Eugene commented on a suggestion that Austria ask for Vidin and Nis (Nish) with words that would later be repeated by others in regard to other Balkan provinces: "I do not find that Your Majesty would be well-served by the possession of these faraway places because their distance and difficult communication would cause more problems than advantages and their situation would demand half again as many obligations."[71]

CHAPTER FOUR

Peace with Turkey,
Alliance with Russia,
1718-1736

Following the Treaty of Passarowitz, the Austrians enjoyed almost two decades of peace with the Ottoman Empire. During that time most of their diplomatic attention focused on serious problems in the West. In 1725 Charles finally reconciled himself to the loss of Spain by concluding the Treaty of Vienna, an alliance between Austria and Spain sealed by the proposed marriage of two of Charles's daughters to sons of the Spanish queen, Elizabeth Farnese. To Charles's surprise, the accord evoked a storm of protest throughout much of Europe. To oppose it, Britain and France, who objected the most vehemently, formed the Alliance of Herrenhausen with Prussia. From then until 1731 feverish international activity surrounded the two alliances; countries took sides, changed sides, issued threats, mobilized armies, and proclaimed neutrality until finally both agreements were scrapped. During this extended crisis, the main concern of the Austrian ministers toward the Porte was, as in 1700-1713, keeping it from aligning with the emperor's enemies. This task proved considerably easier than it had been previously, for throughout these years the Ottomans were engaged in a serious struggle with Persia; consequently, they were as anxious to avoid strife elsewhere as were the Habsburgs.

Nevertheless, important diplomatic exchanges between Austria and Turkey continued after 1718. Immediately following the Treaty of Passarowitz, the two states had to discuss regulating and clarifying its provisions.[1] This necessitated the exchange of great embassies that by now had become

58

a tradition in Austro-Turkish relations. Heading the Habsburg mission to Constantinople was the able Count Virmond, the negotiator at Passarowitz, while the Ottoman delegation to Vienna was led by Ibrahim Pasha, not to be confused with the better-known Ibrahim who was grand vizier at the time.

Despite the peace, Grand Vizier Ibrahim still regarded the emperor as the sultan's most dangerous enemy; at the conclusion of the war, he had even sent letters to the chancellors of Poland and Russia thanking them personally for their refusal to aid the Austrians during the hostilities. Because he feared the Habsburgs, Ibrahim wished his embassy to make a great impression on the Viennese populace and government both in terms of splendor and bribes. Consequently, the trappings of the ambassador and his suite were fitted with all possible finery. The embassy consisted of over 750 persons, 645 horses, 100 mules, 180 camels, and "seven times seven presents" that were "the richest and most magnificent that a Turkish embassy had ever brought to Europe."[2]

The Viennese reaction to all of this brilliance was mixed. One observer was quite unimpressed. "As to the Entry of the Ambassador, I may venture to say, it was magnificent on the part of the Imperial Court; for in Truth the Mahometan's whole Train and Baggage were very inconsiderable. This Ambassador's Name was Ibrahim Basha; he had 600 Men in his Retinue, but they were all shabbily rigg'd." Describing the Ottoman camp he added, "Everything was to the last degree slovenly; the inferior Domestics especially were the most disagreeable Gentry I ever saw; they had not Cloaths to their Backs, but were in Rags and Tatters; . . ."[3] Others were more impressed, including Prince Eugene's antagonist, Count Mérode-Westerloo. While praising the fashions of the Turks, he complained that those of the emperor were ordinary by comparison. He criticized the Habsburg court for not knowing the Turks well enough to awe them with splendor, but at the same time revealed a bit of his own ignorance by implying that the visitors were savages.

The ceremony that took place was, in my opinion, much
too simple for this barbarous people who wish to be
dazzled and to whom one must give an idea of ourselves
conforming to our victories. It is astonishing that, being
so near the Turks as one is here, one is as little informed
of their manners, their nature, and their customs as the
most distant European nation.[4]

Although the Turkish embassy caused much excitement in
Vienna, the real work of clarifying the Treaty of Passarowitz
was performed by Virmond in the Ottoman capital.[5] Vienna
was especially anxious to persuade the Turks to imprison or
to exile the Hungarian rebels who had fled to Turkey following the collapse of their uprising in 1711. Conceding to Virmond's appeals, the Ottomans finally agreed in early 1720 to
intern Rákóczi himself on the European side of the Sea of
Marmara and the other rebels at various places throughout
the Empire. Happy with his success on this and a few other
matters, Virmond completed his work and departed for home
in May of that year.

For the remainder of the 1720s no major issues and few
minor ones affected the relations between Austria and Turkey. One lesser problem involved the Barbary pirates, who
were under the nominal sovereignty of the sultan. In May
1724 Algerian corsairs captured a ship of the Belgian Ostend
Company—a company formed in 1723 with the support and
protection of the emperor—which was loaded with coffee and
bound for Ostend from Mocca. The ship was taken to Algiers,
where the crew was sold into slavery, the cargo distributed,
and the captain imprisoned in the dungeon of the dey. Although the Barbary pirates had raided Neapolitan and Sicilian
vessels before, this was the first time that they had attacked
a ship of the emperor's beloved Ostend Company. Insisting
that such a misfortune not be repeated, he ordered the imperial representative in Constantinople to seek an arrangement with the pirates through the mediation of the Porte.

Responding to the emperor's wish, in 1725 a Turkish

squadron set out for North Africa carrying two Belgian negotiators and some Turkish mediators to talk with the Barbary leaders. They had no luck at Algiers, where the dey
refused to receive them, but they did at Tunis.[6] There they
concluded a treaty establishing an Austrian consulate and ex-
tracting a Tunisian promise not to molest "Flemish, Sicilian,
Neapolitan, or Florentine ships."[7] Following Tunis's example, the dey of Tripoli signed a like treaty in 1726, this one
negotiated in Constantinople between his representatives and
the Austrian resident.[8] The dey of Algiers held out a bit
longer, asking in exchange for his signature a payment of
5,000 gulden. Although Prince Eugene favored investing the
sum in a fleet to send the pirate to the bottom of the sea, the
bribe was approved and the treaty with Algiers completed in
1727.[9] Despite the treaties, imperial ships were still not entirely safe; periodically one would fall victim to a raid in the
Mediterranean. Nonetheless, piracy was by no means a Barbary monopoly even at this late date. In the early 1730s a
representative of Tunis appeared in Vienna to complain of
Sicilian buccaneers raiding the African coast. After Austria
lost Naples and Sicily to the Spanish Bourbons in 1735, the
Barbary pirates for a time lost interest in raiding imperial
shipping, since there was so little of it in the Mediterranean.

Another issue involving Turkey that evoked considerable
interest in Vienna in the 1720s and 1730s was the case of the
celebrated Alexander Bonneval. One of the great European
adventurers of the eighteenth century, Bonneval had begun
his rich and varied career in the service of the king of France
and had achieved fame during the War of the Spanish Succession. When questioned about the use of some funds in Italy,
however, Bonneval deserted his French master and joined
France's archenemy, the Holy Roman Emperor. In Habsburg
service he rose rapidly, largely because of his own ability and
the favor of Prince Eugene, who once described him as "the
foremost commanding general not only among the Germans
but among all the imperial vassals."[10] Undoubtedly talented,
Bonneval was also arrogant, unmanageable, and possessed of

a curious sense of values that enabled him to trample upon the feelings of others while reacting violently to the slightest offense to his own. He was "a man whose whole life from youth to old age seemed to make a mockery of all those limitations with which religion, inhibition, law, tradition, and custom encircle man for his own good."[11]

In the autumn of 1724 Bonneval, piqued at failing to receive an appointment he believed he deserved, became involved in a vigorous verbal dispute with Eugene's deputy in the Austrian Netherlands. The prince regarded Bonneval's attacks as criticisms of his own authority, and, when he protected his deputy, Bonneval turned the full thrust of his scalding tongue on Eugene. The recriminations became so violent that the prince remarked, "If he came in one door, I would go out another."[12] Eugene finally could take no more. He had Bonneval dismissed from the Habsburg service and imprisoned for a year.

Bonneval was not the man to take such a blow to his honor lightly. After his release, he fled to Italy where he conspired against the Habsburgs at various courts. Then, upon hearing that Habsburg agents were intending to murder him, he escaped to Bosnia and demanded asylum from the sultan. His ego still inflated, he wrote to the Ottoman ruler that he came not as a vassal seeking succor, but as a "dispossessed sovereign ready to negotiate an alliance with the Porte."[13] The sultan was not impressed. After first interning Bonneval at Sarajevo, the Porte ordered the local pasha to take him to the Hungarian border and turn him over to Habsburg authorities. But Bonneval again avoided his would-be captors by the clever expedient of converting to Islam; as a Moslem, he became a subject of the defender of the faithful and deserving of his protection. Bonneval wrote to Voltaire, "Either I would lose my head or cover it with a turban."[14] To a man as dedicated to this life and as vague about the next as he, the turban was the only alternative.

After his conversion, Bonneval became an adviser to the Ottoman government in matters both military and diplomatic. Being an able practitioner of the warfare of his day, he tried to introduce Western training in the Turkish army. He achieved only limited success, but Vienna still regarded him as highly dangerous in the service of a potential foe. Habsburg agents tried first to limit his influence at the Porte by heaping discredit upon his name and then to eliminate him altogether through the delicate art of poisoning.[15] At first the Hofkriegsrat allowed the Venetians to try their hand at doctoring his food and, when they failed, employed an engineer named Caroli, who had accompanied Bonneval to Turkey, to do the same. Caroli proposed to poison him by mixing diamond dust in his potage (delicately referred to in the diplomatic dispatches as a "piece of bread"). This plan also failed, and the Hofkriegsrat, fearful that the Turks might discover the plot, did not try again.[16] Bonneval continued to intrigue against the House of Habsburg and to serve his new lord until his death in 1747.

Although Austro-Turkish relations proper produced little of importance in the 1720s and early 1730s, another diplomatic development was to have a profound impact on Vienna's Turkish policy for the remainder of the century: the Austro-Russian alliance of 1726. As mentioned before, the Austrians had developed a growing suspicion of Russia, not only regarding its designs in southeastern Europe but in central Europe as well. In the 1720s, however, Vienna's statesmen recognized that this new power could be a valuable aid in their policies toward other western European states. Harnessed to Habsburg interests, Russia could considerably strengthen the Monarchy's position in both central and western Europe, and at the same time Vienna could keep a watchful eye on the tsar's policies there. Such an arrangement, however advantageous in the West, would have to apply to southeastern Europe as well, and there it would enhance the danger of the tsar using it to draw Austria into a Turkish war, a war that could lead to Russian penetration of the Balkans and the very conditions against which the Privy Conference had warned in the previous decade. If that happened,

Vienna would have to decide whether the alliance were sufficiently valuable to allow Russian aggrandizement at the expense of the Ottoman Empire. But that decision would depend on conditions that did not exist in 1724, when the talks that would lead to the Austro-Russian alliance began.

Negotiations with Russia had become desirable in that year because Austria had run afoul of its traditional friends, Britain and the Dutch Republic. London was annoyed at the emperor for his reluctance to approve the formal cession of the old Swedish possessions of Verden and Bremen to the British monarch, and both London and The Hague expressed concern about the founding of the Ostend Company, which they believed threatened their domination of the East Indian trade. With France and Spain still hostile toward Austria (the Austro-Russian talks began before the Austro-Spanish reconciliation in 1725), the growing rivalry with Britain and the Dutch Republic meant to the conference that "affairs have reached the point where the Emperor does not have one single good friend left."[17] To remedy this situation, the conference suggested an alliance with Russia. When the emperor agreed, the chancellor, Count Ludwig Philip Sinzendorf, began negotiations with the Russian ambassador. For some time little progress was made, however, largely because of the continued opposition of Prince Eugene, who still distrusted the motives of Peter the Great.[18]

In mid-1725 the pace of the discussions quickened as the international situation grew graver. In April of that year Austria concluded the alliance and marriage contract with Spain. The reaction of the other powers was swift and threatening. Britain, France, and Prussia formed the Alliance of Herrenhausen to oppose Austria and Spain and set out to persuade as many other states as possible to join them. In November 1725 a British merchant named Matthew Avison arrived in Vienna and asked for a passport to Belgrade from the Hofkriegsrat. The Hofkriegsrat gave him the document but soon after received word from the Austrian resident at the Porte that the fellow was carrying important papers for the British ambassador in Constantinople, who had scheduled an audience with the grand vizier. The Austrian guessed that the papers contained an invitation to the Porte to become affiliated with the Alliance of Herrenhausen. On the basis of this information, the commander at Belgrade arrested Avison, confiscated his dispatches, and sent them to Vienna. They showed that London was indeed trying to persuade the Porte to cast its lot with the anti-Austrian alliance and "insinuating to the Turks to undertake measures disadvantageous and harmful not only to the interests of His Imperial Majesty but to all Christianity."[19]

The Habsburg ministers, led by Prince Eugene again, immediately set out to counter the British threat. While strengthening the army remained as always the foremost task, the recruitment of allies came close behind. And none was more needed than Russia. Russia could not only provide aid in case of a Turkish attack, but could also put pressure on Prussia and threaten the predominance of the British and the Dutch in the Baltic Sea.[20] Consequently, negotiations with the Russians began in earnest. The talks proceeded throughout the spring and summer of 1726 until the treaty was concluded in Vienna on 6 August. Defensive in nature, it provided that each state assist the other with 30,000 men in case of attack by a foreign power.[21] The purpose of the treaty was to protect Austria from the Alliance of Herrenhausen, and it at least helped to do so. Within three months Prussia withdrew from the Alliance, its king troubled by his opposition to the emperor, seduced by promises of territorial gain in western Germany, and concerned by the Austro-Russian accord. Without Prussia, the Alliance of Herrenhausen appeared significantly less formidable to Vienna.

For our purposes, however, the important question is not the impact of the Austro-Russian accord on events in western Europe, but what it meant regarding the Ottoman Empire. It provided, of course, for mutual assistance should the Porte attack either Austria or Russia. Yet, any border incident could be interpreted as an overt Ottoman attack, and then Austro-

Russian armies could justifiably march into Ottoman territory. Was it then a veiled offensive alliance against Turkey?
For Austria in 1726, the answer was "no." In fact, Eugene
had requested that the treaty specifically exclude military cooperation against the Ottoman Empire. Without such a provision, he feared that the agreement would prompt the Porte
to join the Alliance of Herrenhausen—precisely what he hoped
to prevent. Even as he prepared the army for possible duty in
the west, he sent a personal message to the grand vizier:
"Whereas it is true that His Imperial Majesty is recruiting
soldiers to put his army on a war footing, he has no thought
of beginning a war against the Porte."[22] When the grand
vizier replied that he too wished only peace and friendship,
Eugene was delighted; he dropped his insistence on excluding
the Ottoman Empire from the treaty not only because of Russian objections but also because he believed that war would
not occur anyway. After the conclusion of the treaty, he ordered the Austrian representative in Constantinople to tell the
grand vizier specifically that it in no way endangered the
friendly Ottoman relations with both Austria and Russia.[23]

Despite Eugene's confidence that war with Turkey was unlikely for the present, the treaty still contained implications
for the future. After all, it did provide for common defense
against an aggressor. If the Ottomans attacked Russia—or if
the Russians insisted that they had—Austria would be obli-
gated to come to its ally's aid. The only alternative would be
to void the alliance, thus incurring Russian wrath, a step that
could be taken only when Austria felt secure in its relations
with the other European powers. Whatever the original intention, the alliance could be easily transformed by either
party into an offensive agreement directed against Turkey.

For the time being, however, all of Vienna's attention focused on unraveling the complicated situation in the West.
By 1731 it was finally resolved. The Austro-Spanish accord
was void, good relations—even alliances—with the Seapowers
restored, and the internal affairs of the Holy Roman Empire
pacified. Indeed Austrian diplomacy seemed to be riding a

crest of success; potential enemies were frustrated and friends secured.[24]

In 1733 and 1734, however, this diplomatic prosperity proved a chimera. In February 1733 Augustus the Strong, king of Poland and elector of Saxony, expired, inaugurating another of the many Polish succession crises. The prime candidate to succeed him was Stanislaus Leszczyński, king of Poland under the auspices of Charles XII from 1704 to 1709 and father-in-law of King Louis XV of France. Vienna was much distressed at the prospect of Leszczyński's becoming king, for fear that Poland would then be irrevocably tied to the always dangerous French foreign policy. To contest his election, Austria joined with Prussia and Russia in offering the Poles an alternative candidate, Augustus of Saxony, son of the late king and husband of one of the daughters of Joseph I. The three powers made it clear to Versailles, Leszczyński, and the Polish electors that they would support their nominee with force if necessary. Unfortunately, the threat had precisely the opposite effect from that intended. In September 1733 the outraged Poles met for the traditional election and, in open defiance of the allies, unanimously proclaimed Leszczyński their choice. True to their word, the allies immediately authorized the sending of Russian troops into the country, secured the election of Augustus by a few Polish malcontents, and ejected Leszczyński from Poland altogether.

The Austrian policy-makers hoped that the French would respond to the affair with nothing more than loud protests about insults to their queen's father, but their hopes were ill-founded. Instead of allowing the matter to pass, Versailles used the expulsion of Leszczyński as an excuse to invade the Rhenish provinces of the Empire while France's allies, the Spaniards and the Savoyards, marched into the Habsburg possessions in Italy. Thus began the War of the Polish Succession. At that moment, when it was needed the most, Austria's carefully constructed system of alliances fell apart. Britain and the Dutch Republic, instead of honoring their treaty obligations, proclaimed neutrality; the Prussians, although a party to the deposition of Leszczyński, stalled in sending their troops to the Rhine and in the end contributed little effective aid. The only ally willing to do its part was Russia, which not only secured Poland for Augustus but sent 10,000 soldiers to reinforce the Austrians in Germany. Nonetheless, deserted by most of its supporters, the Monarchy was compelled to fight defensive wars in both Germany and Italy and eventually had to cede a considerable amount of Italian territory to restore peace.

One of Vienna's fears during the War of the Polish Succession was, as one might expect, an attack by the Ottoman Empire. When the conflict began, Eugene dispatched a personal letter to the grand vizier explaining Austrian policy and assuring him that Vienna had no hostile intentions toward Turkey and would make certain that the new king of Poland had none either. He also promised the Porte that the entry of Russian troops into Poland was not a prelude to Russian occupation of that country, and that they would withdraw as soon as Augustus's succession was secure.[25] Despite Eugene's concern, Ottoman involvement in the conflict was most unlikely. The Porte's intermittent struggle with Persia took a decided turn for the worse in the early 1730s, when, revived by an adventurer who took the name Nadir Shah, the Persians expelled the Turks from previously conquered lands and threatened to make substantial inroads into Ottoman territory. Faced by the problems in the East, the grand vizier echoed the prince's request for peace and assured him that the sultan did not intend to mix in Polish affairs.[26]

Yet a real danger of war with Turkey did exist because of the ambitions of Austria's only loyal ally, Russia. Since the late 1720s Russian foreign policy had been the province of Count Heinrich Ostermann, a Westphalian who had risen in the service during the reign of Peter the Great. Ostermann dreamed of achieving an important goal that had eluded his former master: acquisition of the northern coast of the Black Sea. In the early 1730s Ostermann believed his aim realizable. The Ottoman Empire was severely weakened by the war against Persia; Sweden and Poland were no longer serious threats in the north; and the Habsburg Monarchy was an ally. If the Turks could in some way be blamed for an act of aggression, Ostermann could call upon Vienna to honor its obligations under the treaty of 1726, and together Russian and Austrian forces would establish that long-desired Russian foothold on the Black Sea.

The incident Ostermann needed to precipitate his war occurred in June 1733. The Tartar army of the khan of the Crimea, on its way to reinforce the Turks on the Persian front, passed through Daghestan, a province on the western shore of the Caspian Sea claimed by Russia and occupied by Russian troops. When the Tartar and Russian soldiers exchanged shots, Ostermann was ready to declare war on the grounds that Ottoman subjects had violated Russian territory and murdered Russian citizens. Before doing so, however, he had to know if Austria would lend the required aid; therefore he instructed his ambassador in Vienna to broach the question to the Habsburg officials.[27]

As one might expect, the thought of a conflict with the Ottoman Empire just when the War of the Polish Succession was beginning appalled the Austrians. They ardently wished to avoid, not to incite, a struggle with the Turks. Consequently, they notified the Russian ambassador in no uncertain terms that they would aid his country against Turkey only if the sultan interfered on the side of their enemies in Poland. As to far-off Daghestan, the emperor would offer his services in resolving the problem peacefully but would under no circumstances provide military support.[28] Faced with such a resounding Austrian rejection, Ostermann decided not to exploit the issue for the time being. Besides, now he too had to turn his attention to the increasingly serious Polish crisis.

In 1735 the Turks provided Ostermann with a second pretext for war by ordering another Tartar march through Daghestan. By this time the Polish war was close to an end, so Ostermann resolved to act first, before asking for support—or advice—from his allies. In late autumn Russian troops

advanced toward the Crimea, where they planned to lay waste
the Tartar homeland while its defenders were occupied with
the Persians. The effort was a total failure, for the arrival of
winter compelled the Russians to withdraw before they reached
even the entrance to the peninsula. Nonetheless, news of the
operation made it known to all of Europe that Russia intended a full-scale campaign against the Ottoman Empire in
1736. In February of that year Ostermann, in the name of
his sovereign, Tsarina Anne, informed the Austrian ambassador that a Russo-Turkish war was inevitable and inquired
what steps the emperor would take to assist his ally.[29] As in
1715, Vienna was entangled by treaty commitments and had
to determine whether it was in the Monarchy's interest to
abide by them.

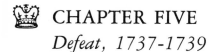 **CHAPTER FIVE**
Defeat, 1737-1739

Like the fundamental issue, the conditions facing the Habsburg policy-makers in 1736 were in many ways similar to those in 1715. Austria was just completing a succession war with France, its treasury was seriously depleted, and its army weakened. Although the fighting in the War of the Polish Succession had ended, the final peace settlement had not been signed, and Vienna feared a resumption of hostilities if the negotiators failed to reach agreement. As in 1715, the Ottoman Empire had not injured Austria directly and seemed to have no intention of doing so. This time no emissary was sent to Vienna, but the Porte repeatedly emphasized to Leopold von Talman, son of the earlier resident and resident himself since 1728, that it wished ardently to avoid any difficulties with the emperor.[1]

There were also, however, some differences. The Porte had not overtly attacked Russia as it had Venice in 1715 and in fact was as anxious to avoid trouble with Russia as it was with Austria. No Russian land was in serious danger of being invaded by the Ottomans, no treaty was violated, and little chance existed that the Porte would turn on Austria. To Vienna and to most of Europe the crisis seemed of Russian, not Ottoman, creation; thus, Vienna could justifiably deny aid to St. Petersburg on the grounds that its ally was engaged in an offensive war, not a defensive one.

On the other hand, this war offered opportunity—as much if not more than the conflict of twenty years earlier. For one thing, this time the Monarchy could fight at the side of a much stronger ally, while the Turks appeared more feeble than ever. In 1732 Count Luigi Ferdinando Marsigli had published a two-volume analysis of Ottoman power in which he concluded that the military establishment had declined to

such a point that the sultan's European possessions were ripe
for the plucking. If Turkey's neighbors would end their animosity toward one another, he wrote, they could relegate "the
impious Moslem sect to the extremities of Arabia" freeing
from Islam not only the European lands but Asia Minor as
well. "Given the slight resistance the [Ottoman] militia can
offer and the state of Ottoman finances, they have only to
march, and, without fighting, each has only to occupy that
part assigned to him by a [future] treaty of alliance."[2] In
1736 Talman endorsed this view of Turkish military weakness and warned that, if allowed to do so, the Russian army
could push the Turks south of the Danube in one campaign.[3]
These assessments were not speculation only; the Turks were
just completing their disastrous war with Persia, which had
resulted in the loss of all the Ottoman conquests made during
the 1720s in the East and had wreaked havoc on the Turkish
army. In early 1736 the Hofkriegsrat learned that the Ottoman position had become so precarious that the sultan had
issued orders to his European pashas to prepare "every man
capable of carrying a weapon" for possible duty in the East.[4]

Although the Austrian army had displayed some weaknesses in fighting against western European foes during the
War of the Polish Succession, no one doubted that it would
defeat the badly battered Turks. Besides, the army now enjoyed the use of mighty Belgrade, which, newly fortified and
populated with German citizens, provided a magnificent base
of operations in the Balkans. Moreover, Austrian control of
the Banat, northern Serbia, and Little Walachia—along with
the construction of a river fleet—guaranteed the security of
much of the Danube by which supplies could go practically
unhindered to columns heading east.

If the military possibilities seemed attractive, the diplomatic situation appeared no less so. While the final settlement of the War of the Polish Succession remained under
discussion, negotiations were proceeding well, and Vienna
knew that renewed trouble with France, while possible, was
unlikely.[5] In the summer of 1736, even Poland seemed des-

tined to quiet down when a "pacifications parliament" accepted Augustus of Saxony as king. Of the other powers, Spain appeared content since the queen, Elizabeth Farnese, had successfully exploited the War of the Polish Succession to secure the kingdoms of Sicily and Naples for one of her sons. As to the Seapowers, neither seemed interested in becoming involved in southeastern Europe beyond offering to serve as mediator between belligerents. In sum, conditions in 1736 seemed favorable for the Austrians to attack the Turks and to extend Habsburg hegemony farther into the Balkans.

Given such inducements, it has often been assumed that Vienna chose to go to war primarily for territorial gain, and there were voices in Habsburg officialdom encouraging such a course. One of the most prominent was Talman, who proposed to the Hofkriegsrat a plan of operations designed to capture all the Ottoman land west of a line running from Ruse on the Danube to Thessaloniki on the Aegean Sea. "Such a border would place the kingdom of Serbia, the greatest part of the kingdom of Bulgaria, the kingdom of Macedonia, Turkish Dalmatia, the whole kingdom of Bosnia, the provinces of Albania, Epirus, Thessaly, Achaya, etc. under the dominion of the emperor."[6] There is no evidence, however, that the Privy Conference considered Talman's plan seriously. Whenever it discussed annexations, the members spoke of compensating the emperor for his sacrifices rather than of extending the Monarchy's frontiers as far as possible.

Essentially, Charles and his ministers were not ready to consider aggrandizement seriously at this time, regardless of how attractive the opportunities might seem. The military defeats, financial sacrifices, and diplomatic rebuffs of the War of the Polish Succession had deeply disappointed the Viennese policy-makers, and they were most reluctant to embark on any further adventures. They hoped instead for a period of calm to assess the damage suffered in the last struggle and to correct the weaknesses that it had revealed in the Austrian army and foreign policy. These concerns clearly offset the favorable military and diplomatic conditions the Russo-Turkish clash offered; the Austrians were not prepared to embark on another Turkish war.

Yet other reasons seemed to compel Austria to participate in the struggle. In the mind of the emperor's secretary and chief foreign-policy adviser, Johann Christoph Bartenstein, participation in the conflict was necessary to preserve the Russian alliance. To him, the War of the Polish Succession had especially revealed the fundamental weaknesses of the alliance system Vienna had so carefully constructed in the early 1730s. Without Russia, the emperor would have had to fight his western enemies alone and probably would have suffered even greater losses than he did. In 1736 St. Petersburg still represented Austria's only loyal ally, and Bartenstein feared that this ally too would be lost if Vienna refused outright to help in the Turkish war. Without Russia, Austria would find itself diplomatically isolated, a condition Bartenstein greatly feared since, although peace negotiations were progressing satisfactorily, his state was still formally at war with France.

Moreover, Bartenstein, like his predecessors, was suspicious of Russian intentions. On the basis of the dispatches from the Habsburg ambassador in St. Petersburg, he could not judge the extent of the Russians' ambitions, but he believed that they wanted more from this war than merely retribution for a Tartar incursion into Daghestan. While pleased with the Russians as allies, he also feared their penetrating the Balkans and establishing a common Austro-Russian boundary that could cause friction between the two powers. Specifically, he did not want them gaining influence in Moldavia and Walachia, the two provinces bordering Habsburg Transylvania and Little Walachia. As he explained to the Austrian ambassador at the tsarist court, "One would rather have the Turks as neighbors than an ally so steadfastly loyal [as Russia]."[7] This refrain nicely summarized the thoughts of those policy-makers before Bartenstein and those who would appear throughout the remainder of the century.

Bartenstein's task, as he saw it, was to keep the Monarchy uncommitted as long as possible while he strove to find out the extent of Russian war aims. He had to make certain, however, that St. Petersburg did not get the impression that Vienna was about to renege on its treaty obligations. He could not allow the Russian alliance to dissolve.

Bartenstein tried a variety of stratagems to discover his ally's intentions, none of which was successful. He first offered Vienna's mediation; if the Russians accepted, diplomatic practice would require them to submit their war aims to the mediator. In the event the offer was rejected, the secretary could assume that St. Petersburg had far more in mind than simple revenge for a Tartar raid.[8] But Bartenstein soon discovered that he had a wily and secretive sparring partner in Ostermann. The Russian minister did not accept or reject Austrian mediation; he sidestepped it, remarking that Austria was beginning to sound untrustworthy as an ally.[9] The initial effort having failed, Bartenstein next suggested a plan of military cooperation, even specifying how Austria and Russia might divide the lands conquered.[10] Although this document leaves the impression that Bartenstein contemplated a war of conquest, he did not. He intended to draw out of the Russians an expression of their war aims. The goals he proposed for Austria did not conform to those later discussed in the Privy Conference, and he purposely omitted mention of Moldavia and Walachia, hoping to discover whether Russian designs included these provinces.

This effort was no more successful than the first. Ostermann did not respond with his own war aims, but remarked that the proposal looked like a new treaty—which, he noted, would be unnecessary if the emperor simply fulfilled his obligations under the treaty of 1726. As to ultimate Russian objectives, he only commented that, when it came time to make peace, the Tsarina Anne "would astound the world with the moderation of her demands."[11]

Bartenstein was thwarted again. The only path remaining seemed to be a firm commitment to aid Russia in the forthcoming conflict. Yet the decision was not his alone. Only the emperor could make war, and he would not do so without the advice of the full Privy Conference. In early September 1736 the conference members gathered to decide the question. Most favored war, largely because they agreed with Bartenstein on the need to retain the Russian alliance and because they assumed that the Habsburg army could defeat the Turks with ease. They did, however, insist that the war last but one campaigning season. The condition of the army and finances demanded that Vienna seek peace after one year's fighting. Such a condition did not seem restrictive at the time, for all assumed that quick Austrian victories would bring the Turks rapidly to terms.[12] Armed with the approval of the conference and the emperor, Bartenstein could now promise the Russians full support in return—he hoped—for a list of their war aims.

What seems so remarkable about this episode is that Austria would commit itself to war as a diplomatic device to discover Russia's intentions. Given the results of the struggle—three painful years of disappointment—the decision seems absurd. To fight on the side of a friend in hopes of finding out what he is fighting for might be acceptable in a tavern, but it appears woefully out of place in the supposedly cautious realm of foreign policy.

One should not, however, condemn Bartenstein and his colleagues out of hand. Their decision was understandable given the information available to them. If the Turks were as weak as Vienna believed, Russia could indeed defeat them easily and advance to the Danube. Moreover, an Austrian refusal to help St. Petersburg might lead the tsarina to break her alliance with the emperor. Vienna was fully aware that a faction at the Russian court was pressing her to abandon Austria for France and would welcome any chance to discredit the emperor in her eyes. If Bartenstein erred seriously, it might have been in his overestimating Russia's value as an ally. St. Petersburg in fact played no role in the Austro-French negotiations concluding the War of the Polish Succession, and there is no evidence that the results would have been different had the Austro-Russian accord dissolved.

Moreover, the expenditure of manpower and resources during the Turkish war made Austria far more vulnerable to Prussia's assault in 1740, and then, when Austria really needed help, Russia did not come to its rescue anyway.

For better or worse, the decision was made, and the ministers began the diplomatic and military preparations necessary for war. The most important was to conclude a pact with Russia that would provide for joint operations. With Vienna committed to the conflict, Bartenstein no longer saw the need to procure a formal list of his ally's war aims because he now believed Russian aggrandizement could be controlled through the mutual planning of the army officers. Omitting any mention of future annexations, the Austrians and Russians concluded on 9 January 1737 an agreement providing for coordinated offensives, exchanges of information, and promises of help in case the Turks attacked one ally with all of their might while leaving only a token force to face the other.[13]

Bartenstein next set out to recruit other allies. The two most likely candidates were the erstwhile members of the Holy League, Poland and Venice. Poland, however, was still recovering from its succession crisis, and King Augustus III, while grateful for Austrian and Russian aid in securing his throne for him, had no intention of risking his tenuous popularity by engaging in a war, even with the infidel. Venice also declined to help because the Senate still resented what it regarded as shabby treatment by the emperor at Passarowitz. Two other sources offered aid. Still infected by the crusading spirit of Clement XI, Pope Clement XII levied a five-year tithe on all Church lands in the Austrian crownlands and contributed additional sums directly from the Vatican treasury. The Diet of the Holy Roman Empire offered 3,000,000 gulden, and some of the smaller German states provided contingents of armed men, although they were to receive their pay and supplies from the Monarchy.[14]

The contributions of the pope and the Holy Roman Empire indicated that the old hatred of the Turks as the dangerous infidels was still alive. In the Habsburg lands, the traditional measures to inspire the people were decreed, including the *Türkenglocken*, the bells rung throughout the land at seven o'clock each morning calling upon the people to pray for a Christian victory over the Moslems.[15] This war would be the last, however, in which such measures would be used; by the next one, they would be considered unenlightened.

Meanwhile, the Hofkriegsrat continued military preparations. Despite the defeats of the War of the Polish Succession, the armed forces were in rather good condition, especially financially. Somewhat to Vienna's surprise, the estates of the crownlands expressed enthusiasm for the struggle, probably because they, like the ministers, believed success would come easily and quickly against the enfeebled Turks. They even voted extra monies, which, along with the grants from the Papacy and the Holy Roman Empire, made the recruitment of men and the purchase of supplies relatively easy.[16]

For the military, the major problem was finding a commander-in-chief. During the previous thirty-five years Vienna had experienced no such difficulty; the choice had always been Prince Eugene. In April 1736, however, the great man had died, and now Charles had to find his replacement among those who had campaigned under his leadership. The choice fell upon Field Marshal Friedrich Heinrich von Seckendorf, sixty-three years old, "a small man, devoid of grace or charm, but intelligent, tough, and endowed with an immense capacity for work."[17] Seckendorf seemed an excellent choice. Not only was he a student of the prince, he was a capable diplomat and an experienced field officer, once described as "one of the best and most effective generals in the imperial army."[18] But he possessed two notable weaknesses: acerbity and an intense dislike of restrictions on his authority, both of which seriously affected his performance in 1737.

Realizing that Seckendorf's appointment would cause ill will among other senior officers who believed that they should have the supreme command, Charles ordered the field marshal to follow a prearranged campaign plan and to consult his fellow officers on all matters requiring major decisions. Seckendorf expressed outrage at these limitations and set out immediately to circumvent them. Without asking his officers or the government, he announced at the beginning of the campaign that he would not lead his army to the fortress of Vidin on the Danube as the Hofkriegsrat had suggested, but instead to Nis on a tributary of the Morava. By the time the news reached Vienna, no orders could be sent to countermand Seckendorf's decision, for the army would already be underway before such orders reached him. The emperor and his advisers could only hope that the field marshal's strategy would prove sound. [19]

At first it seemed that the plan was brilliant. When Seckendorf's forces arrived before Nis, the Ottoman commander surrendered without offering any resistance. With the fortress secure, the field marshal could now advance either on Vidin, at the time lightly garrisoned and inadequately provisioned, or on Sofia along the road to Constantinople. Either choice would have caused the Turks problems in organizing defenses and in maintaining morale. Seckendorf chose neither; he preferred instead to wait at Nis for the Turks to come to him. Almost two months passed in inactivity until news reached the army that one of the subordinate corps operating in Bosnia had suffered a defeat. Despite reassurances from the scene that the setback was not a critical one, Seckendorf left Nis in the hands of a small garrison and marched his army into Bosnia. He encountered no Turkish units of any size, but in his absence the Turks found Nis seriously undermanned. After a few days' siege by a substantial army under the personal command of the grand vizier, the Austrian commander surrendered Nis and with it the only Austrian success of 1737. [20]

While the Austrians wasted their advantages in Serbia, a peace conference attended by Habsburg, Ottoman, and Russian delegates gathered at the Polish town of Nemirov. The conference was a legacy of Bartenstein's effort to use mediation to discover Russia's war aims, and, although nothing was concluded, the deliberations at last revealed those long-sought-after Russian goals. They included precisely what Bartenstein

feared they would: expansion to the Black Sea and a protectorate over Moldavia and Walachia.[21] The Habsburg delegates made clear Vienna's position on such claims immediately, rejecting the Russian demands even before the Turks
could respond. With the Austrians and Russians in disagreement and the Turks sensing a rift between their enemies, a
peace treaty was not possible at Nemirov. In October the
Ottoman delegates finally ended the pointless meetings by
walking out of them.[22]

The collapse of the Congress of Nemirov meant that the
war would continue into 1738, and for Vienna that was a
serious blow. This short war, fought primarily to show good
faith to the Russians, appeared to be evolving into a serious
and protracted struggle. Such a result the emperor and his
ministers ardently wished to avoid. Upon hearing of the collapse of the congress, Bartenstein and his colleagues agreed
that all territorial demands must be dropped and that peace
should be sought purely on the principle of *status quo ante
bellum*.[23] These decisions reached, Bartenstein began to search
for another channel through which to keep the peace talks
going. He found it in mid-November when the king of France
offered to mediate. The Habsburg ministers joyfully accepted
the king's proposal, for they believed that his agents would
have a very good chance of working out a satisfactory arrangement. Vienna was by now on excellent terms with Versailles
and knew that, of all the European powers, the Ottomans
trusted France the most. The only possible obstacle would be
Russian reluctance to accept the French offer, but Bartenstein
believed that, by appealing to Ostermann's good sense, he
could convince St. Petersburg to do so.[24] The Russians did
agree but only after chastising Vienna for accepting the proposal without asking them for approval first.

Despite French diplomatic intervention, there was no peace
in 1738. To everyone's surprise, the Porte wanted to continue
the conflict. Inspired by their successful blunting of the Austrian offensive in 1737, the Turks sensed that in the next
campaign they might be able to carry the war to Austrian

and perhaps even to Russian territory. In December 1737 Sultan Mahmud I appointed as grand vizier his most warlike counselor, Jegen (Devil) Mehmed. Jegen Mehmed believed the emperor's forces weaker and more accessible than those of the tsarina and so decided to launch his major offensive against the Habsburgs. By initiating raids in January and February 1738, he even violated military custom by not waiting until late spring before beginning operations. Here was someone the Austrians would find difficult to discourage.

When it became obvious that the conflict would not be resolved in the spring of 1738, Vienna became resigned to another year of war, and the search began for a new commander-in-chief. The emperor and his ministers hoped to find someone who would have a less difficult personality than Seckendorf and who would, at the same time, be willing to press the offensive. The Turks might be reluctant to come to the peace table now, but, as past experience indicated, one major victory would render them anxious for a settlement. The man selected was Count Lothair Josef Königsegg, another of Prince Eugene's understudies but one who had served the imperial house more notably in diplomatic than military roles.[25] Königsegg fully appreciated the seriousness of his task and wished above all to avoid disgracing himself and his master's arms. Consequently, he tended to be cautious, so cautious in fact that he studiously avoided taking advantage of opportunities that presented themselves.

When Königsegg reached his headquarters, his first task was to lift the Turkish siege of New Orsova, an island fortress in the Danube halfway between Belgrade and Vidin. On the march to his objective he met a major Turkish force at the village of Cornea, some thirty miles north of New Orsova. In the ensuing battle the Austrians inflicted such a crushing defeat upon the Turks that they abandoned their supply train, fled back across the Danube, and gave up the siege. His army inspired by the victory, Königsegg was now in a position to cross the Danube and either to search out the main Turkish army or to besiege Vidin itself. Yet at this point his resolve

failed. Fearful that he might have to fight another battle in
which the outcome might be less fortunate, he decided to
retreat. Neither the protests of his officers nor a second victory over a large Turkish force could alter his intention. He
withdrew farther up the Danube and for the remainder of the
campaign scrupulously avoided contact with the enemy.

Vienna felt at a loss. For the second year in a row a Habsburg commander had begun with a victory and wasted it by
his own indecisiveness or timidity. Moreover, the army was
now being steadily weakened not by enemy action but by
plague. Königsegg's persistent marching and camping about
the Danube marshes had exhausted his men, and more and
more were falling ill. Conditions became so bad that headquarters ordered the construction of special camps for the
plague-ridden, 1,000 steps away from the healthy troops, and
the burning of all possessions belonging to the dead. These
measures retarded but did not halt the epidemic, and soon
officers and men from throughout the Monarchy were ordered
to Hungary to replenish the depleted ranks.[26]

By the end of 1738 Vienna was becoming frantic to restore
peace. The finance minister, Gundaker Starhemberg, remarked: "The condition of things is as bad as could be. The
crownlands are desolate, the treasury deep in debt. One can
do nothing against the Turks. If one battle is lost, all is lost.
It would be a stroke of good luck to make peace by any
means. In another campaign Austria could win nothing, but
might lose everything."[27] Most of the Habsburg statesmen
essentially agreed with Starhemberg, although not with his
eschatological vision. They decided that simple *status quo ante
bellum* might be insufficient to coax a settlement from the
Turks. Consequently, in March 1739 Vienna advised the able
French mediator, Marquis Louis Sauveur de Villeneuve, that
the emperor would return Austrian Serbia and Little Walachia to the sultan in exchange for peace.[28] If accepted, the
proposal would leave Belgrade as the sole Habsburg possession on the Serbian side of the Danube.

By late spring it appeared that the Turks would accept

these conditions, especially since they were accompanied by a Russian offer to restore peace without annexations. The bellicose, but arrogant and self-righteous Jegen Mehmed had fallen from power and had been succeeded by a grand vizier who wished to end the war. The conflict also placed severe internal strains upon the Ottoman regime, and by 1739 the Turks had had enough. All the parties now wanted peace, but to translate that desire into reality—to coordinate proposals, select a conference site, and carry out negotiations— required time, too much time to prevent the onset of another campaigning season. Since none of the parties seemed agreeable to an armistice while discussions proceeded, one more summer of fighting was necessary—a summer in which each hoped to gain some advantage that could be exploited at the conference table.

Reluctantly, Vienna pulled its armies together for another campaign. Sorting through his senior generals for another and, he hoped, better commander-in-chief, Charles selected Count Oliver Wallis, a sixty-five-year-old Irishman with forty years of service to the Habsburgs. While possessing the necessary experience and rank for the job, Wallis regrettably was as jealous of his power as Seckendorf, as unsure of himself as Königsegg, and more secretive and arrogant than both. When the staff officers at the Hofkriegsrat composed a plan of operations for 1739, Wallis objected vehemently on the grounds that he wanted no restrictions on his freedom of choice. When he arrived at his headquarters in Hungary, however, he notified the Hofkriegsrat that he would not allow a single soldier to decamp without specific instructions from Vienna.[29] The orders were sent immediately, but the senior officers and statesmen could only wonder if this campaign would achieve any better results than the others.[30]

Wallis's primary objective was to cover Belgrade. Since Königsegg had virtually abandoned Serbia to the Turks, the grand vizier had been able to place his advance units within a day's march of the fortress. To prevent a Turkish siege, Wallis positioned his men just outside the city and attempted to draw the grand vizier into open battle. On 21 July Austrian reconnaissance patrols reported a Turkish force taking up positions on some hills overlooking the Danube at the village of Grocka, about six hours' march from the imperial camp. Afraid that these troops might be preparing forward redoubts for the advance of the Turkish army to Belgrade, Wallis and his officers decided to take the initiative and drive them from the hills. The imperial army left camp in the late evening of 21 July so that it would be in position to attack the next morning. Only later did Wallis discover that the grand vizier at the same time was also moving his main force to Grocka.

The next morning witnessed the most violent clash of this rather uneventful war. The two armies met face-to-face at Grocka and furiously exchanged fire all day. At nightfall, the Turks, battered and bruised, broke off the engagement and withdrew.[31] In the military understanding of the day, the Austrians, despite heavy casualties, had won because they remained in possession of the field. That night a reinforcing corps of 15,000 fresh troops arrived, and the officers pressed Wallis to pursue the Turks down the river and engage them once more. But Wallis refused. Having fought at the center of the action and obviously shaken by the carnage surrounding him, the commander ordered instead a retreat to Belgrade. On his arrival, he learned that a Turkish force of 16,000 men had gathered across the Danube, hoping to harass Austrian supply lines in the Banat. To frustrate this purpose, Wallis led his men across the river where he crushed that force as well. Fearful that the field army was still exposed to Turkish assaults, he did not return to Belgrade as he should have done, but marched his men thirty miles north, crossed the Danube, and then marched them the same thirty miles south again to take up positions across from Belgrade between the Sava and Danube rivers. By placing the army there, Wallis rendered it virtually incapable of protecting Belgrade from a Turkish advance and, at the same time, completely exhausted his men and disgusted his officers. Vienna's hopes for success were shattered again.

Wallis's strategy mystified the emperor and his advisers. His decisions to retreat after Grocka, to leave Belgrade, and to march about the plague-ridden Danube valley seemed irrational. But Vienna feared even worse. Since the onset of the fighting Wallis had possessed the authority to make peace in the field, and, because the French mediator and a Russian delegate were accompanying the grand vizier's army, the Habsburg ministers assumed that Wallis would eventually meet with them and draft a peace treaty. The commander-in-chief's actions, however, suggested to Vienna that he might cede Belgrade to the Ottomans on the grounds that he could not defend it.[32] To prevent such a possibility, the Privy Conference decided to withdraw Wallis's peacemaking authority and transfer it to one of his subordinates, Reinhard Wilhelm Neipperg.

Neipperg seemed a good choice. Having served in Virmond's mission in 1719, he was no stranger to negotiating with the Turks. He was also an experienced field officer and had commanded the 15,000 men who reinforced Wallis the night after Grocka. Both qualities were needed, for Neipperg would not only have to treat with the enemy but would also have to assess the condition of Wallis's forces. This was most important, because the Privy Conference instructed Neipperg to offer concessions on the basis of the army's capacity to continue the war. If it seemed capable of defending Belgrade, he should suggest to the grand vizier only the terms relayed to the French mediator, namely the cession of Austrian Serbia and Little Walachia. If defense seemed problematical, he was to suggest the destruction of Belgrade's modern fortifications in exchange for the razing of those of the Turkish fortress of New Orsova. If the Belgrade garrison itself seemed too weak to resist at all, he should agree "to allow the Turks to have Belgrade with its walls intact, so that the Danube and the Sava become the borders."[33] With these instructions in his saddlebag, Neipperg conducted his tour of inspection and entered the Ottoman camp on 18 August to begin talks.

With Neipperg gone, the conference decided to send another officer, General Samuel von Schmettau, to Hungary to undertake an inspection of his own. Schmettau reported that both the army and the garrison at Belgrade were in remarkably good condition; as if to prove his point, he organized a small force among the garrison soldiers, led them across the Danube, and reestablished Austrian control of some important redoubts that had fallen to the Turks earlier. Inspired by and perhaps jealous of Schmettau's success, Wallis hurried his men back to Belgrade to assist in its defense. It appeared that the decisive battle the Austrians had hoped for was in the offing.

Once again, however, Vienna was disappointed. On 1 September a courier from Neipperg arrived at Schmettau's headquarters in Belgrade and reported that a treaty had been concluded, surrendering Belgrade to the Ottomans. First Schmettau, then the other officers, and finally Vienna were distraught. But there was little they could do. The peace document had been signed by an accredited plenipotentiary of the emperor and guaranteed by an ambassador of the king of France. To repudiate it would constitute a serious snub to Versailles, and Austria was not prepared at the time to weather a diplomatic crisis with the French. Besides, a condition of the preliminary agreement allowed Ottoman forces to take over certain critical points inside Belgrade—the main gates and the powder magazines—within three days of the signing. Thus, by the time the news of the peace reached Vienna, the Turks had already taken up positions inside the walls, rendering Habsburg resistance difficult if not impossible.[34] Serbia, Little Walachia, and Belgrade had fallen to the Turks. Although reconquered once more later in the century, they would never again become part of the Habsburg patrimony.

The obvious question raised by the war of 1737-1739 is why Austria lost. The prospects of victory seemed excellent at its outset. The Turks were weak, Austria's ally was strong, and no threat existed in the West. In a history he wrote for the future Joseph II in 1762, Bartenstein offered one answer: undoubtedly recalling his Thucydides, he told his pupil that the Monarchy had lost because its cause was not just, as it had been in 1715.[35] Perhaps a satisfactory answer in the divine order of things, it nonetheless smacked of Bartenstein's hope in 1762 that Prussia would receive due punishment for (in his eyes) the unjust invasion of Silesia in 1740.

Another explanation attributed failure in the war to faults in the Habsburg system. The most ardent exponent of this opinion was Maria Theresa, who succeeded her father as ruler of the realm the year after the conflict ended and was immediately beset by seemingly insurmountable difficulties. In her *Political Testament* composed during the winter of 1749-1750, she condemned the Austrian practice of appealing to the estates of the crownlands each year for men and money and explained why she instituted her reforms to end that practice. Whereas the system had held together during the War of the Spanish Succession and during the Turkish War of 1716-1718, it had essentially broken down in the 1720s. The long period of peace from 1718 to 1733 had permitted the estates to reassert their power and consequently to deprive the central government of the money and men that it needed to defend the Monarchy. In the wars from 1733 to 1739, "the general calamities became worse because each minister dared not demand additional sacrifices from the crownland in his trust and contented himself with criticizing others at every opportunity."[36]

Maria Theresa's assessment is, however, colored by her own unfortunate experiences in 1740-1745. The army sent forth in each of the campaigns between 1737 and 1739 was reasonably well-supplied and well-armed and of sufficient strength to defeat the Turks. Raising money for the men and equipment had posed problems, but no more so than in any previous war. In a thoughtful memorandum written to Charles within a year of the war's end, Bartenstein commented that the provinces had actually outdone themselves in supporting the war. "The crownlands were exploited, many millions raised at a modest interest, and numerous and large armies raised [from scratch] and partly enlarged; indeed the Monarchy supported Your Imperial Majesty in the last two wars with more vigor than it has ever done before." The failure, Bartenstein suggested, came when the government squandered the people's efforts. "In one word none of your illustrious forebears had access at any time to as much as was produced, was available, and was sacrificed. And in return we were obliged to see ourselves suffer impressive losses in two unfortunate wars." The government had wasted much that the Monarchy could not replace "immediately or even in a short time. The more one examines the detail of the matter, the more one is impressed by the unvarnished truth of this misfortune."[37]

If the central government and not the system failed, then who within the government bore the greatest responsibility for the failure? The most obvious candidates were the military officers: Seckendorf, Königsegg, Wallis, and Neipperg. Indeed these men were blamed at the time. After the first campaign, Seckendorf was arrested and subjected to a formal investigation at which he was charged not only with deliberate irresponsibility to duty but also with conspiracy to withhold supplies from his men in order to sell them later for personal profit.[38] The following year Königsegg escaped any serious reprimand, but at the end of 1738 he was appointed court chamberlain to the empress, a post that made him, according to Frederick the Great, "a eunuch of the palace."[39] In 1739 Wallis and Neipperg were immediately censured for their actions. In a circular explaining the Treaty of Belgrade to all ministers abroad, Charles blamed the former for his failure at Grocka and subsequent indecision and the latter for surrendering Belgrade and allowing enemy soldiers to enter it before receiving official approval from Vienna.[40] Both were imprisoned and, like Seckendorf, brought before an investigative commission. After hearings lasting almost a year, the commission reached no conclusion, and upon her accession, Maria

Theresa pardoned both officers (and Seckendorf) and restored their honors and property.[41]

There can be no doubt that these officers showed remarkably poor judgment in the exercise of their responsibilities, yet this admission provides only a partial explanation. They had various flaws: arrogance, vindictiveness, timidity, reluctance to take advice, and ambition for great responsibility with an unwillingness to exercise it. All these failings contributed in different measure to the mistakes made, but even they do not suffice for a complete answer. There is the hint of another, perhaps more fundamental, reason in the question that frequently appeared in the correspondence of the men at the time: "What would Prince Eugene have done?" It invariably had an accompanying remonstrance: "We must act like Prince Eugene." This was the first war in over thirty years that the Austrians had fought without their premier commander-in-chief, and the prince's ghost haunted all of their decisions. His genius and his successes had seduced the ministers and the generals into believing that any weaknesses in Austrian government or in the army could be overcome simply by vigorous action at the right moment. They failed to realize that the presence of such genius often masks weaknesses that only appear after it is gone. His fellow ministers and officers at times seemed brilliant as long as they could rely upon the prince's ability to correct their errors and upon his prestige to give them confidence. Without him, they were mediocre at best. The defeat suffered in the Turkish war and that suffered at the hands of the Prussians shortly thereafter forced some—notably Maria Theresa—to realize that, in the absence of genius, one must transform those institutions that enfeeble the state and seek out the competent to replace the deficient.

Although Vienna blamed the defeat largely on failings within the government and the military—and correctly so—it also understood that taking Ottoman land was not as easy for either Austria or Russia as originally thought. The talk of conquering the Balkans with 50,000 men faded after 1739;

and, when Frederick invaded Silesia in 1740, one of Vienna's primary concerns again was to prevent the Turks from joining Austria's enemies and inflicting perhaps a crippling blow on the Habsburg state. The Monarchy still could not withstand attacks in the east, west, and north at once.

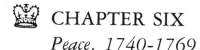

CHAPTER SIX
Peace, 1740-1769

The years 1740 to 1769, while by no means without their times of crisis and concern, represented the longest interval of tranquillity between Austria and Turkey in the eighteenth century. To be sure, on the surface the Ottoman Empire remained Vienna's traditional foe. During the great debates in 1749 concerning the goals of Habsburg foreign policy, many of Maria Theresa's counselors continued to refer to the Turks as Austria's "natural" and "most dangerous" opponents, and in 1755 one of Kaunitz's arguments in favor of an alliance with France was that French influence at the Porte would prevent this implacable enemy from attacking Austria.[1] Moreover, in 1756 when the British ambassador Robert Keith registered disbelief that Maria Theresa was actually negotiating an accord with Versailles, she remarked in the course of the conversation, "I have truly but two enemies whom I really dread, the King of Prussia and the Turks. . . ."[2]

But these sentiments were becoming conventional phrases rather than serious expressions of Habsburg policy. In the debates of 1749 Count Königsegg, while numbering Turkey among Austria's enemies, added: "The Porte in recent times has abjured its eternal strife with the Christians in favor of overriding offers of loyalty and good will so that one can hope that it will not break the peace."[3] At the same time Kaunitz himself expressed doubt that one must always consider the Porte hostile but continued that formulating new policies toward it would be difficult "because it does not act on analyses of the true interests of the state but through fortuitous upheavals, intrigues in the seraglio, or the thoughts of the current grand vizier."[4]

In any case, the invasion of Silesia in late 1740 dramatically vaulted Prussia to the status of Austria's chief enemy.

The two wars it inspired, the War of the Austrian Succession (1740-1748) and the Seven Years' War (1756-1763), dominated Vienna's foreign concerns for thirty years and reduced its policy in the southeast largely to one of preventing the Ottoman Empire from siding with Prussia. As in 1700-1715, Habsburg efforts to maintain good relations with Turkey were successful, and the long period of peace between the two powers established if not feelings of friendship at least those of compatability.

The achievement of keeping the Porte out of the War of the Austrian Succession can in large part be attributed to one of the most knowledgeable and effective Habsburg representatives to serve in Constantinople, Heinrich Christoph Penkler. Like some of his predecessors, Penkler had first traveled to the Ottoman capital as a *Sprachknabe* in the service of Count Virmond in 1719.[5] He remained on the embassy's staff after Virmond's departure and became imperial translator in 1726. After spending the 1730s in Vienna, he served as secretary to Ambassador Corfiz Anton Uhlfeld during his special embassy in 1740-1741 and then remained as resident after Uhlfeld's departure.

Penkler possessed extraordinary gifts as Vienna's envoy. Not only was he well acquainted with the Ottoman language and customs, he also had the rare ability to make friends with many important Ottoman officials. When he returned to Constantinople as Uhlfeld's secretary, he was warmly welcomed by the *reis effendi*, whom he had met during the latter's formal visit to Vienna in 1731 and who not only invited Penkler to his summer home for a private talk but even allowed Penkler's wife to visit his harem, an opportunity permitted to few Western women.[6] During at least two of Penkler's official audiences with the grand vizier and the *reis effendi*, the former dismissed his interpreters in order to converse with Penkler directly, a practice almost unheard of in formal Ottoman receptions.[7] Even Ottoman religious officials became Penkler's associates. In the 1740s one of the chief supporters of Ottoman friendship with Austria was the *seyhulislam*, the principal religious adviser in Constantinople; he kept the resident well informed about events going on behind the scenes at the Porte.

Notwithstanding his friendship with well-placed Ottoman officials, Penkler by no means relied solely on them to keep abreast of Ottoman policy. He recruited paid informants at practically all levels of the Ottoman bureaucracy. Whereas he usually kept the methods employed to gather information out of his dispatches, once in 1746 he told how a contact listened at keyholes and arranged secret meetings as part of an elaborate scheme to find out if the sultan would recognize Maria Theresa's husband as Holy Roman emperor.[8] Penkler had spies in other foreign embassies as well. His reports to the Hofkriegsrat often included copies of correspondence of the British, French, Dutch, Venetian, Saxon-Polish, and Swedish legations. Besides these sources, Penkler also had informants among what one might call the underworld of Ottoman intrigue. He monitored the activities of Bonneval through a number of the latter's servants and especially through a Genoese who was employed as secretary in the Neapolitan legation and who was Bonneval's confidant.[9]

Penkler knew that these people were not always attracted to him by the force of his personality or the worthiness of his mission, for no one appreciated more the venality of the Ottoman court or knew how to use it more effectively. His reports were full of expenses and accounts listing money paid to spies, officials, and hangers-on. On one occasion, in response to a question from Vienna as to whether some diamonds might be sent as gifts to various Turkish officials, Penkler wrote, "In a Christian court one would be honored to receive a precious piece of jewelry, but here everyone wants money because most of the gratuities these ministers pay to the great sultan must be made in money."[10] While Penkler distributed large amounts of cash (10 to 20,000 thalers per year), he expressed considerable contempt for those who accepted his bribes. In one letter he notified Vienna of the appointment of a new *defterdar* (treasurer) who was not a friend of the pro-Austrian *seyhulislam* and thus not likely to remain in his post for long. "In the meantime," he remarked with considerable cynicism, "There is nothing to do but to cultivate him with money and presents just as [we do] all the rest of them."[11] On another occasion he requested an extra 1,000 thalers to add to an earlier 1,000 in order to win some favor from his friend the *reis effendi*, "this well-known money-hungry minister."[12]

After assuming his post in Constantinople, Penkler's most important duty was to monitor and to obstruct French efforts to enlist Ottoman aid against Austria in the War of the Austrian Succession.[13] The task proved easier than one might imagine; Franco-Turkish relations were not particularly good after the Treaty of Belgrade because the French persistently refused throughout the war of 1737-1739 to sign a formal accord with the sultan and because the Porte felt that the French mediator should have secured a more favorable peace with Russia.[14] These relations were not improved by the replacement of the able ambassador, the Marquis de Villeneuve, by the incompetent Michael Ange Castellane, who was intent upon using his post in Constantinople to improve his fortune. Keeping his pocketbook ever in mind, he hesitated to spend money on bribes or gifts, a trait that did not endear him to the Porte.[15] Not until 1747 did Versailles dispatch another official, Roland des Alleurs, to assist Castellane (and to try to loosen his purse strings), but by then the war was practically over.[16]

Although the effectiveness of Penkler's personal diplomacy and the coolness of Franco-Turkish relations played a part in persuading the Porte to avoid the War of the Austrian Succession, undoubtedly the primary reason for its decision was the outbreak of another of its wars with Persia. Although fighting did not erupt until 1743, by 1741 all observers in Constantinople remarked that a conflict between the two Moslem powers was inevitable. Although Uhlfeld completed his mission to settle the border questions in March 1741 (both sides were so anxious to resolve the issues because of other threats that they agreed to a haphazard settlement that required three more years of negotiations to complete and even then caused considerable confusion throughout the remainder of the century), he and his entourage remained in the Turkish capital to catch a glimpse of a huge Persian embassy that arrived in May.[17] This embassy demanded a treaty containing considerable Ottoman concessions, including joint Perso-Turkish "protection" of the Moslem Holy Places. The Porte could never agree to such demands and realized that all the shah wanted was a pretext to open hostilities. Consequently, the Turks desired peace with the Austrians as eagerly as the Austrians desired peace with the Turks. Not only did the Porte quickly reach agreement on the border issues, it also condemned Frederick's invasion of Silesia and refused to recognize Charles VII (Charles Albert of Bavaria) as Holy Roman emperor.[18]

As Austria and Turkey became more deeply involved in their respective wars, relations between the two powers remained uneventful. Then in early 1745 Turkey launched two initiatives that caused considerable surprise in Vienna. The first was an official offer from the sultan to all the belligerents in western Europe to mediate an end to the War of the Austrian Succession; the second was a formal protest from the Porte regarding Maria Theresa's treatment of Jews in Bohemia.

Although it had become customary since Carlowitz for western European powers to mediate disputes between the Turks and their western enemies, no one had even considered the Porte a likely mediator in western European affairs. The reasons were obvious: since the Porte had no permanent representatives at any European court, it was not fully versed in European diplomatic customs and practices, and, as familiar as the Turkish ministers were with the role of belligerent, none had ever served as mediator. Moreover, the Turkish high officials had little or no knowledge of European languages, which meant that they would have to mediate through translators, a handicap of major proportions.

Fully aware of these obstacles to Ottoman mediation—and cognizant that the Porte had never made such a proposal before—Vienna immediately suspected that some intrigue lay behind the offer. Bartenstein, still serving as one of Maria Theresa's chief advisers in foreign affairs, was convinced that he detected a French plot to use the Ottomans to get what Versailles wanted in Germany. If Austria accepted Turkish mediation, he warned, the French would make certain that the Turks supported French demands; if Austria rejected it, Versailles would convince the Porte that the rejection constituted an insult to the sultan's prestige that could be answered only by a Turkish declaration of war on Austria.[19] Others speculated that it was part of some Franco-Swedish scheme to enable the Porte to establish direct correspondence with Berlin which in turn would lead to a Turko-Prussian alliance.[20] In any event, Maria Theresa called it a "really extraordinary" offer that could become "a major event in the universal system of Europe." Although she ordered Penkler to find out more about the move, she never seriously considered accepting it.[21]

While Penkler employed his contacts to discover the source of the offer, Maria Theresa and her advisers sought a way to refuse it without unduly angering the Turks. The solution finally reached was to encourage the Dutch Republic, one of Austria's allies, to reject Turkish mediation; then Maria Theresa could do so as well on the grounds that she could not accept a mediator whom her friends had found unsatisfactory. Agreeing to cooperate, The Hague sent the sultan a document oozing friendship and respect but declining the offer on the grounds that the belligerents had already begun preliminary negotiations which all hoped would lead to a general peace.[22]

After the Dutch response reached Constantinople, Maria Theresa and her advisers dispatched their own rejection. Following the same protestations of friendship as the Dutch communication, the Austrian answer expressed regret that Vienna could not accept Ottoman mediation. Instead of stopping there, however, the note went on to fulminate against the Prussians and to promise no peace until they had been properly punished and Silesia restored to its rightful owner.[23] Penkler was unhappy with the reply, especially with the bellicosity reflected in the anti-Prussian statements, because he feared that the Ottoman ministers would interpret it to mean that Vienna had no confidence in them to achieve an impartial peace. When he met with the grand vizier and the *reis effendi*, he did his best to soften the tone of the letter, but he admitted that he did not know if he succeeded. He confessed that the interview was an unpleasant one and that the *reis effendi* especially believed himself disgraced and his office seriously compromised.[24]

Within a month, however, Penkler reported that the Turkish officials, including the *reis effendi*, were overcoming their damaged pride. The reasons, the Austrian added, seemed to include the liberal gifts that he passed around to soothe Ottoman feelings and, more importantly, bad news from the Persian front. Shortly thereafter, Penkler wrote that the withdrawal of Ottoman forces from Bosnia for service in the east indicated that nothing need be feared in the near future.[25]

The second of the Porte's initiatives in 1745, that protesting Austrian treatment of the Jews in Bohemia, coincided with its effort to mediate. While it was customary for western powers to speak on behalf of Christians in the Ottoman Empire, it was unusual indeed for the Porte to concern itself with the treatment of non-Christians in Christian lands. The protest stemmed from the reception given to Frederick of Prussia by the Jews of Prague when he occupied that city in the summer of 1744—a reception that Maria Theresa considered entirely too warm. To punish them and undoubtedly to fortify her vigorous Roman Catholicism, she decided that all Jews would have to leave Prague by the end of January 1745 and to vacate the rest of Bohemia by June.

In March Penkler reported that the grand vizier had formally remonstrated against the treatment of the expelled Jews in the name of the sultan and had offered them sanctuary in the Ottoman Empire. While his informants speculated that the grand vizier's concern resulted from pressure by Jews in his own household, Penkler thought that monetary concerns might have prompted the protest. "Even if he [the sultan] taxes them only two piasters a head he will get 80,000 more piasters since there are approximately 40,000 Jews."[26]

Whether Penkler believed Maria Theresa's treatment of the Bohemian Jews too harsh or simply hoped to avoid a diplomatic problem, he offered a solution that would ease the Jews' plight and salve his sovereign's Roman Catholic conscience. He informed Vienna that the sultan had recently forbidden Armenian Catholics to attend their churches upon pain of sentencing to the galleys or to the gallows. Since the French, traditional protectors of the Armenians, seemed powerless to do anything about the restriction, Penkler suggested offering the sultan the relaxation of Austrian measures against the Jews in exchange for the relaxation of Ottoman persecution of Armenians. "I see a means to help this people and to restore their religious freedoms: if the Jews of Bohemia are pardoned, in the name of Her Royal Majesty I could intercede [on behalf of the Armenians]."[27]

At first Vienna instructed its envoy to speak for the Armenians without mentioning the Bohemian Jews, for it feared that Austrian recognition of the Porte's complaint would encourage it to assume some sort of protectorate over non-Christian peoples in Austria.[28] Later, however, Maria Theresa ordered Penkler to tell the Porte informally that the Jews could remain in Bohemia for a period to be determined by her, and, even if they did have to move eventually, they would go to settlements in other Austrian lands.[29] Although it may appear that the Ottoman protest influenced Maria Theresa's decision, such was not the case; internal pressure, notably from the Bohemian chancellor Philip Josef Kinsky, was most responsible for saving the Jews from considerable dislocation and distress.[30]

Nevertheless, the willingness of Vienna to respond to the Porte's protest, even in an informal way, opened the door ever so slightly to possible future Ottoman efforts to protect non-

Christian minorities in Christian lands. Had the Porte recognized the potential usefulness of this tiny diplomatic nicety, it might have been able to make Austria and perhaps other western powers uncomfortable when they sought various advantages from the sultans on the grounds of protecting Christians in the Ottoman Empire. Yet, the Porte failed to appreciate the potential benefits of this tactic, and after 1745 there was no evidence that it again tried to intercede on behalf of non-Christians in Austria unless they were Ottoman subjects.

As the Ottoman effort to mediate and the sultan's concern for the Bohemian Jews faded in late 1745, two other matters emerged to tax Penkler's skills. The first involved Habsburg attempts to obtain recognition of Maria Theresa's husband, Francis Stephen of Lorraine, as Holy Roman emperor; the second concerned the negotiation and conclusion of a Turko-Persian peace, which Vienna feared would be a prelude to an Ottoman invasion of Hungary. In both affairs Penkler's principal antagonists were Bonneval and the French ambassador Castellane, and in both the Austrian proved more adroit than either of his foes.

Penkler's efforts to procure the sultan's recognition of Francis Stephen as emperor began as soon as news of the death of Charles VII reached Constantinople in early 1745. Through much of the remaining year, the resident advised Vienna that the Porte was revealing none of its intentions in the matter, but he also warned of endless French efforts to block Ottoman recognition and of their possible success. In late November, however, he reported that the Porte seemed to be growing suspicious of French intrigue and had dropped hints not only that it might recognize Francis Stephen but also that it might be willing to change the time limit of the Treaty of Belgrade from the twenty-seven years prescribed in the document to a permanent peace.[31]

Penkler leaped at this opening and throughout 1746 worked hard to secure the recognition of the emperor and to persuade the Turks to agree to an extension of the treaty. He did encounter a few obstacles. One involved the title "king of Jerusalem," which was part of the long list of titles tradition- ally awarded to a Holy Roman emperor; the Turks objected to it because Jerusalem was an Ottoman possession. A second problem concerned the application of Penkler's suggested words "permanent and eternal" to the Treaty of Belgrade. Whereas the Porte was willing to accept "permanent," it opposed "eternal" as a term with religious meaning and thus unusable in a Moslem agreement with an unbeliever. Penkler, the mas- ter when dealing with the Turks, overcame Ottoman objec- tions to the title by distributing liberal bribes and solved the semantic difficulty by offering to substitute "permanent and perpetual" for "permanent and eternal."[32]

Before these issues were resolved, however, the second of Penkler's problems arose: the Turko-Persian settlement that he feared presaged an Ottoman attack on Austria. When the news of the peace reached Constantinople in November 1746, he noted, the soldiers and the people of the city seemed de- lighted that Moslems could cease killing fellow Moslems and resume killing Christians.[33] His concern increased with the arrival of a new French envoy, des Alleurs, who had served with Bonneval as a volunteer in the Austrian army and had then followed him to Sicily. Versailles hoped that des Alleurs could cooperate more closely with the famous renegade and be more effective than the parsimonious Castellane.[34]

While the arrival of the new French minister disturbed Penkler, the Turko-Persian peace concerned him more. Con- sequently, he found it advisable to inform the Porte of the revival of the Austro-Russian alliance of twenty years ear- lier.[35] Although directed this time primarily against Prussia, the new Austro-Russian agreement did contain an *articulus secretissimus* that bound each state to support the other "with all possible powers" in the event of Ottoman attack.[36] Penkler did not of course divulge the contents of the treaty, and he assured the Porte that it would not prevent Russia, Austria, and Turkey from living together peacefully. Yet he hoped that apprising the Ottoman officials of its existence would at least make them think twice before invading Habsburg territory.[37]

Whatever the effect of the revelation, by the second week in January 1747 Penkler reported that the Turks showed no inclination to move westward.[38] He added that chances were excellent for the Treaty of Belgrade to be extended "forever"; the only remaining obstacle seemed to be the grand vizier himself, a "bizarre" old man with "no passion to leave his name behind him either way: by making war or by signing a permanent peace."[39] The grand vizier's lethargy did not disrupt the talks, however, and after the last minor problems were solved, the final document was signed on 25 May. The renewal of the treaty was not the only agreement reached. At the same time Penkler secured from the Porte treaties of friendship and commerce with Tuscany, Hamburg, and Lübeck, all in the name of the emperor.

The signing of these accords testifies to Penkler's effectiveness as a diplomat. His knowledge of the ins and outs of dealing with the Ottomans and the foreign representatives in Constantinople, his ability to win the confidence of influential Turks, and his mastery of the arts of intrigue and the well-placed bribe all contributed greatly to keeping the Ottoman Empire out of the War of the Austrian Succession and to extending that peace so vital to Habsburg interests. To be sure, other factors also played a role. In the 1740s, the Ottomans experienced considerable internal and external difficulties that helped deter them from adventures against Austria. Yet no one knew better than Penkler that such problems by no means always determined the course of Ottoman policy. Accordingly, he employed every diplomatic subtlety his experience had taught him to carry out the wishes of his superiors. In the end he scored a resounding success that impressed not only Vienna but the other European courts as well. The Dutch secretary at the Porte remarked that " 'It was amazing that he [Penkler] was able to negotiate and conclude secretly a double treaty of perpetual peace at a time when everyone assumed that he was simply on the defensive, parrying those mortal blows that people were trying to inflict upon him from right and left.' "[40] One author has even suggested that the extension of the Treaty of Belgrade was such a blow to Bonneval that he died from the news.[41]

Without doubt the treaty marked the high point of Penkler's diplomatic career, but it was by no means the last of his achievements. While relations between Austria and Turkey remained rather quiet after 1747, they became agitated again in 1756 owing to a determined effort on the part of Frederick the Great of Prussia to enlist Turkish support in the Seven Years' War which began in 1756. In the previous conflict Frederick had not sought direct contacts with the Turks, relying instead upon his French and Swedish friends to represent his interests at the Porte.[42] In May 1756, however, France concluded the Treaty of Versailles with Austria, thus leaving Berlin to fend for itself with the Turks.

With France and then Sweden joining Austria's side, Frederick opened his own contacts in the Ottoman capital. His agent was a man with at least some experience in Constantinople, Gottfried Fabian Haude, alias Karl Adolf von Rexin.[43] Rexin arrived in the Ottoman capital in the spring of 1755, carrying with him the title of privy commercial counselor and the authority to wish the new sultan, Osman III, best wishes upon his accession and to suggest to him a possible trade agreement with Prussia. Unofficially, he was to inquire about the establishment of formal Prusso-Turkish relations of a broader nature.[44] Within a year of this initial probe, Rexin returned to the Porte, this time with a firm offer of an alliance and Frederick's promise that the sultan could have Hungary if he agreed to attack Austria. The offer was prompted, of course, by the Treaty of Versailles, which robbed the Prussian king of his foremost Continental ally and forced him to search for others. Thus began another round of maneuvering at the Porte with the Prussians hoping to involve the Turks in the Seven Years' War and the Austrians trying to keep them out.

In their efforts this time, the Austrians had the aid of Versailles and its ambassador at the Porte, Charles Vergennes, a man far abler than most of his predecessors. Vergennes, however, suffered from a liability more serious than those of the other French envoys, for France was now an ally not only of Austria but of Russia as well. Since the war of 1737-1739, the Porte had viewed Russia rather than Austria as its most serious competitor in Europe, and after 1740 even Bonneval had warned the Ottoman ministers to think less of seeking revenge against Austria and more of protecting their enfeebled empire against the tsars.[45]

A few years before the outbreak of the Seven Years' War, Turkish animosity toward the Russians increased considerably when the Porte learned that they were constructing two new fortresses between Kiev and Ochakov, one thirty hours' and the other seventeen hours' march from the Turkish border. The Porte vigorously protested this threat to the Ottoman frontier, and for a time a Russo-Turkish war seemed in the offing. Complications for Russia elsewhere ended the threat of a conflict, however, and the Russians stopped construction in 1754 to avoid all trouble on their southern flank.[46] Despite this Russian effort to be conciliatory, the Turks remained fearful and distrustful of their northern neighbor. While surprised at France's alliance with Austria, the Porte really resented the French association with Russia. Vergennes wrote that Russia's joining the Austro-French alliance in 1757 made his position at the Porte " 'each day more difficult. One is able to reconcile himself with the Austrians against whom one has no complaint. All the hatred of this nation is directed against the Russians.' "[47]

At this critical time Austria had a new representative at the Porte as well. Penkler had departed for home in 1755 (he would return later) and left his post to Josef Peter von Schwachheim, a man famous in Vienna for his knowledge of Middle Eastern languages. Schwachheim proved to be not only a gifted linguist but a capable diplomat, albeit without Penkler's flair. Owing to the enormous expenses Vienna incurred in the Seven Years' War, Schwachheim worked with a more restricted budget than Penkler had enjoyed. In fact,

upon being received by the sultan, he brought no gifts, a
startling break from previous practice.[48] Nevertheless, he still
had funds to purchase a number of informers in Rexin's
household, and he possessed sufficient savoir-faire to remain
friendly with the grand vizier at the time, the celebrated
Koca Mehmed Ragip Pasha.

Ragip Pasha, a learned and able man, was one of the few
eighteenth-century grand viziers whose administration could
be called distinguished. Aware that the Ottoman Empire was
weaker than appearances indicated, he focused his attention
on internal reforms, especially those that would help the common people. He also realized, however, that a number of
influential officials wished to take advantage of Austro-Russian involvement in the Seven Years' War to restore Ottoman
glory. Thus, he found it necessary to deal with Rexin to make
it appear that he was seriously considering joining the hostilities.[49] His flirtation seduced Rexin totally; the Prussian repeatedly sent Berlin glowing reports of his diplomatic successes, promising at any moment to conclude an alliance with
the Porte that would send Turks and Tartars swarming into
Hungary and the Ukraine. Contrary to his image of a man of
good judgment, Frederick usually believed these reports—
especially when the military situation was going against him—
and dreamed of joint Prusso-Turkish offensives against Austria and Russia.[50] If Rexin (and Frederick) were taken in by
Ragip Pasha, Schwachheim was not. Throughout the 1750s
he advised Vienna that domestic concerns and an unwillingness to engage in foreign adventures would prevent the grand
vizier from advocating war.

Despite Schwachheim's repeated assurances that Vienna had
nothing to fear, Austrian policy-makers became much less
confident of Turkish neutrality after 1760, and for good reason. In that year Frederick, by now fighting for his country's
very existence against increasingly successful enemies, made
an unprecedented effort to draw Turkey into the hostilities.
He promised the Turks that he would guarantee the Banat of
Timişoara to the sultan and would not conclude a separate

peace with his enemies if the Ottomans would declare war immediately. Even more startling, the usually parsimonious monarch authorized Rexin to distribute between 500,000 and 800,000 thalers among the Ottoman officials and even suggested that his minister purchase cartons of Nuremberg dolls to give to the ladies of the harems.[51] In addition to the instructions and gifts, he also sent Rexin the ratification papers to present to the Porte as soon as the alliance was concluded along with military advice on how the Turks should conduct their first offensive. Confronted by this diplomatic onslaught, Ragip opened negotiations with Rexin and concluded a Prusso-Turkish treaty of friendship and commerce on 2 April 1761.[52] Rexin, who had little experience in such diplomatic matters, believed that he had concluded a treaty of alliance and confidently informed his sovereign that Turkey would soon unleash its hordes against Austria and Russia.[53] But Ragip knew exactly what he had signed and assured Schwachheim that it represented no threat to Austria, assurances which Schwachheim sent along to Vienna.

Despite these reports, the news of the agreement disturbed the Austrian policy-makers, especially Kaunitz, who feared that, even if it were not truly a treaty of alliance, it could certainly lead to one.[54] Frederick had the same idea, and, after he discovered that the agreement of 2 April was not what Rexin claimed, he set out to expand it to include military provisions. Instead of relying exclusively on Rexin, whom by now he was calling an "ass's head," the king sent another representative named Dolon to assist Rexin and to find out incidentally if he were truly the fool Frederick now thought he was.[55] Besides the new agent, the king also sent along gifts for his envoys to distribute and an offer to pay the sultan a subsidy of 1,000,000 thalers in exchange for a campaign against Russia and Austria.[56] In March 1762 Rexin presented his sovereign's offer to the grand vizier.

The news of the Prussian proposal disturbed Kaunitz even more than the report of the treaty of friendship, for by the spring of 1762 the international situation had changed considerably. Elizabeth of Russia had died on 5 January, and her Prussophile nephew, Peter III, had ascended the throne. If Russia were now to switch to the Prussian side and Turkey to ally with Berlin and St. Petersburg, Vienna would have no choice but to surrender.[57] But from Schwachheim came the same old assurances that Austria had nothing to fear. Although Prusso-Turkish negotiations were continuing, he consoled Kaunitz, "In my opinion Your All-Highest's affairs at the Porte are today in as excellent condition as anyone could wish." There was not the slightest evidence that the Porte planned a war; no magazines were being filled, no ships constructed, no wood made available for shipbuilding, and "we have already reached the month of May." No war could take place even if the sultan wished it, and Schwachheim guessed that "all the costly gifts that Rexin has passed around have won him nothing."[58]

Despite Schwachheim's confidence, Kaunitz was not convinced. Since Schwachheim had requested to be relieved some time before, Kaunitz decided to replace him with the old master of Ottoman intrigue, Penkler. As Penkler made his way to Constantinople, the chancellor became progressively more nervous about reports from other sources that mentioned Turkish plans to invade Austria. His ambassador in Russia warned of news there indicating that the khan of the Crimea was about to invade Hungary (Frederick had been negotiating independently with the khan since the autumn of 1761) and that Turkish regulars would not be far behind.[59] He sent these and other forebodings to Penkler, warning him that "there is no doubt that a war with the Turks would be the worst thing that could happen to our court and therefore we must do all we can to turn aside this misfortune." Kaunitz even authorized Penkler to distribute cash and promises of cash liberally; "It is better to buy the grand vizier's trust than to begin a new, costly, and highly dangerous war with the Porte."[60]

Upon his arrival in the Ottoman capital, Penkler immediately set to work with Schwachheim to check all available sources about the possibility of a Turko-Prussian military accord. On 15 September he informed the chancellor that, as Schwachheim had declared over and over, there was no evidence that the Porte planned a war with Austria. Using the word *Tranquillizierung* repeatedly, he advised Kaunitz that not only would the Turks remain at peace but so would the khan of the Crimea. To underscore his point, he told the chancellor that he had not even distributed any money to gain this information because all of his sources assumed it to be common knowledge.[61] A month later Penkler assured Kaunitz that on 16 October the grand vizier himself had given Rexin "a completely definitive, straightforward, and clear answer" to Prussia's request for an alliance and that answer was "No!"[62] If that were insufficient, two weeks later Penkler added that Ragip Pasha had personally told him that the sultan wished to live only as Austria's good neighbor. Rexin had received a huge amount of money in October to bribe Ottoman officials, but now, since he had no opportunity to spend it, he was sending it back to Berlin. When an ambassador returns bribe money from Constantinople, Penkler noted, he has indeed abandoned all hope of success.[63]

During no other period was it more essential for Vienna to have able diplomats at the Porte, and the diplomats it had there at this time were surely able. Their genius rested not so much in their ability to counter French and Prussian bribery (for they never had the funds equal to those of their foes), but in their knowledge of the workings of the Porte, where effectiveness did not depend solely—as Rexin believed—on the dispersement of payoffs. Penkler and Schwachheim both knew which persons to bribe, which to trust, what information to gather and from whom to get it, and especially how to interpret the information received. It is true, of course, that the Ottomans had many and varied reasons for not attacking Austria, but no representatives understood those reasons better than the Austrians. In 1749, after the French had failed to formulate a Turko-Swedish alliance against Russia—

a proposal vigorously combatted by Penkler—Frederick had remarked that it seemed to him that " 'the Viennese court knows the Turks better' " than the French.[64] A few years later he was to discover that the Viennese court knew the Turks better than the Prussian court as well.

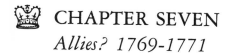

CHAPTER SEVEN
Allies? 1769-1771

Following the conclusion of the Seven Years' War, the attention of Austria and other European powers again turned to events in Poland. The death of King Augustus III in 1763 and the election the following year of his successor Stanislaus Poniatowski, lover and protégé of the formidable Catherine II of Russia, caused considerable commotion in the courts of Europe. Although Kaunitz was not pleased with Poniatowski's success, he realized that there was little Austria could do to oppose it. In April 1764 Berlin and St. Petersburg had concluded a treaty of alliance that meant any confrontation with Russia could lead to a showdown with Prussia as well. As part of a memorandum complaining of what he regarded as Russia's blunderings and inadequacies as an Austrian ally in the past, Kaunitz concluded that it was still essential to prevent Russia from becoming a Habsburg foe. " 'If it [Russia] is almost useless as a friend, it could still cause us considerable damage as an enemy.' " Thus, St. Petersburg must find " 'no opportunity to harm Austria.' "[1]

The election of Poniatowski did not resolve Poland's problems but only intensified them. The antagonism displayed by the Roman Catholic nobility and clergy toward the Protestant and Orthodox minorities prompted protests from Prussia and Russia and finally in 1767 inspired Russia to undertake armed intervention on behalf of the minorities. At first the Russian presence seemed to settle the issue, but in early 1768 it led to even greater violence with the formation of the Confederation of Bar, an armed force of Catholics intent upon expelling the Russians from Poland. The Russians set out immediately to crush the confederates, and for the next year and a half Poland was the scene of widespread conflict.

Kaunitz's policy—approved by Maria Theresa—was for the

Monarchy to remain uninvolved. While he disliked growing Russian influence in Poland, he also planned to undertake no measures that would antagonize St. Petersburg while Russia and Prussia were allies. At the same time, he kept a close watch on the Porte; it seemed quite likely to intervene on the confederates' behalf because it still regarded Russia as its most dangerous antagonist and viewed Poniatowski's election as an ominous extension of Russian influence in Poland. When the Confederation of Bar formed and hostilities erupted, the Porte divided into factions which hotly debated whether the Ottoman Empire should aid the Poles by attacking Russia. The war party was vigorously supported by the French ambassador, whose country wished to see Russia weakened, while the peace party received encouragement from the Russian envoy, who had no desire to see Turkey complicate his sovereign's policies in Poland. The Austrian minister had instructions to play the neutral bystander while keeping a watchful eye on the intrigues of the others.[2]

In mid-July 1768 the scales in Constantinople plunged in favor of the war party when reports arrived of an incident on the Polish-Ottoman border, where the Ottoman town of Balta was razed and its inhabitants massacred by a zealous Russian Cossack detachment searching for Polish confederates. The news caused an uproar in Constantinople, and, despite frantic efforts of the Russian envoy to make amends, the grand vizier summoned him on 6 October and insisted that his sovereign agree to the immediate evacuation of Russian troops from Poland. When the ambassador was unable to give a firm answer to the demand, he and his staff were arrested and taken to the Fortress of the Seven Towers.[3] Another Russo-Turkish war had begun.

Kaunitz was not unduly disturbed by the outbreak of the conflict, but he did wish to avoid Austrian involvement. He still regarded Prussia as the Monarchy's one intransigent foe, and he did not want the Russo-Turkish struggle to ignite an Austro-Prussian conflict in some way. As hostilities opened, he proposed a meeting between Joseph II—the son of Maria

Theresa, who had become emperor upon his father's death in 1765—and Frederick to arrange a tacit understanding that both Vienna and Berlin would remain neutral in the troubles in the East.[4] At first Joseph and Maria Theresa rejected the suggestion because of their intense dislike of Frederick and his state, but, after news arrived of the actual Turkish declaration of war, they decided that Habsburg security demanded such a rapprochement. Shortly thereafter, the Austrian minister in Berlin met with the king, explained that Vienna would remain neutral, and expressed the hope that Prussia would do the same and would join with Austria in declaring the neutrality of the Germanies. Frederick agreed. " 'What does it matter . . . if the Russians and the Turks are in each others' hair? As long as we two, the House of Austria and I, understand each other, Germany has little to worry about being disturbed by war.' "[5] He even accepted the ambassador's offer to arrange a meeting with the young emperor at the next Prussian maneuvers, but, since they were several months off, set no date.

Kaunitz appeared content with Frederick's response and prepared to sit out the war. Only once was his resolve shaken. Within two weeks of Frederick's acknowledgment of mutual neutrality, the Porte proposed an alliance with Austria and Prussia. In exchange for Austro-Prussian aid in expelling the Russians from Poland, the pact would provide for the return of Silesia to Austria and, as Frederick's compensation, the Prussian annexation of Curland and Prussian Poland. The proposal fascinated Kaunitz. In presenting it to his sovereigns he remarked, " 'The thought that the Turk, with the cooperation of the king of Prussia, would ever help Your Majesties regain Silesia is so extraordinary and chimerical, that I had to argue with myself whether I should be so bold—and incur your ridicule—as to lay this proposal before Your Majesties.' "[6] If not ridicule, the proposal did elicit a firm rejection. Joseph raised a number of objections, the most important being that Frederick would never agree to a scheme that demanded sacrifices on his part and then gave him at best only an even trade.[7] When Maria Theresa concurred with her son, the chancellor notified the resident at the Porte to reject the offer, but, so that the Turks would understand Austria's concern about their welfare, to suggest Austrian mediation instead.[8]

For the first eight months of 1769 Vienna continued to observe the struggles in the East. Both Russia and Turkey asked for support, and both received refusals. In August Kaunitz's hoped-for meeting between Frederick and Joseph took place at Neisse in Prussian Silesia. For Vienna the meeting was primarily a formality, the emperor simply repeating earlier statements that the Monarchy did not care to become involved in the Russo-Turkish trouble except as mediator. But to the surprise of Joseph and particularly of Kaunitz, Frederick brushed aside Joseph's innocuous remarks and warned him that something had to be done to stop Russian expansion. The Russo-Prussian alliance was necessary at the moment, he told the emperor, but a time was coming when "all of Europe" must unite to curb Russian aggrandizement. For now, Austria must actively press its offer to mediate because that was the only way to arrive at a satisfactory solution to the war and to the mess in Poland.[9]

Although Kaunitz was initially puzzled by Frederick's warning (and suspicious that it might be a contrivance to heighten Habsburg fears of St. Petersburg), within weeks he became convinced that the Prussian king was right. On 17 September 1769 the Ottoman and Russian armies fought a major battle on the Dnestr River near the massive Turkish fortress of Khotin. The janissaries put up a fierce fight and suffered heavy casualties, but, when the rest of the Turkish soldiers saw that their best troops had been badly mauled, they simply ran away. Not only did the field army flee, but the garrison of Khotin deserted as well, leaving behind only a few men, women, and children to surrender to the Russians. Upon occupying the fortress, the Russians found large numbers of weapons and magazines full of ammunition, food, and other materiel; all Khotin lacked for a vigorous defense was stout-hearted soldiers. With the Turks running before them, the Russians occupied Iasi (Jassy), the capital of Moldavia, on 7 October and entered Bucharest, the capital of Walachia, on 17 November. Some of their reconnaissance patrols watered their mounts in the Danube.

These events had a profound impact on Kaunitz in particular and on Austrian policy in general. Much talk had passed during the century that Turkey was only a shell, weakened by internal strife, incompetent leadership, and an obsolete military establishment. So far, however, that assessment had not been proven. In fact, the war of 1737-1739 had shown the Turks to be vigorous defenders of their lands. The Russian victory at Khotin convinced Kaunitz and others once and for all that the Ottoman Empire was not only woefully weak, but on the verge of collapse. If Turkey fell, Russia would likely take its place in the Balkans unless Austria could prevent it. In early 1770 the chancellor summarized his fears to Franz Amadeus Thugut, his new representative in Constantinople. When the Russo-Turkish war began, he admitted, he had thought the two sides evenly matched and had assumed "that the war would be conducted and ended so that neither side would have any advantage and everything would return to its former balance." In fact, he had thought the war good for Austria. "Nothing could be more helpful for securing and lengthening [our] peace because both sides would require a period of time to recover from their losses and thus would have to postpone their desires to foment new troubles." The Russian victory, however, had shattered these suppositions. "If the Turks are compelled to conclude a disadvantageous peace, the Russian court would win so many advantages through its conquests that it would have little or nothing to fear from the Turks for a long time and would have completely free hands in that area [the Balkans]."[10]

When the news of the Russian victories first arrived, Kaunitz's most pressing concern was to find out how seriously Turkey was damaged in both military might and morale. And here he faced a serious obstacle. The man to send the information was obviously the resident at the Porte, but in June 1769 that officer, Franz Anton Brognard, had unexpectedly died. To replace him, Kaunitz selected Thugut. One of the first graduates of the Oriental Academy and the son of an officer in the war finance office in Linz, he had been chosen for the academy because of his father's faithful service (he had risked his life to save the military and cameral funds when the Bavarians took Linz in 1741) and because he could "speak Italian, French, Spanish, read Greek, and was in all his schools far and away the best [student]."[11] He first went to Constantinople as a translator in 1757 but returned to Vienna later to become an adviser in eastern affairs. As soon as news arrived of Brognard's death, he was ordered to the Ottoman capital to assume the duties of resident.[12]

Thugut would enjoy the most successful diplomatic career of Austria's ministers to the Porte. After his term of service in the Ottoman capital, he would act as ambassador on a number of special assignments and would finally become director of the Monarchy's foreign affairs in 1793. For the moment all of this lay before him. In fact, his tenure as resident had a rather inauspicious beginning. Upon arriving in Constantinople Thugut fell ill—a condition he blamed on the journey—and was unable to gather the information Kaunitz needed. Moreover, the Porte refused to receive him at first because it feared that the populace would interpret such a reception as a sign of the sultan's willingness to accept Austrian mediation, which in turn would mean that he was about to sacrifice Ottoman territory in order to restore peace with Russia.[13]

While Kaunitz waited for Thugut to recover his health, reports from other sources confirmed the chancellor's fear that the campaign had resulted in "the extraordinary and almost complete defeat of the Turkish nation." To Thugut he expressed his concern that the next campaign would lead to an "even worse outcome" for the Turks.[14] "One can only fall back on the hope that the Porte may be able, through secret peace proposals to Russia, to save itself from its dangerous situation or at least to win time to improve it."[15] But it was news from Russia that disturbed Kaunitz the most. In December the Habsburg ambassador there informed him that Catherine had expressed privately the hope that soon her soldiers would seize Constantinople and drive the Turks completely from Europe.[16] If this hope were realized, all of the Balkans would fall to the ambitious tsarina.

Faced by this prospect, Kaunitz and his sovereigns had to formulate a policy to deal with it. They had no wish to see the Russians establish their hegemony in the Balkans, and they were especially alarmed that Russia might expand to the Habsburg borders in southeastern Europe. They still believed in the principle expressed earlier in the century: as a neighbor, they far preferred a weak Turkey to a formidable Russia. Now, however, Austria's worst fears seemed about to be realized. The Russians had already penetrated Moldavia and Walachia, considered by Vienna so vital to Habsburg security, and they seemed about to cross the Danube. In 1770 the Russians inflicted two more serious defeats upon the Turks, one in the sea battle at Çeşme, and one in the land battle at Kartal on the Danube, where one third of the Ottoman army died in the fighting while another third drowned in the river trying to flee. Austria had to find a way to stop Russia with a minimum of risk to itself.

Throughout 1770 and into 1771, Kaunitz, Joseph, and Maria Theresa struggled with this problem, each advocating a different solution. Kaunitz favored strong measures. If Catherine succeeded in extending her power over the northern coast of the Black Sea, the Crimea, Moldavia, and Walachia, he argued, it would be "for the balance of power and especially for the illustrious arch-house a very unfortunate result" that could end in a new "general war."[17] He recommended that an understanding be reached with Frederick to insure his neutrality if not his cooperation; then, while not necessarily declaring war on Russia, Austria should stage a demonstration of military strength along the borders of Moldavia and

Walachia to warn Catherine against annexing those lands and ordering her forces across the Danube.[18]

Joseph, however, warned against taking steps that might appear to the Russians excessively belligerent. When asked by his mother in November 1770 if Austria should resort to arms, he submitted a thirty-four page response emphasizing the prohibitive cost of a single campaign, not counting losses actually sustained. At the end he reminded his mother that the total cost would probably be twice that estimated because Austria would have to pay interest on loans to finance the operations. His conclusion: "All of these reasons, presented here only briefly, convince me how unattractive and unwanted, indeed dangerous and disadvantageous any warlike measures under these conditions and against this enemy actually are."[19]

This reply pleased Maria Theresa, who also wished to avoid conflict with Russia, but she disagreed with Joseph's alternate policy. He suggested (in January 1771) a course reminiscent of that of 1737 and one that, during the next few years, Vienna would find increasingly difficult to resist: the Habsburgs should not oppose Catherine but join her in dismembering Turkey should that country's destruction appear inevitable. "Only in this way can Austria win some advantages from the collapse of the Ottoman Empire and enlarge itself with rich and attractive provinces which, while certainly not as significant as those Russia has conquered, at least will be of considerable importance for the strategic position of the Monarchy." In the meantime, he agreed with Kaunitz that forces along the borders of the Principalities should be strengthened, not necessarily to prepare for war but "to keep Russia uncertain of being attacked, to keep the king of Prussia in doubt of being forced, arms in hand, to declare himself for or against [one side or the other], and to give the Porte hope of being solidly sustained."[20]

The empress herself was in a dilemma. She reluctantly concurred with Kaunitz that Russian aggrandizement on her borders would threaten Habsburg security; yet, like Joseph, she could not approve war with Russia, although not necessarily for his reasons. "I am in agreement with the Emperor not to make war on the Russians. . . . But that which convinced me the most is that the Turks are the aggressors, that the Russians have always been easier for us to manage, that they are Christians, and that they are suffering an unjust war. . . ."[21] At the same time, however, she realized that the Turks, by resisting Russian expansionism, were truly defending the interests of the Habsburgs. Thus, she could not under any circumstances endorse her son's suggestion that the Monarchy participate in the destruction of the Ottoman Empire. " 'Never, never,' " she wrote to Joseph in January 1771, " 'could I join with the Russians to pursue and destroy the Turks.' "[22] For the time being, the only action that all three could agree upon was to reinforce the army in Transylvania. This initiative would, they hoped, impress upon the Russians that Vienna did not wish to see the Ottoman Empire destroyed or its European possessions permanently occupied by the tsarina's troops.

The decision to strengthen the army in Transylvania led to the most unusual, if not the most important, event in the history of Austrian relations with Turkey in the eighteenth century, the so-called Austro-Turkish alliance of 6 July 1771. The archenemy of Christendom, the foremost threat to Austria's being, the infidel that stalked the gates of Vienna— became for a brief time an associate and true friend of the Habsburgs.[23] Although diplomatic relations and official agreements between the Ottoman Empire and the European powers had existed for some time, not until the eighteenth century did formal alliances between them appear. The stumbling block had been religion—no Moslem could, according to Islamic law as interpreted by the Ottoman legal authorites, ally with an unbeliever on an equal basis, and no Christian could rightly ally with a Moslem against a fellow Christian. But underlying and reinforcing the religious obstacle was the image of the Ottoman state as a mighty, aggressive, and alien power intent upon overwhelming Christian Europe. In the

eighteenth century, however, formal military alliances between the Ottoman Empire and Christian powers became, if
not frequent, at least acceptable. One reason was the Enlightenment, which sought out particularly religious animosity as
a blight on humanity and encouraged toleration for all faiths,
including Islam. Thus, an enlightened ruler such as Frederick
the Great could lust after an alliance with the Turks while
giving no thought to their being Moslem. More important,
however, in the growing acceptance of the Ottoman Empire
as a partner in European diplomacy was its obvious decline.
By the middle of the eighteenth century it no longer represented a threat to the existence of Christianity or to the stability of Europe. It presented itself instead as just another
state struggling to survive in the face of growing internal and
foreign pressures. Consequently, in 1740 Sweden became the
first Christian power to conclude a formal military alliance
with the Porte (directed against Russia), and from then on
such accords became more common.

Even in the eighteenth century, however, for Austria to
become an ally of the Ottoman Empire was quite a different
matter than it was for Sweden, Prussia, or even France. After
all, the Monarchy had defended Christianity's frontiers against
Ottoman aggression and had experienced in full measure the
wrath of Islam militant. Moreover, the Habsburg state sym-
bolized to Europe and especially to the smaller German and
Italian states resistance to Ottoman advance. To ally with the
Turks would violate this long and deeply felt tradition and
likely compromise the Monarchy's image in the eyes of some
of its friends. Essentially, the Habsburg decision to reach an
accord with the Turks came down to whether such a tradition
and image could be subordinated to what were perceived by
some Habsburg policy-makers to be the immediate needs of
the state. For a man of the Enlightenment such as Kaunitz,
there was no question that the needs of the state should pre-
vail over tradition; for a conservative such as Maria Theresa,
there was considerable feeling that the state needed most to
maintain its traditions.

The Turks had first suggested a form of alliance with Vienna in the scheme of late 1768 that called for Austro-Turkish-Prussian cooperation to expel the Russians from Poland. When that came to nothing, the Porte offered in March 1770 a plan to expel Russia from Poland and either to elect a new king of Poland or to partition that country between Austria and Turkey.[24] At the time Kaunitz was impressed by the proposal, which he described as "truly extraordinary" and "presumably never before made to a Christian power by the Porte." He added that it must have been inspired by the sultan's "bitterness against and willingness to use every possible means of revenge against Russia."[25] At the time neither the chancellor nor his sovereigns wished such an accord with the Porte and advised Thugut to decline the offer and to encourage the Turks to accept Austrian mediation instead.

In January 1771 when Kaunitz, Joseph, and Maria Theresa were debating the course of Habsburg policy, they decided to reexamine the Porte's earlier proposals, although not in terms the Ottomans would have wished. In the discussions regarding Habsburg forces in Transylvania, one continual concern was the great cost involved. To create a convincing demonstration of military might along the Moldavian and Walachian borders, the Hofkriegsrat would have to transfer troops from the Netherlands and Italy. Moreover, it would be necessary to strengthen the garrisons along the Prussian border. Prussia and Russia were allies, and, if the army facing Prussia remained undermanned, both Frederick and Catherine would perceive that the Austrian demonstration was not serious. All of this would require substantial sums, the most common estimate being 34,000,000 gulden.[26]

Kaunitz suggested that Turkey bear the cost. "Because the Porte can find no salvation from any other power save Her Majesty's, so must it agree to certain reasonable conditions: (1) that we on our side must not bear the expense, (2) that we must be able to proceed with safety, and (3) that for such service we must receive suitable advantages." To procure the Porte's acceptance of these conditions, Kaunitz continued, an agreement must be signed. He realized that such an accord would violate Maria Theresa's sentiments about collaboration with infidels, "but when self-preservation is demanded, such qualities as differences of religion cannot be taken into consideration."[27] Impressed by the financial necessity and persuaded that *Realpolitik* must in this matter take precedence over religion, the empress allowed her chancellor to proceed.

Kaunitz's efforts to gain financial aid (and other concessions, as we shall see) from the Turks in 1771 present a marvelous example of his diplomatic skill, especially his ability to get something while giving practically nothing in return. His initial instructions to Thugut outlined the general political situation, what Vienna proposed to do about it, and finally what the Turks should do about it as well. The main problem, Kaunitz explained, was that Vienna still did not know the exact nature of Russia's goals but had hints that they were broad indeed. Various rumors indicated that they "encompass nothing less than the so-called freedom of Moldavia and Walachia, but in the hands of a prince chosen by Russia, perhaps [Gregor] Orlov, and perhaps also the Morea or a useful island in the Aegean. . . ." Since these conditions were unacceptable to Austria, Kaunitz continued, the time had come for a "tough decision," namely that Vienna promise the Turks not to allow their empire to be overrun. Kaunitz did note the irony: "To save our archenemy is rather extraordinary, and such decisions can be justified only in truly critical situations, such as maintaining self-preservation."[28] Vienna planned to mobilize an army of 100,000 men in Hungary and Transylvania, the chancellor informed Thugut, and at the same time to send reinforcements to the Prussian border to convince Catherine and her Prussian ally that Vienna was truly serious about stopping Russia. Then the Habsburg court would notify both St. Petersburg and Berlin that it would under no circumstances permit Russian troops across the Danube. Meanwhile, the Porte should express its willingness to negotiate with the Russians but should declare categorically that it would never accept a Russian presence on the Black Sea.

All these announcements together, Kaunitz believed, would make Catherine realize that she now faced serious opposition and would inspire Frederick to persuade her to come to terms.

For these efforts on the Porte's behalf, Kaunitz went on, Austria must receive compensation from Turkey, and Thugut should try to obtain all that he possibly could. The bill to present to the Turks should include 34,000,000 gulden (the chancellor told Thugut to inform the Porte that the expenses really came to 50,000,000 to convince it that Vienna was offering a bargain) and Little Walachia, the province won by Austria in 1718 and lost in 1739. Moreover, the Turks should cede to the Monarchy the fortresses of Belgrade and Vidin in exchange for an Austrian guarantee to secure the Danube forever. Finally, the resident was to demand most-favored-nation status for Austria in commercial matters, including the right to sail ships on the Black Sea and an Ottoman undertaking to protect Habsburg vessels from the Barbary pirates.[29]

As these instructions clearly reveal, the agreement Kaunitz had in mind was not an alliance in the strict sense of the term. In fact, he referred to it as a "concert" and specifically told Thugut not to call it an alliance. It provided for no specific numbers of men to assist one another, no plan of joint operations, and no definite promises of military operations. Nor was it designed to bluff Catherine and Frederick into making an early peace. In order to effect such a bluff, Kaunitz would have to hint to them that the accord existed (while revealing no details) and to pretend joint military measures with the Turks against the Russians. But Kaunitz insisted that the agreement remain absolutely secret. He warned Thugut that, if Frederick found out (and if Catherine discovered it, she would surely tell him), the king's "envy and self-interest would bind him ever more closely to Russia." Besides, the news of a Habsburg agreement with the infidel might result in "harmful consequences" among the other Christian courts as well.[30] The military demonstrations along the Moldavian and Walachian borders were bluffs, but the

agreement itself was not, for no one except the parties involved was supposed to know that it existed.[31]

For an agreement that fell short of an alliance, however,
the price was substantial indeed. The chancellor undoubtedly
knew that the Turks would not accept all of his provisions,
but, being an excellent bargainer, he knew that he should
ask for more than he believed he could get so that later he
could concede some items to gain others. During the night
of 27-28 February 1771 (all the meetings were held at night
in order to keep them secret), Thugut laid the details of the
plan before the *reis effendi*.[32] The emperor was willing to prevent the complete defeat of the Ottoman Empire "with force,"
Thugut told him, but would demand significant compensation for doing so. Thugut mentioned Belgrade and Vidin
first, because he feared that these conditions would meet with
the most fervent opposition. He was right.

> The *reis effendi* grabbed me with both hands and asked
> me to swear, by all that I held holy, to say nothing of
> such a demand, because it would make absolutely im-
> possible the fortunate accord, the hope of which was so
> dear to him. . . . Even if the Russians should get Adri-
> anople [Edirne], none of the ministers of the grand sig-
> neur would take the responsibility of advising him to
> purchase an immediate peace through such a concession.

Seeing no chance of progress on that issue, Thugut explained
the rest of Kaunitz's points, to which the Turks seemed more
receptive. They suggested, however, that the Austrians not
conduct operations in Moldavia and Walachia—which would
affect Ottoman citizens—but in Poland, where they could
replace the present king with someone agreeable to Austria
and Prussia or find "another solution," namely the partition
of that country.[33] These remarks showed that the Turks obviously assumed that the Austrians were planning direct military intervention, and Thugut for the moment said nothing
to discourage them.

Three weeks later Thugut again met with the *reis effendi*.

Out of Kaunitz's requests, the Porte appeared willing to go along with some commercial concessions and the cession of Little Walachia, but not at all with Belgrade and Vidin or the 34,000,000 gulden. Claiming virtual bankruptcy of the Ottoman treasury, the *reis effendi* offered instead 18,000 beutels of gold (10,125,000 gulden), a sum considerably less than the chancellor had suggested.[34]

Despite the apparently disappointing response, Kaunitz was not discouraged at all; he knew that Austria would carry out its military demonstrations with or without Turkish funds.[35] A small payment and Little Walachia were better than nothing. He advised Thugut to accept the Ottoman offer if he believed that was the best he could obtain. Before he did so, however, he should try for an additional 3,000,000 gulden by hinting that Austria had been offered—presumably by the Russians—a substantial portion of the Ottoman Empire including "among other places Bosnia, Serbia, Turkish Dalmatia, and [Turkish] Croatia."[36] In order not to frighten the Porte too much and at the same time to impress upon it the bargain it would receive from Austria, Kaunitz advised Thugut to add that Vienna absolutely refused to listen to such temptations. "Even had the eternal peace and policy of the Porte to remain quiet during the last two wars not occurred, the temperate nature [of the imperial house] would not have allowed it to give such proposals the slightest consideration."[37]

Upon receiving the instructions, Thugut went back to work, only to encounter additional Turkish objections. The Porte now specifically insisted that Vienna agree to do more than simply arrange a peace that would leave Turkey with the smallest possible losses. Austria must promise forthrightly to fight the Russians if they did not agree to a full restoration of the boundaries as they stood before the war. Thugut informed the *reis effendi* that he could not accept such a condition since there was "no likelihood" that St. Petersburg, after the stunning Russian victories, would ever accept the *status quo ante bellum*. Besides, he knew that such a provision would virtually obligate the Monarchy to enter the war, something that Vienna would not approve.[38]

Nevertheless, the exchange convinced Thugut that the Turks were slowly but surely realizing that the accord was not a good one for them. Although they were giving up hard cash and territory, they were unable to extract from the Austrians a firm commitment to specific military action, which the Porte wanted and expected. Moreover, the Russians, who were indeed distressed by the display of Austrian might along the borders of Moldavia and Walachia—as Kaunitz had hoped they would be—were avoiding serious operations in those provinces and concentrating on the conquest of the Crimea. Feeling considerably less pressure as a result, the Porte was beginning to question the need for any agreement at all with Austria. But Thugut, who knew how much Kaunitz wanted the subsidy and the land, rose to the challenge. Meeting with the *reis effendi* and other officials for four straight nights in mid-June, the resident engaged in such intense discussions that he "often believed the moment to have arrived when the negotiation of the whole thing could collapse." Finally, through his "earnest arguments," he convinced the Porte that the military and diplomatic situations were still so uncertain that the Austrian proposal was essential to the preservation of the Ottoman Empire.[39]

On 6 July 1771 the agreement was signed. Thugut had procured the cession of Little Walachia (including Habsburg control of both banks of the Olt River), the increase of the Ottoman subsidy to 20,000 beutels of gold (11,250,000 gulden), and the grant of most-favored-nation status for Austrian commerce with the right of Habsburg vessels to sail on the Black Sea. Moreover, he had managed to keep Austria's promises vague: "To deliver, by way of negotiations *or* of arms [Thugut noted proudly to Kaunitz the use of "or" instead of "and"] and to restore to the Porte the fortresses, provinces, and territories which were possessions of the sultan and which have been invaded by the Russians since the commencement of the war." The Habsburg state, the treaty read, would restore the freedom of Poland and the Treaty of Belgrade, *"or,* according to time and circumstance reestablish peace on those conditions which accord with the dignity of and are agreed to fully by the Sublime Porte."[40]

The accord was indeed a resounding success for both Kaunitz and Thugut. In return for commitments ambiguous enough to be interpreted away, the Austrians received territory lost in a previous war and a substantial subsidy to finance a military pose that they would have assumed anyway. To express his pleasure at Thugut's success, the chancellor recommended his promotion to the rank of internuntius. Maria Theresa, while approving the promotion and the treaty, was less certain that the agreement was a good one. It smacked of the immorality she so despised in international affairs because it appeared that Austria was taking goods from the Ottomans while giving nothing substantial in return. " 'I do not like to take money from these people,' " she wrote. " 'God grant us peace this winter.' "[41]

Once the treaty was signed, Kaunitz's primary concern was to insure that the Turks kept their financial commitments. The treaty had stipulated that the Porte would pay 2,000,000 gulden immediately and the remainder "promptly in two parts one after another observing always the necessary precautions for secrecy."[42] Within four weeks, wagons carrying the gold left Constantinople for the Austrian border. To quell the curiosity of the public and the foreign residents concerning the destination and purpose of these funds, the Porte announced that the money was destined for Austria to purchase ammunition and grain.[43] As soon as the first shipment reached Habsburg hands, Thugut insisted that the second set forth. The Porte hesitated, however, explaining that a second wagon train following the first so closely would make the citizens of Constantinople suspect an Ottoman surrender and might provoke them to rebel.[44]

As the summer faded into autumn and the Austrians did nothing diplomatically or militarily that produced results, the Porte began to suspect that Vienna was about to disregard the agreement. Their suspicions were based on Austria's failure to perform two specific acts expected in Constantinople: ratification of the treaty and declaration of war on Russia. Thugut tried to pacify the Ottomans by explaining that Vienna considered the treaty binding, even if it were not formally ratified, and that a declaration of war would involve Austria in a conflict with both Russia and Prussia—a condition definitely not stipulated in the treaty.[45]

The Turks, of course, had sound reasons to suspect Habsburg policy. Even as the treaty was being signed, Kaunitz was beginning to doubt its usefulness and to fear that it might become an embarrassment. In April 1771 St. Petersburg had hinted that it really did not want to establish the tsarina's hegemony over Moldavia and Walachia, and shortly thereafter informed Vienna of the Russo-Prussian agreement to partition Poland.[46] Kaunitz realized that far more might be gained for Austria—in terms of both security and compensation—by negotiating directly with Berlin and St. Petersburg, and as usual he was right. In December 1771, after some months of bluff and bluster, the Russians secretly agreed to return Moldavia and Walachia to the Porte, and Vienna decided to join Russia and Prussia in partitioning Poland.[47]

While Kaunitz and his sovereigns worked out the various arrangements concerning Poland, Thugut continued to appeal for additional funds, and the Porte continued to press the Austrians for strong action. In mid-January 1772 the *reis effendi* brought Thugut before an impressive gathering of Ottoman officials and read him a statement "in the most forceful terms possible" urging Austria to negotiate a general peace immediately or to support Turkey with arms. In the expectation that Vienna would act shortly, the Ottoman foreign minister announced that another shipment of gold would start immediately for the Habsburg frontier. By this time, however, Vienna was no longer interested in arranging a Russo-Turkish peace and had no intention of supporting the Porte in the next year's fighting. After all, Austria had what it wanted: Russian assurances to evacuate Moldavia and Walachia and to leave the remainder of the Balkans alone. The Russians and Turks would still compete for possession of the northern coast of the Black Sea and the Crimea, but Vienna had no interest in that dispute. Thugut therefore put the Ottomans off again with fine phrases about how long and complicated peace negotiations could be.[48]

By the spring of 1772 Vienna was content. Moldavia and Walachia would remain in Ottoman hands, the Russians would stay far from the Danube, and the Monarchy would gain additional land in Poland. Therefore, it had no more use for the convention with Turkey. In fact, because the subject of dividing Ottoman lands as well had come up during the negotiations with Prussia and Russia, the treaty was becoming increasingly embarrassing. Consequently, on 8 April Kaunitz advised his representative at the Porte to inform the Turks that Vienna no longer regarded the Austro-Turkish convention binding. Formal reasons were easy to come by: the Turks had failed to pay the subsidy in a reasonable amount of time; Austria had not promised to fight both Russia and Prussia and under prevailing treaties war with one would bring war with the other; and in its poor condition, the Ottoman army could give Austria little support against a Russo-Prussian onslaught. Kaunitz cautioned Thugut to soften the blow as much as possible, to present the note in friendly terms, and to offer to return the money the Turks had paid up to that time.[49]

Thugut realized that the renunciation of the agreement might incite a violent reaction at the Porte, and for a few days he hesitated to present Kaunitz's message. Armistice negotiations between Russians and Turks in the field were underway at the time, and he hoped that their successful conclusion might make the Austrian action easier for the Turks to accept.[50] When the news of the armistice failed to come, however, he firmed his resolve and, in one of those late night meetings, revealed the Austrian decision. As Thugut had feared, the Turkish officials were outraged. They refused to discuss the matter beyond telling the Austrian that they might pay for the convention's failure with their heads.[51]

After a month's wait—which caused Kaunitz and Thugut some concern—the *reis effendi* called the internuntius to another secret session on 6-7 June to discuss the treaty. While resigned to the abrogation of the agreement, the Ottoman statesman told Thugut that they would have to compose a statement to mollify the legalists so that they would not demand the execution of all the principal Ottoman ministers as punishment for the treaty's failure. After a night's work, a formal declaration was composed—to be issued by the Porte— explaining that, although Vienna had found it impossible to declare war on Russia, it would continue to exert every effort in the forthcoming negotiations to keep Moldavia, Walachia, and the Crimea in Ottoman hands. In other words, it would fulfill all of its obligations under the articles of the convention, short of war. Ever concerned for Austrian interests, Thugut even persuaded the reluctant *reis effendi* to allow the emperor to keep the gold sent to him as a sign of "trust, friendship, and thanks."[52] If Thugut displayed considerable skill in negotiating Austria into the convention, he showed quite as much in negotiating Austria out of it.

The convention was abrogated, but the pronouncement agreed upon still committed Austria to procure a respectable peace for the Ottoman Empire. As Thugut and his Ottoman colleagues were formulating their statement, news of the long-sought Russo-Turkish armistice arrived in Constantinople. Not only did the two belligerents agree to cease hostilities but also to meet at the town of Focşani in Moldavia to arrange a treaty. One of the conditions demanded by the Russians was that no mediators attend the sessions. Although Thugut and the Prussian ambassador journeyed to Focşani to serve as umpires, they were refused admittance to the talks themselves. Kaunitz was delighted, not disappointed, by the exclusion; it meant that the Ottomans had consented not to rely on Austrian aid in the negotiations, and that in turn meant that they had no longer recognized as valid the Austrian agreement to help. Kaunitz was relieved. "If the congress is ex-

ploded or does not reach a successful peace before the end of
the campaigning season, no blame or partisanship can be attributed to us."[53]

The Austrian adventure in courting its former archenemy
had come to an end. Between 1700 and 1790 the agreement
of 6 July 1771 was the only formal Austrian accord with the
Turks in which Vienna promised to help preserve the Ottoman Empire. Since the maintenance of this state as a barrier
to Russian expansion had been long recognized, it is surpris-
ing that an Austro-Turkish alliance was not tried or at least
discussed more often than it was. To some extent of course,
Vienna's reluctance to ally with Turkey resulted from the old
fear and hatred of the infidel, but by 1771 at least these
feelings of animosity were waning rapidly. Kaunitz especially
represented what one might call the enlightened diplomacy
of Europe, which viewed traditional and religious sentiments
as unnecessary obstacles to an intelligent foreign policy. For
him, an alliance with Turkey, as with virtually every other
diplomatic alternative, depended ultimately upon its usefulness in defeating the state he regarded as the new archenemy
of Austria, Prussia. Because an Austro-Turkish compact did
precisely the opposite—that is, because it would alienate Russia,
a power that indeed was necessary to aid Austria against Prussia—it could not be considered seriously for any length of
time.

In 1771 Maria Theresa reflected the religious prejudice of
an earlier era, but she was willing to subordinate her feelings
to her chancellor's *Realpolitik*. However, just as she regretted
the partition of Poland because of its immorality, so she suspected that Kaunitz's dealings with the Turks were funda-
mentally dishonest. If one must treat with the infidel—a
prospect that did not please her—then one must at least treat
with them honestly and in a straightforward manner. She
intensely disliked tricking them into giving the Monarchy
money and land in exchange for vague promises that in the
end would be broken or explained away. As in the partition

of Poland, however, she agreed to the policy her chancellor formulated toward Turkey because she was persuaded that, in this time when all the other powers seemed to be intent on ill-gotten gains, such a policy would better serve the interests of her state.

CHAPTER EIGHT
Partitions Great and Small,
1772-1775

Despite the efforts to discourage Russian expansion in the Balkans, Joseph and Kaunitz never rejected totally the thought that perhaps the Monarchy would be better served by cooperating with the Russians rather than by opposing them. They knew that the military preparations designed to intimidate Catherine could backfire at any moment, perhaps drawing Austria into a dangerous war with Russia from which Vienna feared Prussia would benefit most. As Kaunitz advised Maria Theresa, " 'It is to be assumed that he [Frederick] would not be displeased to see us engaged in a war with that power [Russia], since whatever the outcome of such a war, he would be able to obtain his advantages and run no risks.' "[1] Because Vienna had no wish for war with Russia, a policy of joining St. Petersburg and perhaps Berlin in some sort of partition of the Ottoman Empire and Poland became increasingly attractive. Beginning in 1771, at the same time Vienna was negotiating its convention with the Porte, the Habsburg policymakers began examining a number of plans to reorganize the state structure of southeastern and eastern Europe.

The first detailed scheme to partition the weaker eastern European states was presented by a mysterious Chevalier Massin—knight of Malta, Piedmontese, officer in the Russian navy, and " 'a man full of spirit, enthusiasm, and vivacity, . . . but a hothead, full of the most extraordinary ideas.' "[2] An officer with Alexis Orlov's fleet in the Mediterranean, Massin had met Leopold, grand duke of Tuscany and second son of Maria Theresa, while the fleet was docked for the winter at Livorno in 1771. In private conversations, Massin offered the grand duke several plans to divide the Ottoman Empire; they included granting Serbia and Bosnia to Austria and " 'forming separate countries to give to lesser princes the Morea, the island of Candia [Crete] and all sorts of similar things.' "[3]

When these proposals reached Vienna, Joseph found them especially attractive. After all, it was he who had first suggested to his mother and her chancellor that Austria should be prepared to take its share of the spoils in the event of the demise of Turkey. While calling Massin's proposals "vast and unbelievable," Joseph expressed considerable interest in their details and told his brother to inform Massin that the emperor would be willing to receive him in Vienna.[4] Although Joseph was receptive, Kaunitz was skeptical. He had no doubt that Massin spoke for Catherine but asserted he could not find the "slightest hint" that these proposals were serious; he thought that they were not bona fide offers but a ploy to see how far Vienna would allow Russia to expand.[5] Nonetheless, Kaunitz was not averse to using Massin's suggestions as the basis of his veiled threats to the Turks in April 1771.

For the time being, Kaunitz and Joseph disregarded Massin's suggestions. Later in the spring and during the summer of 1771, however, as news arrived of the Russo-Prussian negotiations to partition Poland, they became increasingly convinced that Austria would have to find some way to obtain a share or be faced with the considerable strengthening of two potential enemies and no compensation for the Habsburgs. Serious discussion of the possibilities began in September, and Kaunitz expressed his belief that Austria's share should not come from Poland but from the Ottoman Empire, notably the provinces of Moldavia and Walachia. Because Vienna would not allow these provinces to pass under Russian control under any circumstances, he suggested to his sovereigns that perhaps the imperial house should try to acquire them for itself. He admitted that traditional policy argued against it. The Principalities were full of the "wildest people," and their "difficult defense would lead to a weakening of Austrian power rather than its strengthening." At the same time, however, he warned that Vienna must always remember the need to maintain a balance of conquests between Austria, Russia, and Prussia. If the Porte were forced to abandon the provinces, Austria would be wise to obtain them.[6]

Joseph preferred a more flexible policy, based on the assumption that two solutions to the Russo-Turkish conflict seemed possible: either Russia would defeat Turkey, acquire advantages at its expense, and leave Prussia and Austria out of the final settlement, or all three powers would receive proportional advantages in Poland and the Ottoman Empire. In the event that Ottoman territory was to be divided, Austria should not claim Moldavia and Walachia but Bosnia and a part of the Adriatic coast; these acquisitions would round off the Monarchy's southern boundaries and provide additional access to the sea. If the powers agreed that only Poland should pay the price of peace, then Vienna should ask for Cracow. In any case, Joseph concluded, Austria must avoid being forced to choose between Moldavia and Walachia or nothing, and to that end Vienna should immediately begin talks with Berlin and St. Petersburg.[7]

Yet Vienna still did not commit itself to the partition of either the Ottoman Empire or Poland. When these discussions took place in September 1771, Russia had not yet formally agreed to evacuate the Principalities—the one condition upon which Austria absolutely insisted, whatever else might transpire. Moreover, Maria Theresa was most reluctant to embark upon a course that smacked of violating international order. Despite objections to the policy her chancellor and her son were preparing to follow, however, she realized that it might be the only alternative to war, which she was determined to avoid at all costs. For now, she could only restrain her advisers' slide toward partition with general admonitions: " 'No war, no defections from our system, no total abandonment of the Turks, and no money.' "[8]

In December 1771 word arrived in Vienna of Russia's willingness to evacuate Moldavia and Walachia and of Frederick's promise to support Russia in any conflict with Austria. Vienna's policy-makers then began to discuss partition in earnest. For the next few years, the idea of preserving the Ottoman Empire as a means of containing Russia seemed forgotten. Instead, the Viennese officials became intoxicated by the thought of acquiring great conquests with minimal or no sacrifices.

In January 1772 several varied plans for partition circulated among the Habsburg policy-makers, the most important being seven plans submitted by Kaunitz to the empress and all based on Massin's suggestions of a year earlier. The first called for a partition of the Ottoman Empire between Austria and Russia—the former to receive Serbia, Bosnia, Dalmatia, Macedonia, Albania, and the Greek coast to the Morea, and the latter all other Turkish possessions in Europe including Constantinople and the Straits. Such a solution would produce what the Austrians had for some time wished to avoid: a number of poor provinces added to the Monarchy and a common frontier with Russia. But with so many gains in prospect, traditional reservations receded into the background.

This first plan—despite the scope of its ambitions—was a rather conventional division of spoils. The second, however, was truly imaginative. It called for the creation of a new kingdom in the Southeast, incorporating Macedonia, Albania, Thrace, and the Aegean islands with Constantinople as the capital and with Catherine choosing the ruler. The plan is obviously similar to her more famous Greek Project of 1782, but the grandson whom this later scheme envisioned as heir to the Byzantine emperors was still unborn in 1772. Instead, as ruler of this new state, she had in mind Gregor Orlov, brother of the Russian naval commander and at the time her favorite lover.[9] Because the new state would be a Russian creature, Catherine would restrict her own acquisitions to the northern coast of the Black Sea.

Of the remaining parts of the Ottoman Empire, the second plan awarded Little Walachia, Bosnia, Serbia, Turkish Dalmatia, and Belgrade to the Habsburgs. Kaunitz, who at the time was becoming increasingly interested in the commercial potential of the Danube, told the empress that such acquisitions "would make the Danube the foundation of the Austrian Monarchy." The provinces were, he admitted, "in terrible condition" in terms of population, economy, and culture, but "an intelligent administration could draw from this land such advantages, that no power in Europe could compare to the illustrious archhouse."[10] But Kaunitz was not finished. Crete, Cyprus, the Morea, and some Aegean islands could be formed into another independent Habsburg kingdom, although the chancellor did not name the archduke he thought might serve as sovereign. He did recognize, however, that so much land ceded to the Habsburgs might cause jealousy among other powers and suggested accordingly that perhaps the Morea should go to Venice, but only in exchange for the Venetian provinces of Istria and Frioul.

The plan truly whets one's appetite for speculation. What would have been the course of Habsburg—and European—history had it come to pass? Would the Monarchy have been able to absorb all of the eastern and Orthodox Slavs into its western and Roman Catholic body politic? In the nineteenth century, could the Habsburgs have channeled the nationalism of these people into areas compatible with the needs and interests of the Monarchy? Would the Monarchy have become a federal state? Would the showdown between the Germanic and Slavic worlds have occurred before 1914 or not at all?

Since such questions have no answers, perhaps others would be more appropriate: did Kaunitz believe that such a plan could be realized at that time? Did he think it a good one for Austria? Even these questions are difficult to answer. He did discuss possible objections to the second plan more thoroughly than he did those to the first. For example, he knew that Prussia's approval would be necessary and that Prussia would have to be placated with Polish lands. To compensate the Poles for their losses and to avoid the Austro-Russian boundary that he feared, Kaunitz suggested awarding Moldavia and Walachia to Poland.

The chancellor apparently considered this second plan seriously enough to send it to his ambassador in Warsaw, who was to show it to Polish officials for their reaction. Although anonymous, the document sent to Poland resembled almost exactly the proposal submitted to Maria Theresa but with more detailed discussion of its advantages and disadvantages. These instructions, unlike the memorandum sent to the empress, admitted that the Turks would accept no partition without a fight, and that, despite the weakness of the Ottoman Empire, the difficulties of conducting operations in the Balkans might obstruct the military successes necessary to implement such a scheme.[11]

This evidence does not prove that Kaunitz really believed that such a complete overthrow of the territorial system in southeastern Europe was possible or beneficial at that time. Although such an overthrow had at times been suggested in the earlier part of the century, Vienna had rarely considered it a likely possibility. Could Kaunitz have decided that now it was not only possible but an acceptable solution to the twin problems of Ottoman decline and Russian ascendancy? Unfortunately, the archives lack the thorough Kaunitzian memoranda one might expect on the meaning of the Ottoman Empire's disappearance for the European state system and Austria's place within it. Perhaps the omission can be explained by the chancellor's relief that the waiting of 1771 had at last ended. Russia had conceded the issue of the Principalities and, by doing so, had considerably lessened the likelihood of an Austro-Russian confrontation. In addition, the prospect of partitioning Poland or the Ottoman Empire as a solution to the whole eastern European dilemma might have appealed to the chancellor as a new challenge to his skill in foreign affairs. He could now abandon the previous year's policy of waiting for the concessions of others and resume an active role in the European game of thrust and counterthrust. The absence of serious danger might have made the partitions especially attractive. So many courses of action appeared open, that if trouble emerged in one, another was readily available.

In addition to the two plans already discussed, Kaunitz presented five other proposals to Maria Theresa on the same day, but only one dealt significantly with the Ottoman Empire, calling for considerably fewer acquisitions for all parties, with Austria's share being Turkish Dalmatia, Serbia, and Bosnia. The remaining four provided for territorial arrangements among Austria, Russia, and Prussia not in the Ottoman Empire but in Germany and Poland.

Kaunitz's partition proposals were not the only ones offered by Austrian ministers nor were they the most extensive. Another submitted about the same time came from *Hofrat* Baron Friedrich von Binder and exceeded all those of the chancellor in its dreams for Habsburg expansion. Whereas Russia, Prussia, Poland, and Austria would receive largely the same territory outlined in Kaunitz's second plan, Binder suggested that Macedonia, Albania, Greece, and the Morea be organized into a kingdom ruled not by a Russian, but by a Habsburg. Constantinople, the prize for everyone, would be a free city, and flags of all nations would have the right to sail freely through the Straits. Crete, Cyprus, and the remaining Ottoman islands would be given to Austria's "friends (presumably Venice if its behavior met with Vienna's approval)." In an exuberant flight of fancy Binder noted that such an arrangement would require a change of titles: Catherine would rule from then on as "Empress of the East" and Joseph and Maria Theresa as "Emperor and Empress of the West." He even suggested changes in court protocol to reflect the exalted ranks of the sovereigns.[12]

In the end Vienna discarded all the proposals for dividing Ottoman lands. The reason was the opposition—indeed, the righteous indignation—of Maria Theresa. To her, acquisition of territory belonging to a neighbor whom she had formally promised to protect was a violation of honor among states and, worse yet, smacked of the kind of thing Frederick II would do.

> We want to act like the Prussians and at the same time retain the appearance of honesty. By doing so, we are deluding ourselves as to the means, and are confusing

> appearances and events. . . . Should they [the proposals]
> win for us the district of Walachia, Belgrade even, I
> would regard them as always purchased too dearly—at
> the expense of our honor, the glory of the Monarchy,
> and our good faith and religion.[13]

In late January and early February 1772, during the early
stages of the talks that would eventually lead to the partition
of Poland, Kaunitz tried to persuade the empress to change
her position, but she steadfastly refused.[14] Ironically, Maria
Theresa made her decision because of the Austro-Turkish accord, which she had originally opposed but which Kaunitz
had persuaded her to accept. Had it not existed—had Kaunitz
not sought subsidies for military operations the state would
have undertaken anyway—Maria Theresa might have consented to a territorial arrangement in the East that would
have involved partitions of both Poland and the Ottoman
Empire.[15]

For the remainder of the spring and throughout most of
the summer, Vienna's attention focused on the negotiations
to divide Poland. The agreement finally reached in August
defused any threat of war among Russia, Austria, and Prussia,
but it did not end the Russo-Turkish war. The congress at
Focşani, at which Thugut had tried to serve as mediator,
collapsed over the issue of the independence of the Crimea,
which Russia demanded and which Turkey rejected. Because
neither side wished to end the talks, they moved to Bucharest, where each hoped the other would become more tracta-
ble.

In the meantime, the Partition of Poland and the abrogation of the Austro-Turkish convention considerably eased the
tension in Vienna. Now that Austria had won some territory,
Kaunitz returned to his earlier conviction that the Ottoman
Empire must be saved. He informed the empress that Austria
must not allow Catherine to cripple Turkey. " 'It would be
against all decency . . . against all good faith and trust,
contrary to the policies of most of the European courts and

contrary to our own interests to permit Russia to destroy or to weaken the Porte.' "[16]

These were noble sentiments indeed from the man who six months earlier had proposed the partition of Turkey and had abandoned the convention that had given the Porte some hope for a respectable end to its war with Russia. In fact, Kaunitz was now less interested in ending the Russo-Turkish war than he had been earlier. He advised Thugut not to take part in the negotiations at Bucharest or even to go there to observe. Whatever Thugut might say, he warned, could cause ill will between Austria and one of the parties involved.[17] The chancellor proposed simply to wait to see how the talks in Bucharest progressed.

Before the talks concluded, however, the ever-watchful Kaunitz noticed another opportunity to gain some territory, although nothing as extensive as Galicia, which was Austria's main share of the Polish lands. He had in mind Little Walachia, which he had tried to win as part of the convention of 1771 and which Austrian troops still occupied even though the convention had lapsed. The news from Bucharest indicated that the Russian demands included a substantial reparations payment, which the depleted Ottoman treasury would be unlikely to raise. Kaunitz suggested to Maria Theresa that she offer the sultan "5-6,000,000" gulden for Little Walachia which he could then use to pay the Russians.[18] Apparently bewildered that the chancellor wanted this province and that he was willing to pay so much for it, the empress told him that she was not sure "if I agree with it or not." Yet she authorized him to proceed if he thought it best.[19]

She informed her son of the proposal, and he thought it downright extravagant. The "financial, military, commercial, and political advantages" of Little Walachia were "far too small" for 6,000,000 gulden. Moreover, he reminded his mother, the final amount would substantially exceed 6,000,000 because Austria would have to borrow the money and pay interest on it. Given these liabilities, Joseph suggested send-

ing someone to Little Walachia to find out more about the
province, especially how much it was actually worth.[20]

Joseph chose himself to conduct the inspection. In the late
spring and summer of 1773 he made an extensive tour of
Little Walachia, Transylvania, and Galicia. Of Little Walachia he wrote, ". . . I am convinced that the acquisition of
the Walachia surnamed Austrian would be more a liability
than an asset," but did suggest that Austria secure the nearby
Ottoman town of Orsova on the left bank of the Danube.[21]
Its possession, Joseph believed, would deprive the Turks of
an important post jutting into Habsburg territory and would
help the Austrians control "sanitation affairs, contraband,
banditry, as well as many other things."[22]

Within a few weeks, however, Joseph discovered what he
really wanted: the Bukovina. During his inspection of Galicia, the emperor learned that the way from eastern Galicia
into Transylvania was blocked by mountains. To build roads
through the passes would be extremely expensive, and the
winter weather would make them impassable for much of the
year anyway. The best route connecting the two provinces lay
along the valleys of the Siret (Sereth) and Suceava (Suczawa)
rivers, which ran through the Bukovina, at that time part of
Ottoman Moldavia. Without doubt, Joseph informed his
mother, the acquisition of this territory would "facilitate our
communications and our commerce as well as win for us the
passageway for our troops in case of war from one to the other
of our provinces who would otherwise have to make a terrible
detour to join together."[23]

As the emperor's desires became known, Kaunitz sent them
to Thugut. In late February 1773 he forwarded to the minister his own wish to acquire Little Walachia for Austria, then
in June cancelled this demand and passed on Joseph's request
for Orsova. Finally in July he dispatched instructions to persuade the Turks to cede the Bukovina.[24] All these requests
caused Thugut considerable concern. Securing these lands would
not be as easy as Vienna seemed to think. First, he told the
chancellor, the Turks would not give up anything without

compensation, and Austria had little to offer in exchange.[25] Second, the Porte would not cede territories that had mosques (such as Orsova), because it would be contrary to Islamic law. Third, Austria could not claim any reward for showing friendship toward Turkey in 1771—as Kaunitz had suggested—because Vienna had unilaterally abrogated the convention.[26]

What disturbed Thugut the most, however, was that Vienna seemed to be overlooking what he considered the truly important issue in Ottoman relations. Being a Turkish specialist since he entered Habsburg service, the minister had firm ideas about Austrian policy toward the Ottoman Empire, and he did not hesitate to express them to Kaunitz. For Thugut, the greatest danger was the spread of Russian hegemony, and Austria's primary objective should be to block that danger, even if it necessitated some sort of cooperation with the sultan. At this time, Kaunitz to him seemed to have forgotten the danger that Russia represented. At Bucharest, he reminded the chancellor, the tsarina had asked for an independent Crimea, acquisition of the fortresses of Kerch and Enikale at the mouth of the Sea of Azov, unrestricted Russian shipping on all Ottoman waters, the right to establish consuls throughout the Balkans, and recognition of Russia as protector of all "schismatics" within the Ottoman state. If these demands were met, Thugut emphasized, Russia would become so formidable that Turkey could not contain it. The tsarina could launch a raid with only 10-12,000 men from Kerch and "with the support of a general rising among the Greeks [Orthodox] would raise the Russian eagle on the walls of Constantinople."[27] A treaty based on Russian wishes "would mean the end of the Ottoman Empire, at least in Europe, and Russian power would become established within a short time in such a strong position . . . that no other state would be able to oppose it."[28]

These warnings, sent in the spring of 1773, did not elicit the response Thugut expected from Kaunitz; in fact, they were ignored. In September, after studying the request to pry

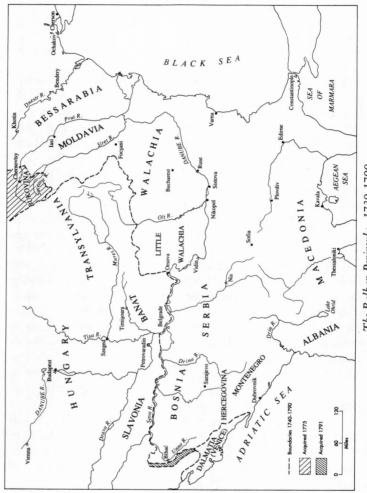

BLACK SEA

SEA OF MARMARA

Ochakov? Cherson
Bendery
Dnestr R.
Khotin
BESSARABIA
Prut R.
MOLDAVIA
Iasi
Siret R.
Chernovtsy
BUKOVINA
Suceava
TRANSYLVANIA
Focsani
WALACHIA
Bucharest
DANUBE R.
Ruse
Sistova
Nikopol
Varna
Constantinople
Edirne
AEGEAN SEA
Plovdiv
Kavala
MACEDONIA
Olt R.
LITTLE WALACHIA
Orsova
Vidin
Sofia
Thessaloniki
Lake Ohrid
Mures R.
BANAT
Timisoara
Belgrade
Nis
SERBIA
Drin R.
ALBANIA
Tisa R.
Szeged
Petrovaradin
Drina R.
Sarajevo
HERCEGOVINA
MONTENEGRO
Dubrovnik
HUNGARY
Budapest
DANUBE R.
Vienna
SLAVONIA
Sava R.
BOSNIA
Drava R.
DALMATIA (VENICE)
Bihac
Una R.
ADRIATIC SEA

Boundaries 1740-1790
Acquired 1775
Acquired 1791

0   60   120
Miles

The Balkan Peninsula, 1739–1790

the Bukovina from the sultan, Thugut sent to the chancellor a long and rambling assessment of the political future of the Ottoman Empire and what he believed Habsburg policy should be. After the usual warnings about the Porte's almost certain resentment at such a demand, Thugut adopted a new ploy to get Kaunitz to look more carefully at Vienna's interests in southeastern Europe. Abandoning his earlier pleas for Austria to come to Turkey's aid, he now declared that the end of the Ottoman Empire was "quite near." The portents were clear: weakness of the military, the ease with which enemies could now cross the important rivers, internal strife, and the coming extinction of the House of Osman. The old sultan was ill, his brothers probably would be unable to have children, and, if they died soon, the throne would pass to Selim, a boy who was unlikely to be able to hold the empire together.

When this collapse occurred, Thugut advised, Austria could annex all of the Turkish possessions in Europe. In terms reminiscent of Fleischmann and Talman, he argued that, with a good fleet on the Danube, efficient organization, and a force of 60-70,000 men, Austria "could achieve the greatest things;" in fact, it could become "the true Roman Empire." Until that time, Vienna should not discuss minor acquisitions, but instead "employ every means . . . to arrange a peace that will keep the Ottoman lands unpartitioned and the Porte in at least some position [of power]." This should be Austrian policy "until the right time for the illustrious archhouse to appear, in conjunction with the approval and cooperation of other Christian courts concerned for their own existence, to save [Turkey] from Russian greediness."[29]

In this rambling epistle, Thugut was trying to muster all the arguments he could think of to persuade Kaunitz to return to the spirit, if not the letter, of the Austro-Turkish convention. It is difficult to determine whether Thugut was serious in suggesting that Austria be prepared to take over the entire Ottoman Empire in Europe. Given the tenor of the rest of this report and of his dispatches up to early 1774, he was apparently trying to persuade Kaunitz to let Austria at least return to the peace negotiations as mediator and to try in that capacity to support the Ottomans. Clearly Thugut feared Russian aggrandizement and believed that Vienna must take measures to stop it. To him, Kaunitz's policy of cooperating with Russia instead of opposing its expansion was a highly dangerous one. Since the authorities in the Habsburg capital seemed concerned primarily about acquisitions, he hoped to show that more extensive gains could be achieved by protecting Turkey, rather than by nibbling at it.

Thugut's brief caused a bit of a stir in Vienna. When it arrived, Kaunitz was vacationing in Moravia; in his absence another minister read it and recommended to Maria Theresa that she tell Thugut exactly what Vienna's policy was. When the chancellor returned, however, he did not go so far. Addressing Thugut as a teacher does a pupil, he carefully reassured the internuntius that things were not as bleak as he thought. Turkey was not an old friend, as Thugut seemed to think, and Russia was not an old enemy either. Besides, the military situation did not seem likely to produce more stunning Russian victories. In essence, Kaunitz advised Thugut to calm down, to continue following his orders and giving helpful advice on certain matters, and to trust that his chancellor was following a policy in Austria's true interests.[30]

In his general policy toward the East, Kaunitz was for now following a waiting game, and he expected Thugut to go along with it. The chancellor wanted the Russo-Turkish war to end, but he dared not do anything to bring it to a close. He feared that any Austrian action might be interpreted as hostile in St. Petersburg, and any ill will between Vienna and St. Petersburg would be greeted with pleasure in Berlin. For Kaunitz, the potentially dangerous enemy was not Russia—and certainly not Turkey—but Prussia, and the negotiations leading to the Partition of Poland reminded him of that fact. He outlined his hopes and his policy not to Thugut but to the more experienced and trusted Count Florimund Mercy d'Argenteau, his ambassador at Versailles. He feared that a continuation of the Russo-Turkish war would lead to "new manifestations of the audacity and success of the Russians on the one hand and of the ineptitude of the Turks on the other," which in turn would encourage the king of Prussia to engage in further "political knaveries." Despite these unfortunate prospects, Vienna for now could take "no part either against the Porte or against Russia" but must remain strictly neutral in their hostilities and deliberations.[31]

In the meantime Thugut, chastened by Kaunitz's veiled reprimands, undertook his assignment of wresting Orsova and the Bukovina from the Turks. For the remainder of 1773 and the first few weeks of 1774, the internuntius could not approach the Porte because the Turkish ministers dared do nothing while they waited for the old sultan to die. He did so on 21 January and was succeeded by his brother Abdul Hamid I. The new sultan made an immediate—and poor—impression on Thugut. He "considers the details of business as unworthy of him," the internuntius advised Vienna, and, whenever his ministers asked him for orders, "this man, a great admirer of Mehmed the Conqueror, simply told them to do what Mehmed's government would have done." Thugut believed that for the moment there was no way to assess Austria's chances of winning the Bukovina and Orsova, but he did not think "the new sovereign, his advisers, or anyone he is likely to choose for his ministers" would accede to Austrian demands. If Vienna really wanted those territories, Thugut advised, Habsburg troops should simply occupy them. "Real possession" would be much easier to argue at the Porte than requesting any formal cession.[32]

A month later Thugut repeated his counsel with new emphasis, noting that the Turks were becoming increasingly unfriendly. In a conversation with the grand vizier, Thugut had expressed again Austria's desire to take part in the Russo-Turkish peace talks (an expression that had become merely a formality by this time) and had suggested that continued exclusion from them represented an insult to the Habsburgs. To Thugut's surprise, the grand vizier had replied to this routine statement by emptying "the full pot of his political-logical bile against the inconsistent, now pro-Turkish, now pro-Russian, now pro-Polish, now anti-Polish, now neutral Viennese policy."[33] This reaction on the part of the senior Ottoman minister indicated that since 1770 the Turks had hoped for some form of cooperation with Austria to resist Russian aggrandizement. The Porte knew that in this situation Ottoman and Habsburg interests were the same: to stop the Russians from obtaining a formidable position of power in southeastern Europe. The Ottoman ministers could not appreciate why Austria refused to recognize that fact and persisted in following what seemed to them a haphazard policy designed to gain insignificant territories while ignoring the danger that loomed so ominously beside them. While Thugut undoubtedly sympathized with this Ottoman assessment of Habsburg policy, he obviously could do nothing more than follow his orders from Vienna. Consequently, following the grand vizier's outburst, he told Kaunitz that for now Austrian influence in Constantinople had practically vanished. If Vienna wanted anything from the Porte, it must take it by force or the threat of force.

Kaunitz prepared, as far as possible, to act on Thugut's suggestion. Since he and his sovereigns wished to avoid hostilities, they could not take Orsova, which was defended by Ottoman troops. The Bukovina, on the other hand, was held by the Russians. They had occupied it at the outbreak of the Russo-Turkish war and in 1774 were still there awaiting a peace settlement. Kaunitz had already inquired indirectly if the Russians would object to being replaced by Austrian troops as they departed, and they had agreed, provided it could be done surreptitiously.[34] In early May, as rumors spread of an approaching Russo-Turkish treaty, Kaunitz informed St. Petersburg of Austria's intention to occupy the Bukovina and asked Catherine to allow Habsburg forces to move in while her soldiers evacuated.[35]

Shortly after the news of the signing of the Treaty of Kuchuk Kainarji that ended the Russo-Turkish war reached Vienna, Kaunitz sent a high-ranking officer to the Russian commander-in-chief P. A. Rumiantsev to coordinate the Russian withdrawal with the Austrian occupation.[36] No convention was to be negotiated, merely an understanding between general officers. "For the easing of all this," the Austrian was to present to Rumiantsev a diamond-studded dagger and 5,000 ducats and to distribute an additional 1,000 ducats to other important officers.[37] Vienna had no trouble securing Russian cooperation; on 20 August Austrian troops entered the Bukovina, and six weeks later Kaunitz notified Thugut that the forces there could "hold it secure from all insults of the Moldavians and even of the Turks."[38]

Now Thugut had to persuade the Turks to accept the *fait accompli*. There was no point in trying to justify the occupation, he told Kaunitz, for "to make such claims understandable to this nation is completely impossible."[39] Nor should Austria offer to exchange the region for a guarantee of its future friendship. The "favorites and ministers" of the sultan "in no way concern themselves with the future" because none is sure that he will be part of it. Instead, Thugut suggested reaching an agreement with the *hospodar* of Moldavia, Gregor Ghika, who had just won reappointment to his post from the sultan. Ghika alone, Thugut believed, knew the true value of the Bukovina (earlier Thugut had asked for information and maps concerning that province because the Ottoman ministers "possess not the slightest knowledge of geography"),[40] and he alone could persuade the Porte that it would be all right to concede it to Austria. In fact, Thugut suggested, an arrangement might be worked out solely with Ghika "so in this fashion [we could] bring the whole business to an end without it being necessary to involve the Porte itself. . . ."[41]

Ghika had been openly pro-Russian and anti-Austrian in the past, but Thugut did not anticipate problems for two reasons. First, he planned to appeal to Ghika through his father-in-law Jacob Riso, who represented the *hospodar* in Constantinople and was friendly toward Austria. Second, Thugut believed that Ghika could be bribed.[42] Accepting the

assessment of the internuntius, Kaunitz authorized him to
offer Ghika either a single, substantial gift or a "life-long
pension," something he might find attractive given the notoriously short tenure of most *hospodars*.[43]

These temptations proved ineffective. In early January 1775
Thugut learned of a letter written by Ghika to the Porte
declaring that the Bukovina was the richest of all the Moldavian lands, that the people were begging the sultan to stop
the Austrian piracy, and that, if the Porte could do nothing,
he should permit the Moldavians to appeal to a power that
could, specifically Russia. At the same time Riso brought
Thugut a personal note from Ghika telling him that the letter
was only a device to calm Moldavian boyars who risked losing
property in the Bukovina. Thugut found this business rather
unsettling and expressed to Kaunitz his fear that the matter
could not be resolved easily.[44]

By this time, Kaunitz was anxious for a speedy settlement
of the affair. By early 1775 the Austrian occupation had caused
rumblings in other courts, and the Turks themselves were
sending reinforcements to Belgrade and the Principalities in
case of trouble with Austria. Kaunitz instructed Thugut to
tell the Porte that Vienna was not impressed by this activity
and that its forces would continue to occupy the Bukovina;
beyond that, he had no advice to send.[45]

In mid-February Thugut decided upon a simple but direct
step. He presented to the Porte a formal demand that the
sultan cede the Bukovina to Austria. "I clothed the demand
for the Bukovina as well as the other matters [Orsova and
some commercial privileges] in the friendliest terms . . . but
in my oral presentation [I used] all the force and seriousness
that could serve the promotion of the whole affair."[46] The
oral presentation must have been forceful indeed. Within a
month talks began, and on the night of 2-3 April the *reis
effendi*, a group of Ottoman legalists, and Thugut reached an
agreement. The Bukovina would become Austrian but Orsova, which possessed mosques, would remain Ottoman. In
reporting the meeting, Thugut remarked that he never thought

that the Turks would yield and was not certain why they did so.[47] In fact, the Porte believed that it had no choice, being unfit to fight another war to save a far-off province and to run the risk of losing more.

On 7 May 1775 Thugut and some Ottoman officials formally signed the agreement, the first article of which declared that the Porte agreed to Austria's possession of the Bukovina as "proof of its unequivocal friendship, affection, and good neighborliness."[48] The treaty did not firmly settle the boundaries, but it did provide for the creation of a commission to work them out.[49] After the signing, Thugut again received congratulations from Kaunitz and his sovereigns, and the internuntius sent to Vienna his accounts listing all the bribes he had had to pay. For Riso he recommended an additional gift of 1,000 ducats because he had provided much useful information from inside the Porte, but he advised nothing for Ghika, "that two-faced Greek."[50]

The acquisition of the Bukovina earned Thugut and Kaunitz considerable acclaim both at the time and later on. Frederick II called it a "masterpiece" of Austrian diplomacy, and a nineteenth-century historian labeled it a feat "worthy of a Kaunitz and a Thugut."[51] A prominent scholar of our own day described it as "the most successful single move in Kaunitz's foreign policy," for he kept Russia out of Moldavia and Walachia and essentially got paid for doing so.[52] It was quite an achievement. Austria gained a province which connected Galicia and Transylvania and which cost virtually nothing to obtain. While wild and depopulated when acquired, it became a model province of the Monarchy in the nineteenth century, extolled by some scholars as proof that eastern European nationalities could live and work in harmony under the rule of the Habsburgs.

At the time of the annexation, however, two persons expressed reservations about it, one being Maria Theresa. Although she congratulated Kaunitz when the treaty was finally concluded, some months before she had revealed her dismay at taking another piece of property to which she had no right.

"I am not going to speak of affairs to you," she wrote to Marie Antoinette, but "they are disagreeable; those of Poland and Moldavia [the Bukovina] are quite contrary to my way of thinking; but I cannot separate from the other two powers [Russia and Prussia] without risking a war, and I certainly do not want to do that."[53] The other reservation came from Thugut. Of all the Austrian ministers at the Porte during the eighteenth century, Thugut expressed the most sympathy for and the most understanding of his beleaguered hosts. Indeed, even more than Kaunitz or Joseph, he appreciated the importance of the Ottoman state in the future of the Habsburg Monarchy. Keeping the Ottoman Empire intact would far better serve Austrian interests in the southeast than the acquisition of a few provinces here and there to round off territories or improve communications. Moreover, the annexation of such provinces would only encourage further Russian (and in Poland Prussian) expansionism because it would show to St. Petersburg that Austria could be bribed into supporting such expansionism with tidbits of territory. Besides, Kaunitz's abandoning the Austro-Turkish convention of 1771 and then wrenching property from the sultan again harmed Habsburg status as an upholder of international respectability. Like Maria Theresa, Thugut complained that this matter "has renewed the ancient reproaches regarding our conventions. . . . It is a great evil, but what can be done?"[54] Some Habsburg officals still believed in the importance of ethics in foreign policy, but they were obviously a beleaguered few.

CHAPTER NINE
Taming the Bear, 1774-1786

Recent scholarship has identified the Treaty of Kuchuk Kainarji, which ended the Russo-Turkish war, as the beginning of the Eastern Question.[1] According to its provisions, Russia annexed the northern coast of the Black Sea between the Bug and Dnepr rivers, the fortresses of Kerch and Enikale in the Crimea, and part of Kabardia; the Crimea became independent and thus open to Russian intrigue; Russian merchants won the right to sail freely on the Black Sea; and the Russian sovereign received vaguely worded rights to protect the Orthodox in the Ottoman Empire, rights that would later be used to meddle in Turkish internal affairs.[2] The importance of the treaty and its implications were recognized not only by historians tracing the causes of Ottoman decline, but also by many observers at the time. They saw it as a stunning victory for Russia and a possibly fatal blow to the Ottoman Empire. In fact, the Turks themselves, encouraged by the French, delayed implementing some provisions of the treaty because they realized what fearsome damage to Turkish security and prestige it represented.

The treaty impressed Kaunitz in particular. Not only had Russia won the war, it had won the peace as well. To Thugut he remarked that the Russians had secured "an advantageous and glorious peace" and had done so in the face of adversity. Hindered by war-weariness at home, by considerable expenditure of resources, and by the Pugachev uprising in the east, the Russians had nonetheless pressed home their victory "with dagger in hand and with perseverance."[3] While admiring the Russian success, the chancellor also seemed to think that the Turks deserved what had happened to them. " 'The Turks . . . have earned the fate that they have received,' " he told the British ambassador. " 'This people is destined to oblivion, and a small but good army can expel them from Europe right now.' "[4] Which army Kaunitz had in mind was unclear.

Kaunitz's admiration for the Russian achievement was not shared by his minister at the Porte. To Thugut Kuchuk Kainarji represented tragedy for Turkey and danger for Austria. Virtually every provision, he warned, contained grim omens for the future. The acquisition of the Black Sea coast and the Crimean fortresses would make it possible for the Russians to launch an amphibious assault directly at Constantinople. "As soon as one in Petersburg finds it convenient, . . . [Russia] can bring 20,000 men to the walls of Constantinople in 36 or even 24 hours." Time-consuming, difficult, debilitating campaigns in the Ukraine and the Principalities would no longer be necessary for the Russians to inflict total defeat upon the Turks. Moreover, Thugut did not underestimate the provisions granting the Russians the status of protectors of the Orthodox. Calling the terms full of "dangerous consequences," he guessed that St. Petersburg would exploit them by sending agents throughout the Balkans to prepare a general Orthodox rising against Ottoman rule. When the time was right, Thugut emphasized, the Russians would coordinate an amphibious assault at the Ottoman capital and a Balkan revolution, neither of which the Turks could resist. "With the news of a successful [Russian] landing, the sultan will have no choice but to leave his palace, flee deep into Asia, and abandon the throne of the Eastern Empire to his successful conquerer." Then European Turkey, the Aegean islands, and Constantinople would fall to Russia. The supreme danger, Thugut concluded, was that this victory could be achieved "before the news of a Russian move even reached the borders of Christianity." Vienna would not hear of the total destruction of the Ottoman Empire until it was an accomplished fact. Kuchuk Kainarji was not merely a terrible blow to the Ottoman Empire, but "to the rest of the world."[5]

While not as Russophobic as Thugut, Kaunitz knew that Kuchuk Kainarji would add a new element in the formulation of Austrian policy toward Turkey. The fundamental problem remained the same: how could Austria restrict the aggrandizement of Russia and at the same time avoid a confrontation with St. Petersburg? The new element was the possibility that now Russia could inflict a sudden, perhaps fatal blow upon the Ottoman Empire and annex all of its possessions without asking for Austria's permission or help.

Two years after Kuchuk Kainarji, Kaunitz developed a set of guidelines for eastern policy that he hoped Vienna could follow for some time to come. He presented these principles to Joseph who was about to depart for Versailles, so that the emperor would have a firm grasp of Kaunitz's ideas when he visited his sister, Marie Antoinette, and her husband, King Louis XVI of France. There was no question, Kaunitz began, that Catherine's goal was the destruction of the Ottoman Empire. Nor was there any question that, given Turkey's current weakness, she would achieve her goal. If Austria assisted her in that venture, the House of Habsburg could acquire "great conquests, such as Turkish Dalmatia and Croatia, Bosnia, Serbia, Walachia, Moldavia, and still more Turkish provinces on our borders." Nevertheless, Kaunitz strongly advised against such a course for numerous reasons. Because the Porte feared Russia, it desired only friendship with the Monarchy; consequently, it presented a minor threat as a neighbor. If Russia should acquire the eastern Balkans and Constantinople, it would become too strong for Austria to resist. Then, Russia might cooperate militarily with Prussia against Austria, and the Habsburgs would face "a prospect too horrible to imagine." Yet if Austria joined the Russians in dismembering Turkey, Prussia would have to be included, because it would not sit by and watch its neighbors grow stronger without compensation. This compensation would have to come in Poland and would far surpass in value any Austrian acquisitions in the Balkans which would consist of "depopulated, distant lands that would diminish rather than augment our internal strength."[6] Moreover, Habsburg participation in a partition of the Ottoman Empire would alienate Austria's most loyal ally, France.

The only solution, as Kaunitz saw it, was to preserve the territorial status quo as long as possible. While the Austrians dared not aid the Turks in improving their defenses against Russia, they should encourage the French to help. If, in the meantime, St. Petersburg appealed to Vienna for assistance against the sultan, the Habsburgs should emphasize strongly that Prussia, not Turkey, was Austria's primary enemy and should not commit themselves to the dismemberment of the Ottoman Empire. However, they must also be careful to say nothing that might cause the Russians to draw closer to Berlin.[7]

This Kaunitzian analysis, which would be repeated in various forms to various officials for the next four years, reflected the problem foreseen since the second decade of the century. A weak Turkey was a welcome neighbor; a strong Russia was not. Even if Austria could secure a large share of Ottoman spoils, they would not compensate for the threat that increased Russian strength would present. Now the problem was growing more serious because Kaunitz could find no way to slow Russia's potential aggrandizement. In 1716 Austria was Turkey's primary foe; thus Vienna could restrict Russian expansion by rejecting offers of aid. In 1737 Vienna hoped to control Russia's conquests by manipulating operations plans, although this proved unnecessary in the end because of severe logistical problems that hampered the Russian army's marches to the south. In 1776 Russia did not seem to need Austria as it had in 1737; it seemed capable of crushing Turkey all by itself. Even if the Monarchy did assist Russia, St. Petersburg would get the choice morsels and Vienna the scraps when the partition occurred.

There was one alternative to Austria's policy: rapprochement with Prussia. An Austro-Prussian accord, supported by France and by Turkey, would likely keep Catherine in her place. But for Kaunitz an understanding with Prussia was unthinkable. Securing Frederick's neutrality and actually seeking an alliance with him were for the chancellor entirely different matters. And in this conviction he was supported by

Maria Theresa, who would never agree to an accord with the "Monster" of the North.

Given his absolute refusal to cooperate with Berlin, Kaunitz believed that he could delay but not prevent the strengthening of Russia at Turkey's expense. His only consolation to Joseph was that Russia's losses in the last war and the depredations inflicted by Pugachev would postpone any decisive Russo-Turkish war "for 20 years or more." In the meantime, Kaunitz advised being ready for all eventualities in order to gain what was best for Austria "by declaring for or against the Porte."[8]

Kaunitz's hopes for a long delay before the next Russo-Turkish conflict were almost dashed in 1777. The creation of an independent Crimea by the Treaty of Kuchuk Kainarji had actually bred more problems than it had solved. Soon after independence, a power struggle broke out between two members of the ruling Girey family, one pro-Russian and the other pro-Ottoman. In November 1776 Catherine decided to assist her protégé by sending Russian regulars into the Crimea to establish his firm control over the country.[9] In response, the Porte announced that it too was thinking of military intervention, ostensibly to preserve Crimean sovereignty, but in fact to resist the Russians. Another Russo-Turkish war seemed in the offing.

In Vienna the news of such a possibility reopened the debate about what Austria should do in case war erupted. Joseph offered largely the same assessment as he had in 1772:

> Concerning the Porte, one can do nothing bad and nothing good; we cannot save it, and its demise, if nothing else happens, will be more unfortunate than useful. Nonetheless, we must be ready for all eventualities, so we must look around a little to see what is going on in the [Ottoman] lands bordering ours to find out what and how much will be useful to us.[10]

Besides offering these thoughts, Joseph asked the senior Austrian military adviser, Field Marshal Franz Moriz Lacy, to suggest action which the Habsburg army could take should Turkey "completely evacuate its possessions in Europe." On 2 May Lacy submitted a plan of operations calling for the conquests that he believed would be the easiest to defend. Resembling closely the proposal submitted by Talman in 1736, his plan recommended occupation of Little Walachia, the Danube to Nikopol (Talman had suggested Ruse), and then all the lands west of a line running from Nikopol to the Aegean, including Greece. The invading columns would proceed from Transylvania southward, using the Danube as a supply route and Sofia as the main base of operations with additional support in Dalmatia and Greece from warships and transport vessels dispatched from Trieste and Fiume. The campaign should be concluded in one season, Lacy warned, because Russia would take Constantinople very quickly and because Vienna must not give the other European powers time to organize a meaningful protest.[11] Lacy's proposal became the subject of considerable debate among the policy-makers in Vienna, but no one questioned the assumption that the Ottoman Empire would collapse in a war with Russia.

The plans and arguments were, of course, similar to those in 1772 and, as long as international conditions remained the same, would be repeated at every similar crisis. This time, however, Maria Theresa, who had always disapproved of talk of partitions, passionately stated her opposition not only to the proposals of Joseph and Lacy but to the whole course of Austrian policy toward the Ottoman Empire since 1771. In doing so, she also revealed what she thought the true value of the Ottoman lands the Monarchy might acquire would be.

> Of all the enterprises the most hazardous and most dangerous will be the partition of the Ottoman Empire, whose consequences we have the most to fear. What can we gain from such conquests, even to the gates of Constantinople? Provinces unhealthy, depopulated, or inhabited by treacherous and ill-intentioned Greeks [Orthodox]—they would not strengthen the Monarchy but

weaken it. Even more, the credit that my house has always been so eager to preserve would be lost forever and this would be an irreparable loss . . . even more critical than [that from] the partition of Poland. . . . Without a fatal combination of unfortunate circumstances, I will never prepare myself for the partition of the Ottoman Empire, and I hope that our descendants will never see it expelled from Europe.[12]

To Maria Theresa's relief, the "fatal combination of unfortunate circumstances" did not occur. The Turks made a half-hearted effort to land troops in the Crimea, but, when the attempt was repulsed, decided to keep the peace. Russia, which had not sought war in the first place, did not press the issue, and in 1779 both powers concluded an agreement recognizing the Russian candidate as khan of the Crimea for his lifetime.[13]

Despite the attention paid to the Russo-Turkish confrontation in 1777, the settlement resolving it went largely unnoticed in Vienna, for by 1779 Austrian policy-makers had other, more pressing matters on their minds. During the night of 29-30 December 1777, Elector Maximilian Joseph of Bavaria died without male issue. Within a week his successor recognized Habsburg claims to parts of Bavaria and the Upper Palatinate, and shortly thereafter Austrian troops marched into the ceded areas. Fearing the greatly increased influence the Bavarian lands would give Austria in German affairs, Frederick convinced the new elector's heir presumptive to reject the Habsburg claims and mobilized some of the lesser German states to resist Austrian annexation of those lands. In the ensuing War of the Bavarian Succession, the "Potato War," the Austrian and Prussian armies glared at one another in Bohemia while both ran out of food. The war was a short one, largely because France declared itself unwilling to support Vienna while Russia was willing to support Berlin. Consequently, the Monarchy accepted the joint mediation of St. Petersburg and Versailles and in May 1779 concluded the

Treaty of Teschen, which gave the Habsburgs only a fraction of what they had hoped to obtain.[14]

Although it might seem unrelated, the War of the Bavarian Succession had a decided impact upon Austria's eastern policy, for it reinforced Kaunitz's hatred and fear of Prussia. While the chancellor expressed considerable hostility toward Berlin throughout the 1770s, after 1779 this expression became substantially more strident. Consequently, the concerns about Ottoman collapse, a dangerous and mighty Russia on Austria's eastern flank, and annexing lands that would be liabilities rather than assets became subordinated in Kaunitz's mind to the desire to seek revenge against Prussia. From then on he seemed willing to support Russian aggrandizement in the southeast if Russia would join him in destroying Prussia.

And after 1779 Kaunitz faced less opposition from the throne in pursuing that goal. Maria Theresa would die in 1780, leaving Joseph the sole ruler of the state. Joseph presented a less formidable obstacle to the chancellor's policies than his mother had, because he lacked her experience and her strong principles. Yet, Kaunitz could not always manipulate Joseph easily. The emperor regularly rejected the chancellor's advice and on occasion suggested policies that Kaunitz detested. Nonetheless, the chancellor was usually able to convince Joseph of the wisdom of his proposals, most of which were directed toward the defeat of Prussia.

The War of the Bavarian Succession also reemphasized to Kaunitz that, without Russia actively assisting Austria, the defeat of Prussia was unlikely. Not long after the Treaty of Teschen, the chancellor instructed his ambassador in St. Petersburg to suggest to the tsarina that an alliance with Vienna was more valuable than the one with Berlin, because Prussia would block Russian expansion in the north while Austria could aid Russian interests in the south.[15] Catherine was quite receptive to such a notion, because at that time, her ally, Frederick, still fearful that Kaunitz and his sovereigns would renew the Austro-Prussian conflict at the first opportunity, was pursuing a whimsical alliance that would unite Prussia,

Russia, and the Ottoman Empire against the Monarchy.[16] Catherine made it clear to the Prussian king that she would not conclude an alliance with Turkey, a power that she intended to dismember, but Frederick—in many ways just as narrowly antagonistic toward Austria as Kaunitz was toward Prussia—persisted in his efforts.

The first significant step toward an Austro-Russian accord came not from Kaunitz, however, but from Joseph. Apparently without the knowledge of his mother or the chancellor, he advised the Russian ambassador in Vienna that he desired to meet Catherine because he had heard that she was about to visit her western provinces.[17] For Joseph, the purpose was both to learn more about this enigmatic woman and " 'to stimulate the bile of the dear Frederick so that he dies of it.' "[18]

Catherine granted Joseph his wish. The first meeting of these two great personalities (opposed of course by Maria Theresa, who found considerable fault with the Russian empress's personal life) took place in the spring of 1780 at Mogilev, a city awarded to Russia in the first partition of Poland. Kaunitz and Joseph had no doubts that at the meeting Catherine would ask for Austrian aid in expelling the Turks from Europe, and both agreed that Joseph should answer in the affirmative, but then should add that Austria must receive a substantial share of the spoils and that no corresponding compensation should go to Prussia.[19] The informal conference consisted of subtle fencing between the two monarchs and some open negotiations between the current Russian favorite, Prince Gregor Potemkin, and the Austrian ambassador, Louis Cobenzl. Although no firm commitments were made, the company was sufficiently pleasing and the exchanges sufficiently promising for Joseph to journey with the empress to Moscow and to St. Petersburg before returning to Vienna.

When the tour ended, each side had made clear what matters it considered most important, even though no formal agreements were concluded. Joseph knew that Catherine wanted Constantinople. "Her project of establishing an empire in the

East rolls around in her head and broods in her soul."[20] Likewise, Joseph had emphasized that Austria feared Prussia and would not agree to any strengthening of the Hohenzollern state even if it resulted from a partition in which all parties received comparable gains. Indeed, Joseph had implied that Russia and Austria should resist, with force if necessary, Prussian efforts to share in any Ottoman spoils.[21] In addition to clarifying their positions, both monarchs found that they liked one another, a diplomatic success of considerable importance.[22]

For the moment the Austro-Russian rapprochement consisted of social pleasantries and expressions of friendship, but after the death of Maria Theresa in November 1780, the two monarchs set out to give their relations a substantive form. Had the old empress lived, an Austro-Russian alliance would probably have come about but not perhaps in the tight form that eventually emerged.[23] The initiative came from Russia, which proposed a treaty similar to one suggested during the conversations of the summer, namely a mutual guarantee of each other's territorial gains.[24] Kaunitz sensed in this proposal an opportunity to secure an anti-Prussian commitment from St. Petersburg; instead of accepting immediately, therefore, he suggested a full-blown defensive alliance providing for mutual assistance (in the amount of 30,000 men) in case either state were attacked by a third power. Kaunitz's offer closely resembled the treaty of 1726, but that pact had been aimed at western Europe while this time the target was Prussia. In fact, the chancellor had wanted to ask simply for a renewal of the alliance of 1746, which had been directed primarily against Prussia, but he feared that the Russians would reject this suggestion and so offered a modified version of the agreement of 1726 instead.[25]

The Russians declined his proposal anyway. Instead, they offered a more elaborate plan, essentially calling for each side to support the other in case of attack, but only with 12,000 men. If the Ottoman Empire were the attacker, however, the support would be unlimited.[26] Such an agreement was undoubtedly to Russia's advantage, and Kaunitz and Joseph knew it. Austria would be committed to an all-out war with Turkey while Russia would provide minimal support in case of a Prussian attack on Austria. But Kaunitz and Joseph also believed that their need for Catherine was greater than her need for them. Both agreed that Turkey would fall sooner or later and that they could do nothing to stop it. If they tried, St. Petersburg would simply call upon Berlin to keep the Habsburg army occupied while Russia carved up Turkey's possessions. To preserve some semblance of balance in southeastern Europe, Vienna would have to resort to Bartenstein's policy in 1737: alliance with Russia in an effort to control its aggrandizement through mutual agreement. The Ottoman Empire might have to be sacrificed if Austria were to enlist the Russians in a crusade against Frederick II.

Although the negotiations leading to the accord revealed no serious disagreements on its substance, they soon became snarled in the question of the "alternative." When a treaty was concluded, diplomatic practice required that two copies be made, one listing one party first with the second listing the other party first (hence the "alternative"). In treaties with the emperor, however, his name and title came first on both copies. In these negotiations, Catherine insisted that the "alternative" be practiced, which would in effect recognize her title as equal to Joseph's. Vienna of course resisted, and it appeared for a time that the talks would founder on this issue. They were saved, however, when Catherine suggested that, instead of a formal treaty, the two sovereigns exchange personal letters listing the promises to one another. After some discussion, Vienna found the solution acceptable, and Joseph dispatched his letter containing the provisions of the agreement.[27]

Kaunitz insisted that the accord be kept secret. If the article promising Russia full Austrian support against Turkey leaked out, he feared, it could precipitate a Prusso-Turkish-French agreement that would leave Vienna and St. Petersburg "greatly embarrassed."[28] Moreover, he expressed concern that the solution reached about the "alternative" would make other courts suspect that the accord contained more extensive commitments than it did, because they would never believe that the emperor had given up his precedence for so little.[29] To keep the agreement confidential, the Russian and Austrian policy-makers engaged in an elaborate deception, to the point that Joseph told his brother and heir, Leopold of Tuscany, that the negotiations had collapsed, while Catherine said nothing of it at all to her son and heir, Grand Duke Paul.[30] Many suspected the existence of the treaty, but it did not become common knowledge in the other European courts until 1783.

Although secret, the agreement inaugurated obvious expressions of Austro-Russian friendship. In the autumn of 1781 the grand duke and duchess of Russia set out on a European journey that took them to many Habsburg courts, while conspicuously avoiding those of the Hohenzollerns.[31] About the same time Joseph joined the League of Armed Neutrality, a device created by Catherine to protect neutral shipping during the War of the American Revolution.[32]

Another gesture of Austro-Russian amity had consequences unforeseen by Vienna. In the summer of 1782 another revolt erupted against the Russian-sponsored khan of the Crimea, who as usual appealed to Catherine for aid. Suspecting Ottoman complicity, the empress informed Joseph of the event and advised him that she would take "the necessary precautions to protect my frontiers against the incursions to which they are exposed."[33] In a romantic and fanciful reply, Joseph called her "my empress, my friend, my ally, my heroine," and promised to support her in "all possible exigencies that the trouble in the Crimea . . . might occasion."[34] To Vienna's surprise and consternation, this chivalric epistle elicited a personal letter from Catherine to Joseph setting forth the famous Greek Project. The tsarina proposed to establish a new Greek empire with its capital at Constantinople and her grandson Constantine as emperor; to form a kindom of Dacia under a Christian ruler—presumably her lover Potemkin—out of

Moldavia, Walachia, and Bessarabia; and to divide the remainder of Turkey's European possessions between Austria and Russia.[35] This proposal has, of course, caused considerable interest among historians, but for Vienna it was neither startling nor new. The establishment of a Russian-sponsored Greek empire based on Constantinople had its origins in Massin's plans, and the proposal for an independent state in Moldavia and Walachia had been offered in 1771. To be sure, Catherine had never combined the two projects before, but that caused no particular concern in Vienna.

What disturbed the Habsburg court was not the plan itself, but Catherine's suggestions that the European situation was now right for the Austro-Russian division of the Ottoman Empire. The only power likely to oppose the partition, she had argued, was Prussia, but Frederick would not act without French or British support, and they were embroiled in the War of the American Revolution. Should Frederick decide to attack Austria by himself, the combined Austro-Russian armies would be sufficient to defeat him. Besides, Catherine concluded, Frederick would be most reluctant to intervene, since he wished to end his reign in "peace and tranquillity."[36]

Kaunitz rejected Catherine's assessment of European affairs out of hand. It was, he remarked to Joseph, based on assumptions "partly unlikely and partly that can be shown to be false very easily." The obstacles to the fulfillment of her dreams could be summed up in two words, Kaunitz noted: "Prussia and France." Berlin especially would never allow Vienna and St. Petersburg to undertake such expansion unless it were included, and Austria would never agree to that because any Prussian gain would negate Austria's advantages. Kaunitz did not want to maintain a balance with Prussia, but to make his state superior to it. He cited several measures that would be necessary to deal with Prussia: St. Petersburg and Vienna would have to secure France's friendship, assign 100,000 troops to the Bohemian frontier, dispatch 30,000 Russians to stations "as near to the Prussian border as possible [meaning inside Poland]," reach an accord with the elector of

Saxony by promising him the throne of Poland, and recruit
as many German allies as possible. All of these steps would
be essential to implement the Greek Project, Kaunitz concluded, and none was likely to be realized.[37]

Notwithstanding his reservations, Kaunitz advised Joseph
against rejecting Catherine's project outright. If Vienna did
so, she would only seek Prussian support, and Austria would
find itself at the mercy of both powers. Vice-Chancellor Philip
Cobenzl remarked to the emperor that Catherine probably
offered the alliance to Austria rather than to Prussia only
because she liked Joseph personally more than she did Frederick. Should the emperor reject her offer, she would not
hesitate to propose it with appropriate modifications to Frederick. The emperor's acceptance of the Greek Project would
make Austria's situation "if not better than it is now, at least
not as bad as it could become if Your Majesty did not respond
favorably to the attention of the Empress, who is perhaps
governed only by the preference of an intimate liaison with
us to that of the king of Prussia."[38] In many respects the
situation of 1737 had repeated itself. Because Vienna needed
an alliance with Russia more than St. Petersburg needed one
with Austria, the Habsburgs were on the verge of entering a
Turkish war that they truly wished to avoid.

Joseph's reply to Catherine accepted the project with some
modifications and promised support—but hedged by insisting
that Catherine was misreading badly the international situation. France and Prussia would be more formidable opponents
than she might think, he warned (echoing Kaunitz's words),
for Prussia could invade Bohemia while France attacked
Habsburg possessions in Italy and the Netherlands and possibly the Russian fleet in the Mediterranean. Consequently,
the emperor would support the project only if the Russians
placed between 60,000 and 80,000 men in Poland and agreed
to let France have Egypt.[39] As the emperor explained to his
ambassador at the Russian court, "without both [conditions]
you know very well that I will not budge. . . ."[40]

While Vienna awaited the reply to Joseph's letter, good

news arrived from Constantinople. When the Crimean crisis became serious, Catherine had asked Vienna to instruct its representative at the Porte to issue a note jointly with the Russian ambassador demanding, among other things, that the sultan cease interfering in Crimean affairs.[41] Vienna had agreed, but the ministers assumed that the Porte would reject the note and precipitate hostilities. In late December, however, the Porte accepted it. Joseph and Kaunitz immediately seized upon the acceptance as a way out of the crisis altogether. They instructed their ambassador in St. Petersburg to play up the Ottoman concession as an end to Russian concerns about the Crimea and, of course, as an end to further talk of the Greek Project.[42]

To Vienna's consternation, St. Petersburg ignored the Porte's action completely. As a result, Joseph and Kaunitz concluded that Catherine intended to make war on the sultan regardless of any conciliatory gestures. Because the conflict would certainly involve the Habsburg Monarchy, Joseph implored Catherine to accept the Turkish concession; to Louis Cobenzl Kaunitz lamented

> how much the general hostility [toward Austria and Russia] would increase, how much the great jealousy of many courts would rise, how much the Prussian intrigues would be made easier, how inevitably the participation of France [in a partition] would be made more difficult, how much the proposed project would be in apparent danger, and what unfortunate consequences would threaten especially our state.[43]

After two months of anxious waiting, Vienna—and the rest of Europe—learned the Russian response: the annexation of the Crimea. On 8 May the Russian ambassador handed Kaunitz the announcement, asked for Habsburg support, and invited the emperor to take equivalent territory with Catherine's blessing.[44] The chancellor advised Joseph to applaud publicly the Russian step because passivity or opposition would ruin the alliance. He also suggested that Austria occupy Mol-

davia and Walachia as the Habsburg "equivalent" to the Crimea. Such a move need not lead to war with Turkey, Kaunitz
explained, especially if the Austrian envoy at the Porte explained that Vienna was taking the Principalities "in no unfriendly manner" but simply because it had become necessary
"under the present circumstances."[45]

Joseph thought that his adviser had taken leave of his senses.
To occupy Moldavia and Walachia would precipitate the very
war that he had been trying to avoid. The sultan might not
fight for far-off Crimea, but he would surely fight for the
Principalities. Then Austria would attract "the onus of all of
Europe for flippantly starting a war." The only solution, he
informed the chancellor, was to tell Catherine that he would
support her diplomatically but would avoid arms if at all
possible and would take no "equivalent" for himself.[46] He
wanted no conflict with France, Prussia, and Turkey together.

From this exchange to the end of the crisis, Kaunitz and
Joseph disagreed seriously concerning the course that Habsburg policy should take. To Kaunitz, Russia's annexation of
the Crimea while Austria received nothing would reveal to
Europe a fact that he had hoped to disguise: that Russia was
the dominant partner in the Austro-Russian friendship. When
Joseph refused to order the occupation of Moldavia and Walachia, Kaunitz urged him to seize some other land, primarily
near Bosnia, simply to save face.[47] Joseph, on the other hand,
merely wanted to avoid war and to maintain his alliances with
Russia and France. He could not understand the chancellor's
insistence that Austria should seize territory only for the sake
of seizing it. By following Kaunitz's recommendations, he
told his brother:

> I would have the Ottoman masses alone on my neck and
> quite probably the king of Prussia and perhaps even the
> Bourbon courts in the Low Countries, on the Rhine and
> in Italy, and in the end risk everything in order to gain
> a miserable, deserted morsel of Bosnia or of Serbia. I am

unable to conceive how this man of intelligence has been able to get this into his head.[48]

It is difficult to judge which policy was the correct one. Perhaps Kaunitz, in addition to his fear of exposing Austrian weakness, actually wished to precipitate a war with Prussia. France and Britain were just ending their American war, and both would be likely to avoid any difficulties on the Continent for the time being. Accordingly, Austria and Russia might have been able to catch Prussia alone. In fact, Frederick had recognized his country's isolation and was in the process of creating the League of German Princes, which would cause Vienna considerable grief in 1785. Yet there is no evidence that Kaunitz now wished to challenge Prussia; indeed, he based his vigorous criticism of Catherine's Greek Project on the grounds that it would lead to war with Prussia—a war that he did not then want.

In the end Vienna adopted the policy toward the annexation of the Crimea upon which Joseph insisted. He promised the Russian empress his support, but rejected her invitations for him to take something for himself, to conclude a joint plan of operations, or to engage in any direct action against Turkey. Moreover, he assured Versailles that he did not want war and that he would not demand Moldavia and Walachia as an "equivalent." He did, however, reject a French request that he join a coalition to force Russia to rescind the annexation.[49] Nonetheless, not even he wanted to come away empty-handed. While the crisis was in progress, the internuntius at the Porte, Peter Herbert-Rathkael, sought some commercial advantages for Austria along with acquisition of the left bank of the Unna River, for which Joseph was willing to pay 1,000,000 gulden.[50] Herbert won the commercial privileges, but, when it became evident that Vienna's request for the lands on the Unna might jeopardize those privileges, he dropped it at Joseph's orders.[51]

Joseph fulfilled his promise to assist Catherine in persuading the Turks to concede the Crimea. On 7 December 1783

Herbert presented a note to the Porte declaring that Austria approved the Russian annexation and reminding the Turks that, although the emperor wanted only peace, he was an ally of the tsarina and, if pressed, would honor his commitments to her.[52] The Porte, by now aware that France and Prussia would offer no aid and fearful that Austria might attack, formally accepted the annexation.

As all Europe recognized, Vienna provided major assistance to St. Petersburg in the Crimean affair. But Austria still had no real desire to see Russia on the Black Sea. The hatred for Prussia, however, restricted Habsburg policy toward the Ottoman Empire and essentially forced it to support almost anything that the Russians wanted to do. In the midst of the crisis, Herbert summed up best the way Prussophobia had hamstrung Austrian policy. " 'The greatest blow the king of Prussia has dealt us is not the taking of Silesia but having chained our activity by rendering us simple spectators of all that happens in Europe instead of [letting us] choose each time a role in accordance with the interests of the Monarchy.' "[53] Herbert's assessment would prove even more accurate in the next few years, for Austria's animosity toward Prussia would soon pull it into another unwanted Turkish war.

CHAPTER TEN
Austria's Last Turkish War, 1787-1790

After the Crimean crisis, affairs in the East became briefly quiet again, so that Joseph could pursue Austrian interests elsewhere. He now believed that he could do so more effectively, since his role in aiding Catherine's acquisition of the Crimea had placed her considerably in his debt. Immediately following the conclusion of the Crimean affair, he took steps to secure two diplomatic objectives: the exchange of the Austrian Netherlands for Bavaria and the opening of the Scheldt River, which had been closed to overseas shipping since the sixteenth century. The more important was the exchange project, which Vienna knew would most certainly be opposed by Prussia, and here Joseph intended to ask for Russian assistance. Catherine, he wrote to his minister in St. Petersburg, should not only help him to persuade the small German courts to accept the project but should also promise that, if Frederick went to war, "Russia would recognize it as an unjust aggression" and would assist Austria "with all its forces, as I was prepared to do if the Turks declared war over the Crimea."[1]

Grateful indeed for Austria's role in the Crimean affair, Catherine supported Vienna's plans, but no one else in Europe did. By the summer of 1785 Joseph had to abandon the exchange project in the face of opposition from Prussia and France. In addition, in July 1785 the League of German Princes formed under Prussian leadership and agreed to oppose the exchange of all German territory, by force of arms if necessary. Confronted by an almost united German front, Joseph had to issue a proclamation promising not to pursue the exchange project.[2] Vienna fared only slightly better in the Scheldt affair; the river remained closed, but the Dutch agreed to pay a considerable indemnity, officially to "purchase" the Habsburg claim to the city of Maestricht.[3]

In Vienna the failure of these two projects made Kaunitz more Prussophobic than ever. He condemned the League of German Princes as "one of the most heinous things envisioned by the evil will of the court of Berlin" and focused his attention more and more on finding the means to gain revenge on Prussia.[4] Joseph, on the other hand, began to doubt the efficacy of Austria's traditional anti-Prussian policy. Simply assuming Berlin to be the enemy, regardless of the circumstances, seemed to him to restrict seriously Habsburg options in foreign affairs. Joseph came to the opinion that an Austro-Prussian rapprochement would perhaps be more beneficial to Habsburg foreign affairs than continuing the Austro-Prussian enmity. Although he had toyed with the idea as early as January 1785, he did not suggest it to Kaunitz until December of the following year, shortly after learning of the death of Frederick II. The king's passing, Joseph told the chancellor in the most persuasive terms he could muster, might be the occasion for an Austro-Prussian reconciliation and an end to the anti-Prussian albatross that hung around the neck of Habsburg policy.

> If the houses of Austria and Prussia ally and follow similar policies, they have nothing to fear, either from any single power or from an alliance of powers. They would become the arbiters not only of Germany but of all Europe. . . . They can gather for themselves all possible advantages and apportion favors to other powers at their pleasure. These are indisputable truths, which one can calculate mathematically.[5]

Kaunitz was not ready for a diplomatic revolution of such enormity. Composing a reply "with all the tools of his political experience," he argued so mightily against Joseph's suggestion that the emperor withdrew it.[6] The chancellor's success came from the vehemence of his objections rather than from the persuasiveness of his arguments. Joseph still believed that Prusso-Austrian harmony should be the goal of Habsburg policy and shared his idea with Kaunitz's two principal subordinates, Vice-Chancellor Philip Cobenzl and Court Counselor Anton Spielmann. Both agreed that a reconciliation with Prussia would be advantageous but also that it was not the time to suggest such a course to Kaunitz, who would resist it vigorously.[7]

By this time Kaunitz, not Joseph, was essentially formulating Habsburg foreign policy. Although the emperor had not avoided arguments with his chancellor over foreign affairs in the past, his defeats over the Bavarian exchange and the opening of the Scheldt had apparently caused him to question seriously his ability to judge conditions and formulate policy. Joseph often could not muster the confidence to defy Kaunitz, even when his intuition told him that the course being followed might not be the best one for Austrian interests. Kaunitz continued to dominate Habsburg foreign policy until 1790, when Joseph died and was succeeded by his brother Leopold, who had fewer qualms about challenging the illustrious chancellor's control of affairs.[8]

It was Kaunitz's commitment to the defeat of Prussia that essentially drew Austria into its last war with the Turks. The Austrian involvement in the conflict came about because the chancellor assumed that the Russian alliance was essential to his objective of humiliating Prussia. In fact, his goal following the failure of the Bavarian exchange was to convince Catherine and her advisers that any Russian aggrandizement at Ottoman expense could only be achieved with Austrian cooperation and that such cooperation was impossible without the defeat of Prussia. If Russia hoped to partition Turkey, the first step must be to reduce substantially Prussian might.[9]

To persuade Catherine to accept this interpretation of international affairs, Kaunitz needed an opportunity to present his case, and in late 1786 his chance came. The tsarina invited the emperor to meet with her at Cherson in order to inspect Russia's new settlements in the lands won from Turkey in 1774. Joseph, concerned about his health and displaying a certain weariness of politics, did not want to go, but Kaunitz encouraged him, arguing that the trip would be immensely flattering to Catherine and would guarantee her friendship "for life."[10] Persuaded by Kaunitz's words and his own promise some time before to meet the empress again, the emperor decided that he had no choice but to accept the invitation.[11]

His reception at Cherson was a grand one. While traveling with a small and inconspicuous personal entourage, he was magnificently received by Catherine, her court, and the diplomatic corps, including his own envoys to Russia and Turkey.[12] While the two sovereigns toured the countryside, serious negotiations took place among the ministers who attended them. The more aggressive were the Austrians, who followed closely their instructions from Kaunitz. Aware that the Russians desired a firmer commitment of Habsburg aid against the Turks, Kaunitz's agents did their best to persuade their Russian counterparts that no Russian or Austrian aggrandizement was possible anywhere "without the diminution of Prussian power."[13] The Russians listened politely but were not convinced. They had reduced their ambitions in the Ottoman Empire considerably since the Greek Project of 1782, for now they talked only of acquiring Ochakov, the massive Ottoman fortress that blocked the entrances to the Bug and Dnepr rivers and that could harass shipping passing to and from the newly established Russian port at Cherson. In any case, the Russians assured the Austrians that they had no present intention of starting a war with Turkey.[14]

The meeting at Cherson ended innocuously enough. No plans to partition the Ottoman Empire changed hands, and no new agreements were concluded. Indeed, both sides sensed that their desires in foreign policy were not identical, but at the same time there were no truly serious differences. No one questioned that the alliance should continue.

Yet the meeting of the two sovereigns roused uneasiness in other quarters. The Porte suspected that it was a prelude to an attack on Turkey, and, since St. Petersburg had been pressing a number of issues in Constantinople, it had good reason to think so. The first few months of 1787 had witnessed growing Russo-Turkish disputes over what Herbert described as "no great problems but a multitude of little ones, accumulated over a long period of time."[15] They included border clashes in the Caucasus, the deposition and flight northward of a Russophile *hospodar* of Moldavia, harassment of Russian consuls in Ottoman cities, refusal of the Turks to return certain Cossack deserters, and what the Russians claimed was an Ottoman abuse of the right to mine salt in Russian territory for the garrison at Ochakov.[16] Before Herbert left for Cherson, he reported from the Ottoman capital that, despite numerous warlike gestures, he believed that various internal problems and the unpopularity of the current grand vizier would keep the Turks at peace.[17]

When he returned from Russia, however, Herbert noted that the meeting of the two sovereigns at Cherson had decidedly changed the atmosphere in Constantinople.

> Upon arriving I have found the state of affairs seriously deteriorated during my absence; some enemy courts [Prussia and Britain] have represented the interviews of the two imperial majesties . . . in the most alarming terms. The grand vizier, the *reis effendi*, and the new *kahya* protest the bad faith of Russia, exaggerate its demands, rave about the danger to the Ottoman Empire and the necessity of using arms against such an ambitious neighbor.[18]

Whether the Porte wanted war, however, seemed to Herbert problematical. As it had done frequently in the past, the Porte appeared to be stirring up public hatred of Russia in order to distract attention from the country's pressing internal problems. The danger was that the inflammatory rhetoric might make it difficult for the Turkish ministers to agree to compromise on some of the outstanding issues between Russia and Turkey without loss of face. In the meantime, Herbert

could only "emphasize the greatest firmness and most intimate union between the two imperial ministers [himself and
the Russian ambassador, Jakov Ivanovic Bulgakov] because it
will be infinitely difficult to temper such buffeted spirits by
the maxims of an equitable solution."[19]

Herbert failed to quiet the Porte's "buffeted spirits." In
mid-August the grand vizier called Bulgakov to a conference
in which he demanded that Catherine return the Crimea to
the Ottoman Empire and renounce all agreements since the
Treaty of Kuchuk Kainarji. The ambassador refused, and the
grand vizier ordered him incarcerated in the Fortress of the
Seven Towers. While Herbert still claimed that the breach
was caused primarily by "the little injustices in detail," he
acknowledged that in the end the divan and the sultan were
carried away "by the fanaticism of the grand vizier and the
reis effendi."[20]

For the third time in the century, the Habsburg policy-
makers found an ally involved in a Turkish war that they
would have preferred to avoid. The Austrians did not regard
Turkey as a particularly dangerous threat nor did the Porte
look upon Austria as its primary foe. This time, however, the
Turks did not plead as strongly for Austrian neutrality as they
had done in the past. After all, the Austro-Russian alliance
was well-known in Constantinople, and Herbert had reminded the Porte repeatedly that Vienna would act on Russia's behalf. After declaring war on Russia, the Turks did ask
for an Austrian declaration of neutrality, and they apparently
harbored a faint hope that the request would be honored because they knew of growing anti-Habsburg dissidence in the
Austrian Netherlands and of Vienna's fear of Prussian interference. Yet; Herbert thought the request more formal than
sincere, and the Turks seemed reconciled to its being rejected.[21]

Just as the Turks did not plead so strongly for Habsburg
neutrality this time, so too Vienna hesitated considerably less
about committing itself to war. On 30 August, shortly after
the news arrived of the Ottoman decision, Joseph dispatched

a personal letter to Catherine promising his support in the forthcoming hostilities. To him the decision was unavoidable, given the terms of the Austro-Russian alliance. The sultan had clearly declared war first without any overt Russian aggression. As he told his brother, "It puts me in an absolute case of *casus foederis* because they attacked Russia."[22]

It was Kaunitz who placed the decision within the perspective of the international situation. "Provided the bombs must go off sooner or later," he wrote to Louis Cobenzl, "it appears that the state of the present political situation is more favorable than unfavorable." France would probably not protest because the Turks were the aggressors and because French financial affairs were becoming increasingly chaotic. Moreover, French involvement in a Dutch political crisis had led to a confrontation with Britain and Prussia that would make Versailles most reluctant to embark on any adventures in the East. As to Prussia, Berlin's policy since the death of Frederick had appeared vague and uncertain, and his successor "had shown himself in all matters weak and vacillating." Besides—and here Kaunitz reiterated the fears of Bartenstein in 1737 and his own in 1777—if Austria did not participate in the war, "Russia will achieve its goals to the degree that all that will remain for us is to wait in fear and anxiety to see which party will control that court in the future and if that party will use its newly won advantages not to support us but, according to time and circumstance, to turn against us."[23]

As in 1737, Austria wanted both to preserve the alliance with Russia and, at the same time, to do what it could to limit Russian aggrandizement or at least to gain equal compensation for Austria. The only way to achieve these goals, as Bartenstein and Kaunitz saw them, was to join Russia in a war against the Turks. In both 1737 and 1787 it was an unwanted war for Austria, but the alternative—losing Russia as an ally and allowing its unlimited expansion—was a policy Austrian leaders could not accept.

Of the three eighteenth-century Austro-Turkish wars, the prospects for Habsburg success seemed the brightest in this

one. In late 1787 the military and diplomatic situations suggested that Austria would be able to inflict a crushing defeat
upon the Turks. The Ottoman Empire appeared as weak or
weaker than it had in 1716 and 1737, and for the previous
two years Herbert had sent reports of the growing inability
of Constantinople to govern its provinces or even to control
its soldiers. A Mamluk rebellion in Egypt had occupied considerable forces and the pasha of Scutari (Shkodër), Mehmed
Pasha, had ignited a civil war with the sultan by trying to
extend his personal power into Bosnia and Herzegovina.
Moreover, the regular troops appeared unreliable and ineffective. In mid-1785 Herbert had written that "all the corps of
the army are in the worst possible condition . . . ," and
nothing had occurred since then to indicate any improvement.[24]

Besides the weakness of the Ottoman forces, the Austrians
did not anticipate any sudden advances on the part of the
Russians, at least in the first or second campaigns. Despite
continued concern over what many believed to be overwhelming Russian military power, the fears expressed by Thugut in
1774 and by Lacy in 1777 of a Russian strike on the Ottoman
capital followed by the immediate collapse of Turkish resistance had been dispelled by 1787. During Joseph's visit to
Cherson, he and his retinue had looked closely at Russian
military potential and had discovered some glaring deficiencies. The Austrian ambassador agreed with his sovereign that
some Russian ships might reach Constantinople "to throw a
few bombs at it," but the navy was by no means ready to
challenge Turkish superiority on the Black Sea.[25] Even the
Russian army seemed unlikely to advance rapidly. Notwithstanding a number of reforms, it appeared disorganized, and
crop failures in southern Russia meant that a shortage of supplies would hamper operations. Before the Ottomans declared
war, Louis Cobenzl had suggested that "given these conditions, it is unlikely that one here [St. Petersburg] wants an
all-out war, and therefore I believe that during this year and

the next the empress must be quite opposed to anything being undertaken against the Turks."[26]

In contrast to the condition of the Russian and Turkish forces, the Austrian army seemed as strong and as well-prepared as at any other time in the century. At the outset of the war, the official strength was 245,000, of whom 140,000 would take the field against the Turks in the spring of 1788.[27] Although more men had been under arms during the War of the Bavarian Succession, one scholar has described this force as "the strongest and best-equipped army that Austria had possessed up to that time."[28] Moreover, in 1786 Wenzel Brognard—military officer, son of a former resident at the Porte, and graduate of the Oriental Academy—had journeyed from Constantinople to Vienna via the Danube, mapping and describing Turkish military installations along the way.[29] The Austrian army was not only stronger than that of Turkey, it possessed far greater intelligence about its enemy's capabilities.

The Austrian forces also seemed likely to receive more help from Ottoman subjects than in the previous wars. In the 1780s Vienna had become aware of growing discontent among the Serbs in the Ottoman Empire and had established extensive contacts among them. When the war began, Austrian military officers organized approximately 5,000 Serbian malcontents into *Freikorps*, placed them under the command of *grenzer* officers and their own leaders, and sent them into battle against the Turks.[30] Vienna also established contacts with others who might foment trouble for the Ottomans. The *hospodar* of Moldavia asked for a force of 8,000 men to occupy his land as quickly as possible and promised the full support of himself and his Christian subjects, who "expect their liberation, good fortune, and existence only from the imperial-royal court."[31] Some Montenegrins offered their assistance, and some Greeks promised to rebel if they received naval support. Joseph sent agents to the Montenegrins, but he declined the Greek offer because "the expense would be too high and the distances too great to make it of any value."[32]

Of all the possible Ottoman dissidents, the emperor was most interested in Mehmed Pasha. The first agents sent to him reported that he demanded considerable sums and would probably provide little aid, but Joseph believed that the rebellious pasha could make a significant diversion. Accordingly, Vienna sent two additional agents to him with instructions to give him 100,000 gulden and to reach an agreement with him providing for mutual support. The treacherous pasha accepted the subsidy but decapitated the agents and sent their heads to the sultan as a gift.[33] Vienna was understandably outraged, Kaunitz calling the act "abominable" and wondering why "this miserable pasha of Scutari would want to add this horror to his infamy."[34]

The diplomatic situation seemed as promising for Austrian success as the military. Traditionally France had expressed considerable opposition to any Austro-Russian offensive against the Ottoman Empire, but in the autumn of 1787 Versailles virtually extended its support. While Mercy reported French feelers for closer relations with Russia, Louis Cobenzl in St. Petersburg wrote that the French ambassador there had told the court that his country had completely changed its policy toward the Turks. "If it should come to the complete destruction of the Turkish Empire," he reported the Frenchman as saying, "this would not be offensive to his court or contrary to its interests."[35] Although suspicious of this change of heart, Vienna also knew that Versailles was seriously concerned about affairs in the Dutch Republic and about trouble at home and might wish to maintain Austrian and Russian friendship so much that it would sacrifice Turkey. Prussia remained a potential enemy, but for the moment seemed anxious to take advantage of the Austro-Russian involvement in the East to promote its own interests in the West, particularly in the Dutch Republic.

Unlike its course in 1716 and 1737, Vienna did not appeal to any of the lesser states for aid. Neither the smaller German states nor the Holy Roman Empire were likely to offer help anyway because the Prussians and their friends would oppose assistance for Austria. From the old anti-Turkish ally, Venice, Kaunitz wanted no support because he had his eye on incorporating that state into the Habsburg Monarchy and wished to avoid any promises that he might later regret.[36] The pope was ignored; in this war there was hardly a hint of the old cry of gathering the Christians to strike the Moslems. Everyone politically aware knew that the infidel was a shadow of his former self and probably doubted whether Joseph and Catherine were truly Christian. All in all, the chance to pose an Austrian answer to the Eastern Question seemed at hand. "It would be very unfortunate," Kaunitz reflected, "not to take advantage of this opportunity, which may never return. . . ."[37]

Within a few months, however, Vienna's fond dreams seemed to vanish. The first blow came before war was even declared. In December 1787 the deciphering service intercepted and decoded a letter from the Prussian chief minister, Count Ewald Friedrich Hertzberg, to his ambassador in Constantinople, a letter that contained the famous Hertzberg plan, a fanciful proposal by which Prussia would gain the important Polish cities and areas of Danzig (Gdańsk) and Thorn (Toruń) at the expense of Austria, Poland, and the Ottoman Empire. In exchange for Prussian efforts to restore peace, the Turks would cede Moldavia and Walachia to Austria; Austria would return Galicia to Poland; and Poland would give Danzig and Thorn to Prussia. In the plan, only Prussia would sacrifice nothing to gain additional territory. It seemed to prove that Vienna's assessment of Berlin's preoccupation with the West was wrong. Not only were the Prussians interested in affairs in the East, they appeared ready to exploit the situation to strengthen themselves and to weaken the Habsburgs. To Kaunitz, the revelation demanded some precautions on Vienna's part; thus, he sent a note to St. Petersburg requesting an agreement providing for joint Austro-Russian action should Berlin try to implement the Hertzberg plan by force.[38]

If Kaunitz believed that the Hertzberg plan demanded additional precautions, Joseph was convinced that it had seriously altered the whole international scene. Prussia, not Turkey, was the true enemy, and Austria had to prepare itself to face the serious danger Berlin offered. To his ambassador in Russia he wrote:

> Rather than allow the king of Prussia to possess a single village, much less realize this grand project in its entirety, I would rather fight a war to destruction; and if you are unable to procure for me perfect assurances on the part of Russia that it will never consent to allow the king of Prussia to reap any advantages from this war, I will not hesitate a moment to reach an immediate arrangement with the Porte . . . and leave Russia all alone in order to turn all my forces against the king of Prussia.[39]

Joseph did receive the assurances that he demanded from Catherine, and thus could not turn his attention away from the Ottomans and toward the Prussians. With considerable concern that he was marching against the wrong enemy, he set off to join his splendid army in pursuit of the Turks.[40]

Despite the growing uncertainty of the diplomatic situation, the prospects of military success still seemed bright. The Habsburg plans called for offensives of five separate armies from the Adriatic to Galicia, with the main force under the emperor's personal command striking at Belgrade and then advancing into Serbia. By the end of 1788 the Austrians hoped to have all of Moldavia, Walachia, Serbia, and most of Bosnia in their possession with a thrust into Albania to follow in 1789.[41] The plans, however, were predicated on the belief that the Russians would advance before the Austrians. Just as in 1737, the Austrians assumed that Russian forces would bear the brunt of the fighting because Russia was Turkey's principal antagonist. But, just as in 1737, the Russians delayed for some months, and, when they finally moved, they did not attack on a broad front but concentrated their efforts on Ochakov.[42] The Turks, who had been equally tardy in gathering their troops, did not advance to meet the Russians but turned instead to challenge the nearer Austrians—the very thing Vienna had hoped would not happen.

Worried by Russian lethargy and uncertain about Turkish plans, the Austrian command spent the spring of 1788 simply waiting to see what would occur. Joseph has since received much of the blame for this timidity, but, of all the senior officers at headquarters, he was the most anxious to launch an offensive. To Kaunitz he repeatedly complained of the excessive caution of his general officers, and to his brother he lamented, "I must say to you with chagrin that I find neither will, nor zeal, nor energy in our generals. All are reluctant to make war; they want to be comfortable in their lodgings, and no one wants to do anything he is not forced to do."[43] As emperor and commander-in-chief, Joseph could have ordered them to act, but, having by this time lost much of his confidence in military matters as well, all he did was wring his hands. As the soldiers sat in defensive positions and waited, they were attacked by the Balkan enemy in many ways more dangerous than the Turks: disease. By the end of May more than 5,300 men in Joseph's 66,000-man army were ill, and the number increased daily as the summer approached.[44]

As disease spread and the Austrians dawdled, the Turks suddenly launched an offensive. They crossed the Danube at Orsova and lunged into the Banat, easily breaking through the extended Habsburg line. Joseph and his senior officers rushed as many men as they could to the Banat, but the forces there remained in such a state of confusion that they were unable to construct defensive positions to stop the enemy. The Ottoman onslaught finally stalled, not so much because of Habsburg resistance but because the Turks overextended their supply system. After laying waste part of the countryside, they retreated back across the Danube. Their effort had, however, considerably shaken the already wavering resolve of the emperor, whose growing ill health further dampened the morale of his officers. Finally, at Kaunitz's urging he returned to Vienna, this time to stay.

The military effort of 1788 was a great disappointment to Vienna, and news from the diplomatic front promised additional setbacks as well. In June 1788 the Prussians and the British concluded the Treaty of Loo, an arrangement primarily designed to maintain the status quo in the Netherlands but also providing for joint Anglo-Prussian mediation in the Turkish war.[45] When reports of the accord reached Vienna and St. Petersburg, the statesmen in both capitals immediately suspected it to be part of a Prussian effort to solidify support for the implementation of the Hertzberg plan.[46]

A few weeks later, additional intelligence further heightened concern in Vienna. In late August the deciphering service intercepted two more letters from Hertzberg to his ambassador at the Porte suggesting a Prusso-Turkish military alliance to be followed by a joint invasion of the Habsburg Monarchy. These letters frightened Joseph in much the same way that news of the Spanish invasion of Sardinia had frightened his grandfather in 1717. In a pleading, scolding letter to Kaunitz, the emperor claimed that the intercepted notes forecast a Prussian and possibly an Anglo-Prussian entry into the war. If Austria should have to fight on two fronts,

> the Monarchy is lost, because it will be necessary to diminish the number of troops on the Turkish front to prevent the king of Prussia from occupying all of Bohemia and Moravia and marching to Vienna. But in diminishing the actual forces against the Porte we are no longer in a state to defend ourselves, and consequently a great part of Transylvania, the Banat of Timişoara, and Slavonia will be lost with 2,000,000 inhabitants, and the ravages will not be compensated for a century.

To prevent such a catastrophe, Joseph continued, Kaunitz must ask for specific means by which Catherine would guarantee Austrian security from Prussian attack. If she could not comply, "she must at least allow me the liberty to try to conclude my own {separate peace}."[47]

Joseph's letter greatly disturbed Kaunitz, who feared that

the policy it suggested might destroy the Austro-Russian alliance. If Austria negotiated a separate peace with the Porte, St. Petersburg would abandon its Habsburg ties for closer relations with Berlin. Then the House of Austria "would find itself in a situation that would put it in much greater danger for the future." Essentially, Kaunitz emphasized in his reply to Joseph's memorandum, the only way by which Vienna could avoid future diplomatic complications was for the army to conduct a vigorous offensive. Victories over the Ottomans would force them to the peace table, and peace would decrease even the remote likelihood of Prussian interference.[48]

This time, Joseph did not passively submit to Kaunitz's arguments. He avowed that the chancellor was underestimating the Prussian danger and insisted that he pursue peace negotiations with the Porte or acquire guarantees that Russia and France would use all of their forces to defend Austria should Berlin attempt aggrandizement anywhere.[49]

This disagreement between Joseph and Kaunitz regarding Austrian policy in the Turkish war would continue until the emperor's death in February 1790. It centered upon the Prussian threat. To Joseph that threat was immediate, and the only way to meet it was to withdraw from the Turkish war as quickly as possible and to dispatch troops to the Austro-Prussian border. To Kaunitz the threat had to be considered within the broader context of international affairs. Allied with France and Russia, the House of Habsburg seemed capable of parrying any Prussian diplomatic or military blow. And to remain allied with Russia, it was essential to prosecute the war with Turkey. As to Bartenstein in 1737-1739, there appeared to Kaunitz no alternative to war.

Throughout the remainder of 1788 and into 1789 the emperor and the chancellor continued their disagreement on the course of Habsburg policy. At times, however, Joseph exerted his authority as sovereign. On 7 November 1788 he ordered Kaunitz first to persuade the Russians to join a search for peace and then to open talks with the Turks. "This is the only way to bring the king of Prussia and his ministry to their senses, forestall his supporters, and stop all those who plot against me."[50] As to the terms of a settlement, Joseph suggested the time-honored solution of *uti possidetis* used in 1699, 1718, and 1739. The Austrian army had taken one notable objective, the fortress of Khotin, which would go to Austria under such terms. Joseph may have been hoping to secure some token conquest, perhaps to placate Kaunitz, who had maintained that to fight the hapless Turk and win nothing would severely tarnish Habsburg prestige throughout Europe.

No one knew better than the chancellor that the road to peace would be a difficult one. His first task was to persuade Russia to join Austria in seeking a settlement. This effort proved less embarrassing than he imagined. In December 1788 Potemkin had taken Ochakov, and Catherine announced that she would accept a general peace if she could retain the fortress and receive an indemnity from the Turks. She would even permit the Austrians to conclude a separate settlement if they would promise to transfer Khotin to Russia after they had procured it from the sultan.[51] While not entirely happy with these conditions, Kaunitz knew that they could have been worse and so proceeded to open talks with the Turks through the French ambassador in Constantinople.

Negotiations, however, took time, and, as the summer of 1789 approached, Vienna realized that the talks would not make enough progress to prevent another season of campaigning. If anything, in early 1789 the prospects of peace were fading. Word had come from the Ottoman capital that the Prussian representative there was "moving heaven and earth" to get the Turks to accept Anglo-Prussian mediation and hinting broadly that Prussia might ally with the Porte to implement some sort of peace based on the Hertzberg plan.[52] Meanwhile France, the power Kaunitz had depended upon to check Prussia in the West, was collapsing into revolution. In April Neckar told Mercy that there seemed little likelihood France could meet its treaty obligation to defend Austria in case of an attack by a third power.[53] While this news dimmed hopes for peace, they were extinguished by the death in April of Sultan Abdul Hamid I and the accession of his nephew Selim III, described as "rash, decisive, and much more war-like than peaceful."[54] Vienna learned that the new sultan was indeed bent upon prosecuting the war in June, when he firmly rejected Austria's peace proposals.[55] Kaunitz wrote to Joseph that the only available course was to "conduct military operations with the greatest vigor and force an immediate peace with a decisive blow. . . ."[56]

As much as he hated to face another campaign, Joseph knew that the chancellor was right. This time, however, his health would not permit him to lead the army personally. As poor as his health was in early 1788, it had been further weakened by the campaign of that year. As his replacement, he initially chose Field Marshal Andreas Hadik (Hadek), "an old, unimaginative man" who himself became ill and unable to carry out his duties.[57] To succeed him, Joseph then appointed Field Marshall Ernst Gideon Laudon (Loudon). Although the famous veteran of the Seven Years' War, he was almost as old as Hadik (Laudon was seventy-two, Hadik seventy-eight) and his own health was "doubtful."[58] At first Laudon seemed as reluctant to act as the officers of the previous year. Although the plans called for laying siege to Belgrade, Laudon did not believe the army adequately prepared and advised the emperor that he would not advance unless he received direct orders to do so. On 23 August Joseph dispatched the orders, and the field marshal's hesitancy vanished.[59] Crossing the Sava immediately, he opened the siege in mid-September.

While Vienna awaited reports of Laudon's progress, signs that the tide was turning in favor of the imperial allies began to arrive from Moldavia. On 30 July an army under the joint command of the Austrian Josiah von Saxe-Coburg and the celebrated Russian Alexander Suvorov scattered a large force of Ottoman reserves and irregulars at the town of Focşani. Fearing an Austro-Russian thrust across the Danube, the grand vizier advanced to meet the joint force at the village of Martineşti (Martineshti) on the Buzău (Boza) River, where his troops were crushed by an enemy with one-quarter their numbers. It was the decisive battle Kaunitz had desired, for it shattered the Ottoman field army and rendered hopeless any Turkish attempt to relieve Belgrade, some 350 miles to the west.

Meanwhile, Laudon pressed the siege with a vigor and dedication reminiscent of Prince Eugene. In fact, when the aging officer heard that an Ottoman relief army might appear, he told his fellows: " 'Here is the place where we must be victorious or die. I will not withdraw. I have the order to take Belgrade from the enemy. I will do all that I can to fulfill that order.' "[60] Martineşti made relief impossible, and on 8 October the fortress surrendered. With the Turks in disarray, the Austrians and Russians pressed on. Within six weeks the important fortress of Bendery fell to the Russians and the city of Bucharest to the Austrians.

Not even Kaunitz could have asked for greater successes than these. Indeed, it seemed that the long-delayed partition of the Ottoman Empire might be possible. A few days before the fall of Belgrade, Kaunitz wrote that the army must now press on to greater victories and that Austria must insist on a peace based on *uti possidetis*, which now would require substantial Ottoman concessions. But the emperor was not interested in great annexations. While pleased with the army's successes, Joseph did not believe that they in any way lessened the danger from Prussia, and he declared Kaunitz's proposal excessive. It would "frighten [the Turks] into throwing themselves into the arms of the king of Prussia and signing an alliance with him which for the present and future would serve to our greatest disadvantage."[61]

If Joseph felt burdened by his fear of Prussia, in late 1789 another crisis added its weight to his shoulders. Strife in the Austrian Netherlands, simmering since 1787, boiled into open conflict between Belgian insurgents and regular troops. The regulars proved incapable and the concessions of the ministers insufficient to quell the rising, and in early December the imperial government and its forces fled for the safety of Luxembourg.[62] The upheaval seemed particularly ominous because the National Assembly had by now firmly established its hold in France and had made it clear that it would not come to Austria's aid in case of war with Prussia.[63] To his brother Leopold Joseph summarized Austria's numerous woes: "Given the impotence of France and even her ill will, the exhaustion of Russia, the revolt in the Low Countries, the same spirit instigated by the Poles in Galicia and even [rumors of upheaval] in Hungary, and finally our own weakness, it will take a miracle to get us out of this safe and sound."[64]

Vienna's effort to get out of its difficulties "safe and sound" continued into 1790 but with little success. In order to undercut Prussian influence in both Constantinople and London, Kaunitz offered the Turks an armistice lasting for one or two years and the British a rapprochement. Neither was accepted. Instead, the situation deteriorated. News reached Vienna in January of a possible Prusso-Polish accord and in February of a Prusso-Turkish alliance.[65] Having received this information, the chancellor believed that his efforts to arrange a peace had failed. Austria's only alternative was "to deal [the Turks] a decisive blow before they can gather their forces, and at the same time to make every effort to turn [more Austrian troops] toward Prussia and Poland."[66]

This admission represented the bankruptcy of Kaunitz's policy. Faced with turmoil in Belgium, discontent elsewhere, and a possible two-front war, Austria needed to resolve some of its problems to deal effectively with the others. But Kaunitz advised only that Vienna continue struggling with all of them.

The answer to the problems posed by the Austro-Turkish war, the threat from Prussia, and the internal upheaval eventually came from the chancellor's sovereign—not from Joseph, who had died in despair on 20 February 1790, but from his brother Leopold, who had become emperor on Joseph's death. Since 1787 Leopold had warned his brother against becoming involved in a Turkish war and against underestimating the seriousness of internal discontent.[67] The way to resolve the Monarchy's domestic difficulties, he believed, was to resolve its foreign ones first, and the way to do that was through the rapprochement with Prussia suggested by Joseph in 1785. Two weeks after arriving in Vienna, Leopold sent to the king of Prussia a letter expressing his hope for peace and renouncing all Austrian annexations of Turkish lands.[68] When King Frederick William's encouraging reply reached the Austrian capital from Berlin, Leopold called a meeting of his most important advisers in matters of war and foreign policy on 26 April.[69] While ostensibly arranged to discuss the Prussian answer, the meeting in fact was designed to overturn Kaunitz's policies. It succeeded. The most prestigious member of the gathering after Kaunitz, Field Marshal Laudon, declared that the Monarchy must conclude peace with Turkey as soon as possible and with no annexations if that were the condition that would please Prussia. The council agreed despite the chancellor's objections, and the appropriate memoranda were composed to send to Berlin.[70] Realizing that his policy of many years had been repudiated, Kaunitz offered his resignation. Within a day, however, he withdrew it, undoubtedly convinced that this time his monarch would accept it.

Austria's policy had now changed dramatically. In June 1790 Prussia and Austria concluded the Convention of Reichenbach, by which Vienna accepted Anglo-Prussian mediation in the Austro-Turkish peace negotiations and agreed to conclude a treaty on the basis of *status quo ante bellum*.[71] Not long afterward, Herbert left Vienna for the village of Sistova (Svishtov) on the Danube near Nikopol to meet the Turks. For all intents and purposes, the last Austro-Turkish war was over.

👑 EPILOGUE

Although the convention at Reichenbach ended the Austro-Turkish war in fact, it still had to be concluded formally. This was the task of the Austrian and Turkish delegates and the Prussian, British, and (by everyone's consent) Dutch mediators who gathered at Sistova. The town itself, chosen because it would require minimal expenses and had been the birthplace of the current grand vizier, was succinctly described by the British representative as "the world's end."[1] Although the congress opened in the last week of December 1790, it failed to issue a final treaty until 4 August 1791. One cause for the considerable delay was the effort of Herbert to salvage some token Habsburg advantage from this frustrating war. He wished to procure frontier changes along the Unna River and to acquire the long coveted town of Orsova.[2] This time Herbert succeeded. On the same day that all of the delegates signed the Treaty of Sistova, Herbert and the Ottoman plenipotentiaries concluded a separate convention—not guaranteed by the mediators—that ceded to the Monarchy Orsova, on the condition that it not be fortified, and a stretch of land on the upper Unna approximately six miles wide and seventy-five miles long.[3] Although the separate convention obviously violated the Reichenbach accord, which had insisted upon *status quo ante bellum*, the mediators did not object to the minor frontier changes. In fact, they encouraged the Turks to accept them so that the peace conference could end.[4] Without the support of the mediators, the Turks had to concede because they were still at war with Russia and wanted to antagonize no other powers. The treaty itself, besides restoring the other prewar boundaries, called for the release of all military prisoners, a provision included in no previous Austro-Turkish treaty.

While the delegates negotiated at Sistova, their masters in

the respective capitals worried still about the ongoing Russo-Turkish war. St. Petersburg had sent no envoy to Reichenbach or to Sistova and therefore had made no commitment either to restore the *status quo ante bellum* or to cease its war at all. In fact, as soon as they heard of it, the Russians made it clear that they would reject the solution agreed upon at Reichenbach. "The sensation caused by the news," the Austrian ambassador wrote when the convention became known in St. Petersburg, "has convinced me that here one would much prefer war to such a sacrifice [*status quo ante bellum*]."[5] However, Berlin and London insisted that Catherine accept the settlement as the basis for ending the Russo-Turkish war and even mentioned military operations to force her to do so.[6] As the possibility of a Prusso-Russian clash became increasingly likely, both sides asked the Habsburg court what its policy would be should hostilities erupt.

The Austrian policy-makers now found themselves in an enviable and, for the eighteenth century, unusual position. For the first time it was the sought-after power in the eastern European triangle. And an alliance with either Prussia or Russia offered significant advantages. If Vienna joined Berlin, it could arrange a Prusso-Austro-Turkish coalition supported by Britain that could make war on Russia with an excellent chance of victory. As the price for its cooperation, the Monarchy could demand territorial concessions from the Turks and additional land in Poland. Moreover, success in the field might do away with the Russian menace to the Balkans for some time to come. By restoring the Crimea, the northern coast of the Black Sea, and a portion of the southern Ukraine to the Ottoman Empire, Austria and its allies could undo a whole century of Russian expansion to the south.

If joining Prussia offered numerous opportunities for Austria, joining Russia instead offered none fewer. By establishing and then keeping the peace with the Ottoman Empire, Austria would be free to unite with Russia in the all-out offensive against Prussia that Kaunitz had desired for so long. The Prussian army was just as large as it had been in the days of Frederick the Great, but he was now dead, and his nephew showed no sign of having inherited his military genius. A joint Austro-Russian offensive against Prussia might restore Silesia to the Monarchy and in the process reduce Prussia to a second-rate power. Then all of eastern Europe would be at the mercy of the Habsburgs and the Romanovs.

Despite such temptations, the leading policy-maker in Vienna, Leopold II, had no taste for either adventure. He had no desire to join Prussia against Russia because he knew that the geography of Russia made victory unlikely. When the Prussian ambassador suggested that Leopold persuade Catherine to accept *status quo ante bellum* because Prussia, Britain, Sweden, and "even Spain" intended to force her to do so, the emperor replied "that Russia, owing to its power, its resources, and its strategic location, has nothing to fear from them. . . ." Moreover, Leopold told the Prussian envoy that he could not understand Berlin's insistence upon *status quo ante bellum* since Catherine had already made it clear that she wanted no extensive conquests but only Ochakov and the land between the Bug and Dnestr rivers, both already in Russian hands.[7]

While rejecting a coalition with Prussia against Russia, the emperor also had no wish to join Russia against Prussia. Such a conflict might reopen hostilities with the Ottoman Empire, which in turn would revive all of those dilemmas and dangers that the court had faced in the last years of Joseph II. Moreover, there was no evidence that Catherine really wanted to fight Prussia, and, if she did so in a half-hearted manner, Austria might again receive the brunt of the enemy's onslaught.

To assume, however, that Leopold made his decisions by weighing the advantages and disadvantages of different aggressive foreign policies misses the mark. The Monarchy's essential task, as Leopold saw it, was the restoration of internal order. A war against Russia, Prussia, or the Ottoman Empire, regardless of the opportunities for aggrandizement, would aggravate unrest throughout the Habsburg possessions

and result in worsening upheaval. Pacification was uppermost
in the emperor's mind, and pacification would not occur if he
demanded greater sacrifices from a war-weary population. The
Austro-Turkish war had been the undoing of many of his
brother's reforms, and he had no intention of allowing another conflict to frustrate his efforts to restore tranquillity to
the Monarchy.

Essentially, Leopold wanted no war at all to occur between
Russia and Prussia. He wanted to irritate neither side by
declaring for the other or to irritate both sides by declaring
his neutrality. Since at this time Berlin seemed more belligerent than St. Petersburg, the emperor decided to side ten-
tatively with Russia. He hoped that Frederick William would
be persuaded to back down but that Catherine would not be
encouraged to become more bellicose. He hinted to both that
he would honor his continuing treaty obligations to St. Petersburg but would not say how he would do so. "I have my
engagements with Russia, which I will never fail to honor,
but, because once the war begins the consequences and results
are unknown, I cannot say in advance what I would do in
such a case."[8] To Louis Cobenzl Kaunitz wrote that Austria
would continue to honor the Russian alliance but "without
declarations or demonstrations on our part" in order to provoke "no rupture between us and Prussia."[9]

In the end no war erupted. Not only was Berlin unsure of
Austrian policy, but it could get no firm commitment of
support from London. Consequently, it simply watched as St.
Petersburg concluded its own peace with the Porte at Iasi in
January 1792 (the treaty confirmed the provisions of Kuchuk
Kainarji and the subsequent Russo-Turkish agreements and
granted Ochakov and the lands between the Bug and the
Dnestr to the Russians). Not long afterward Prussia and Rus-
sia resolved their differences by partitioning Poland again, a
partition in which Austria did not participate.

The eighteenth century offered the Habsburg Monarchy
the opportunity to solve the Eastern Question to its own advantage. Between 1683 and 1718 the Ottoman Empire had

revealed its weakness and seemed to invite the Habsburgs to mount a thrust that would strip it of its European possessions and to subject its Christian residents to Western government and culture. After 1718 the Austrians possessed a foothold on the right bank of the Danube that provided a superb strategic base for further campaigns to the south and east. The Monarchy seemed about to mount drives that would eventually reach the Aegean, the Black Sea, and possibly Constantinople itself. Had the Habsburgs annexed the Balkans, they might have become truly a Danubian dynasty, and the presence of a large Orthodox population might have encouraged the liberalization and federalization essential to its survival.

Yet the opportunity was never seized. One reason was the poverty and backwardness of the lands to be had. The policymakers in Vienna looked upon southeastern Europe as the poorest region of the continent economically and culturally. If conquered, those provinces would have required enormous investments. The experiences of the government in improving small regions such as the Banat of Timişoara, where the Habsburgs spent huge sums of money settling German colonists amid the indigenous population and introducing economic improvements with minimal results, revealed that doing the same for larger provinces in the Balkans would demand vast and possibly bankrupting expenditures. Annexing such lands and peoples, many in Vienna believed, would weaken the state, at least for the immediate future, and possibly for the distant future as well.

Another reason for the failure of the Habsburgs to advance into the Balkans was religion. Despite the growing appreciation of religious toleration at the highest levels of the Habsburg government, there remained substantial prejudice against non-Catholics in general and against the Orthodox in particular. In eighteenth-century Austria, religion was still considered the determinant for patriotism. Protestants were suspected of being loyal to the king of Prussia, Jews to the sultan of Turkey, and Orthodox to the tsar of Russia. Only Roman Catholics could be unswervingly loyal to the Habsburgs, and, to many Austrian advisers, the incorporation of large numbers of Orthodox in the Monarchy would have been dangerous indeed.

To a great extent, such reasons for leaving the Balkans as they were camouflage a more fundamental cause. After the great war of 1683-1699, Vienna returned largely to the defensive in the southeast. From 1700 to 1740 this defensive posture was tempered by occasional and largely opportunistic thrusts for gain, especially during the wars of 1716-1718 and 1737-1739, but even then Vienna chose to go to war for reasons other than simply to add Ottoman lands to the Habsburg patrimony. The Prussian invasion of Silesia in 1740 solidified this defensive policy because it revealed to the Habsburg statesmen how fragile their state was and how dangerous their rival to the north had become. The Austrian obsession with Prussia after 1740 precluded any expansion to the southeast unless it could be undertaken—as in 1773 and 1774—without war or even the serious threat of war elsewhere. Even then the assumed value of the lands to be gained was of considerable importance. The Monarchy dared not acquire territories that might require considerable immediate investment, even if they promised substantial return in the future. To challenge Prussia, the government had to husband its resources for the moment and could risk no expenditures on developing lands that might strengthen the state only at some later time.

Whereas the Austrians viewed the growing feebleness of the Ottoman Empire as decreasing the danger on the Monarchy's southeastern flank, the Russians looked upon it as an opportunity—first to expand to the Black Sea, then into the Balkans, and finally to Constantinople. Early in the century Vienna recognized that such expansion could ultimately lead to an Austro-Russian confrontation, which would pose as great a threat to Habsburg security as that offered by the Turks in the previous century. Opposing Russian expansionism in the southeast, however, precluded Austria's opportunity to use tsarist might to threaten the Monarchy's enemies to the west and north. To their chagrin, the Habsburg statesmen found that enlisting Russian support against other enemies demanded that they tolerate and at times sustain Russian designs on the Ottoman Empire. Twice, in 1737 and in 1788, this policy resulted in unwanted Turkish wars, both of which made Austria inviting prey to the Prussians.

To some extent, Russia and Austria viewed the Balkans differently because of their different geographical positions. Whereas Austria had enemies or potential enemies on all sides, the Russians faced them only to the west. Since Sweden and the Ottoman Empire had fallen on hard times in the eighteenth century, the only powers Russia had to fear were Austria and Prussia. And, since these states were mutual enemies throughout most of the century, Russia could exploit their rivalry to secure what it wished.

To preserve the Ottoman Empire and to restrict Russian advances to the south, Vienna had to reach a rapprochement with Prussia. But for Maria Theresa and Kaunitz, such an act was unthinkable. Within the confines of irreconcilable Austro-Prussian enmity, Vienna's statesmen had to juggle their policies to preserve the post-1718 status quo in the Balkans as best they could. In the particulars they did poorly. In 1739 Belgrade and the surrounding area were lost, and Belgrade was the most important fortress on the lower Danube. While the Austrians could penetrate no farther south than the Danube, they also could not prevent the Russians from winning control of most of the northern coast of the Black Sea. In general terms, however, Vienna enjoyed some success, although it was largely fortuitous. Eighteenth-century warfare was not that of blitzkrieg, and the Russian—and Austrian—armies often fell short of the overwhelming victories forecasted by many. When the armies did enjoy grand successes, as they did particularly in 1789, other pressures, either from European powers or from internal difficulties, prevented the victors from exploiting their gains to the fullest. The governments of eastern Europe rarely possessed the stability and resources to weather serious storms of domestic upheaval or international protests. Consequently, even stunning victories were often followed by moderate acquisitions. By the end of the century, Russia was indeed on the Black Sea, but its armies still remained outside of the Balkans and its southern border away from the Danube.

Seventeen ninety-one concluded an era in Austro-Turkish relations, not only because it marked the end of the last Austro-Turkish war, but also because the stunning events of the French Revolution transformed for a long time the major issues and concerns of all the European powers. When the era of the Revolution was over, the Eastern Question reemerged with new complications, circumstances, conditions, and statesmen to deal with them. Moreover, in the new century, more powers believed that they had a stake in its outcome. In the eighteenth century, the Habsburg policy-makers recognized the nature of the Eastern Question, but lacked the resolve to solve it to the Monarchy's advantage. In the nineteenth century, the solution was not theirs to find.

Notes

INTRODUCTION

1. Hans Sturmberger, "Türkengefahr und österreichische Staatlichkeit," *Südostdeutsches Archiv* 10 (1967): 139.
2. Karl Otmar von Aretin, *Heiliges Römisches Reich, 1776-1806*, 2 vols. (Wiesbaden, 1967), 1: 18.
3. The most recent studies are Thomas M. Barker, *Double Eagle and Crescent* (Albany, 1967) and John Stoye, *The Siege of Vienna* (New York, 1964). For older works see W. Sturminger, *Bibliographie und Ikonographie der Türkenbelagerungen Wiens 1529 und 1683* (Graz, 1955).
4. Adolf Beer, *Die orientalische Politik Österreichs seit 1774* (Prague, 1883).

THE ART OF DIPLOMACY

1. For detailed descriptions of two journeys of grand Habsburg embassies to Constantinople, see Gerard Cornelius von Drietsch, *Historische Nachricht von der Röm. Kaiserl. Grossbotschaft nach Constantinopel . . .* (Nuremberg, 1723), and Gerhard Fritsch, *Paschas und Pest* (Graz and Vienna, 1962).
2. Peter Meienberger, *Johann Rudolf Schmid zum Schwarzenhorn als kaiserlicher Resident in Konstantinopel, 1629-1643* (Bern, 1973), p. 96.
3. Ibid.; Viktor Weiss von Starkenfels, *Die k. k. orientalische Akademie zu Wien* (Vienna, 1839), p. 3; Paul Wittek and Friedrich Kraelitz-Greifenhorst, "Introduction" to *Mitteilungen zur osmanischen Geschichte* 1 (1922): 5.
4. The first such school for *Sprachknaben* in Constantinople was established by the Polish embassy in 1621. Its most illustrious graduate was John Sobieski, king of Poland from 1674 to 1696. Wilhelm Anton Neumann, *Ueber die orientalischen Sprachstudien seit dem XIII. Jahrhundert mit besonderer Rücksicht auf Wien* (Vienna, 1899), p. 46.
5. Anonymous (but certainly Kaunitz) to Maria Theresa, April 1753, Vienna, Haus- Hof- und Staatsarchiv, Staatskanzlei,

"Interiora," 55 (Orientalische Akademie). Hereafter cited as HHSA, with appropriate category and carton number.

6. Bertold Spuler, "Die europäische Diplomatie in Konstantinopel bis zum Frieden von Belgrad," *Jahrbücher für Kultur und Geschichte der Slaven* 11 (1935): 186-87.

7. Wolfgang Klesl, "Leopold von Talman" (Ph.D. diss., University of Vienna, 1966), p. 79.

8. Joseph von Hammer-Purgstall, *Geschichte des osmanischen Reiches*, 10 vols. (Pest 1827-1835), 8: 379.

9. Fritsch, *Paschas und Pest*, p. 67.

10. Thugut to Kaunitz, 17 June 1772, "Türkei," II, 59, HHSA.

11. Gümec Karamuk, ed., *Ahmed Azmi Efendis Gesandtschaftsbericht als Zeugnis des osmanischen Machtverfalls und der beginnenden Reformära unter Selim III* (Bern, 1975), p. 117.

12. Spuler, "Europäische Diplomatie," p. 204. At the end of the century the British ambassador Spencer Smith married the daughter of the Austrian internuntius. Joseph von Hammer-Purgstall, *Constantinopolis und der Bosporos*, 2 vols. (1822; reprint, Osnabrück, 1967), 2: 39.

13. Lady Mary Wortley Montague to the Countess of Bristol, n.d. but probably 10 April 1718, in Lady Mary Wortley Montague, *Letters from the Levant during the Embassy to Constantinople, 1716-1718* (1838; reprint, New York, 1971), p. 213.

14. Hammer, *Geschichte*, 8: 326-29. Living in Pera and avoiding Moslems did not mean that the embassy staff was enamored with the Christian population either. Hammer complained that the Orthodox of Pera were a disreputable lot and that they should have been called "not Peraites but pirates." Hammer, *Constantinopolis*, 2: 113.

15. Herbert to Kaunitz, 15 December 1787, "Türkei," II, 94, HHSA. His friend Philip Cobenzl advised him to be philosophical about it. "If you ever go to the Seven Towers, say that you have always wanted to try a little of everything. . . ." P. Cobenzl to Herbert, 4 September 1787, "Türkei," V, 19, HHSA.

16. Thugut to Kaunitz, 3 June 1774, ibid., II, 63.

17. Schwachheim to Colloredo, 1 September 1762, ibid., II, 39.

18. Hammer, *Constantinopolis*, 2: 125.

19. Hammer, *Geschichte*, 7: 21.

20. For published copies of documents freeing slaves and serving

as passports to allow freemen to return to Habsburg land, see
Karl Jahn, *Türkische Freilassungserklärungen des 18. Jahrhunderts
(1702-1776)* (Naples, 1963).

21. The right was guaranteed by article 13 of the Treaty of Carlowitz. Gabriel Noradounghian, ed., *Recueil d'actes internationaux de l'empire ottoman*, 4 vols. (Paris, 1897-1903), 1: 189.

22. For an excellent description of border diplomacy, see Osman
Aga (Utman Aga Ibn-Ahmad), *Zwischen Paschas und Generälen*
(Graz, 1966).

23. A fine discussion of the ins and outs of delimiting borders is
Ebu Sehil Numan, *Molla und Diplomat* (Graz, 1972).

24. Edlen von Mosel, *Geschichte der kaiserlich-königlichen Hofbibliothek zu Wien* (Vienna, 1835), p. 152.

25. Franz Gall, "Türkisch-österreichische Beziehungen in der Geschichte der Wissenschaft," *Internationales Kulturhistorisches Symposion Mogersdorf 1969: Österreich und die Türken* (Eisenstadt, 1972),
p. 88.

26. J. G. von Harrach to Penkler, 22 May 1753 in Josef Kallbrunner and Melitta Winkler, eds., *Die österreichische Staatsverwaltung* (Vienna, 1925), pt. II, vol. 2, pp. 421-22.

27. For an example of the hotels and provisions provided by the
Habsburg government for a Turkish embassy, see Johann Baptist Schönwetter, *Ausführliche Beschreibung. . . .* (Vienna, n.d.).

28. Joseph to Leopold, 9 June 1774 in Alfred von Arneth, ed.,
Maria Theresia und Joseph II: Ihre Correspondenz, 3 vols. (Vienna,
1867-1868), 2: 36.

29. Joseph to Leopold, 16 June 1774, ibid., 2: 37.

30. Kaunitz to Koch, 25 April 1750 in Hanns Schlitter, ed.,
*Correspondance secrète entre le comte A. W. Kaunitz-Rietberg . . . et
le Baron Ignaz de Koch. . . .* (Paris, 1899), p. 6.

TURKEY IN AUSTRIA'S "WORLD WAR," 1700-1714

1. In early 1704 Prince Eugene wrote of Austria's defenses in
Hungary: "The condition of the army and garrisons is well
known to Your Imperial Majesty. The majority of troops are
naked and unprotected, without money, and the officers are as
poor as beggars; many are almost crippled with hunger, want,
and false expectations. . . . On all sides one hears nothing but
lamentations and desperation, the cries of which reach heaven

itself." Eugene to Leopold I, 12 January 1704, in *Feldzüge des Prinzen Eugen von Savoyen*, 20 vols. (Vienna, 1876-1892), 6: supplement, p. 18 (Hereafter cited as *Feldzüge*).

2. In 1700 the principal Austrian advisers, when discussing plans for the forthcoming War of the Spanish Succession, recommended that a substantial military force remain in Hungary both to discourage a Turkish invasion and to guard against a Hungarian uprising. Conference Protocol, 19 July 1700, in ibid., 3: 395-97.

3. For the former reason see William Slottman, "Austro-Turkish Relations: Carlowitz and the Rákóczi Rebellion" (Ph.D. diss., Harvard University, 1958). For the latter see Alfred von Arneth, *Prinz Eugen von Savoyen*, 3 vols., 2nd ed. (Gera, 1888), 1: 195.

4. John P. Spielman, *Leopold I of Austria* (New Brunswick, N.J., 1977), p. 202.

5. An envoy was appointed at this time largely because of British appeals for Austrian aid in combatting French efforts to involve the Ottomans in a war with Austria. Slottman, "Austro-Turkish Relations," pp. 484-85.

6. Ibid., p. 531.

7. G. Stepney to Secretary Hedges, 22 August 1703 in Ernö Simonyi, ed., *Angol diplomatiai iratok*, 3 vols. (Pest, 1871-1877), 1: 36.

8. Eugene to Leopold, 21 February 1704 in *Feldzüge*, 6: supplement, pp. 39-40.

9. Eugene to Leopold, 26 February 1704 in ibid., p. 40.

10. Eugene to Leopold, 21 February 1704 in ibid., pp. 39-40. Leopold added to the prince's admonishment, saying that the Turk should be turned away "without any pretext to go back disgusted."

11. Talman to Hofkriegsrat, 21 April 1704 in Eudoxiu de Hurmuzaki, ed., *Documente privitóre la Istoria Românilor*, 19 vols. (Bucharest, 1876-1922), 6: 22-23.

12. At this time Tiell was Eugene's trusted subordinate in Turkish matters. When Tiell became seriously ill in the late summer of 1705, the prince expressed great concern about his health because "of all people, the *Herr Hofkriegsrat* is the best-informed." Eugene to Hofkriegsrat, 28 August 1705 in *Feldzüge*, 7: supplement, p. 346.

13. Tiell to Eugene, 21 July 1704 in ibid., 6: 771-72.

14. Eugene to Tiell, 30 July 1704 in ibid., supplement, p. 122.
15. Eugene to Tiell, 19 September 1704 in ibid., p. 177.
16. Slottman, "Austro-Turkish Relations," pp. 494-501.
17. *Feldzüge*, 8: 32.
18. Slottman suggests that Joseph may have regarded bribing public officials as somehow immoral. Perhaps he was trying to create that impression as a warning to his own venal ministers. Slottman, "Austro-Turkish Relations," pp. 513-15.
19. Hofkriegsrat to Talman, 5 April 1705 in Hurmuzaki, *Documente*, 6: 27. Despite Vienna's parsimony, Talman did have some funds to disperse, given to him by the British ambassador.
20. See Spuler, "Europäische Diplomatie," p. 74. The French pamphlet is printed in Hurmuzaki, *Documente*, 6: 37ff.
21. Guillaume de Lamberty, *Mémoires pour servir à l'histoire du XVIIIe siècle*, 14 vols. (The Hague, 1724-1740), 1: 42-46. Comte de Saint-Priest, *Mémoires sur l'ambassade de France en Turquie, 1525-1770* (1877; reprint, Amsterdam, 1974), pp. 246-52.
22. The details of the incident at Kecskemét and the ensuing negotiations concerning it are told by the marvelous Turkish autobiographer, Osman Aga, who served as translator to the pasha of Timişoara. Osman Aga, *Zwischen*, pp. 58-60.
23. Talman to Hofkriegsrat, 13 October 1707 in *Feldzüge*, 9: 17.
24. Charles Ingrao, *In Quest and Crisis: Emperor Joseph I and the Habsburg Monarchy* (West Lafayette, Ind., 1979), p. 146.
25. He remarked to the Venetian ambassador that he would personally like to lead a Christian army against the Turks. Slottman, "Austro-Turkish Relations," pp. 524-25. Daniel Dolfin to the Senate, 9 December 1708 in Alfred von Arneth, ed., "Die Relationen der Botschafter Venedigs über Österreich im 18. Jahrhundert," *Fontes Rerum Austriacarum*, series 2, vol. 22 (1863): 36.
26. Joseph to Hoffman, 28 December 1707 in Alfred von Arneth, *Das Leben der Kaiserlichen Feldmarschalls Grafen Guido Starhemberg, 1657-1737* (Vienna, 1853), pp. 462-63. See also Max Braubach, *Prinz Eugen von Savoyen*, 5 vols. (Vienna, 1963-1965), 2: 211; and Ingrao, *In Quest and Crisis*, pp. 162-63.
27. Talman to Hofkriegsrat, 19 January 1708 in Hurmuzaki, *Documente*, 6: 64-68.
28. Eugene to Joseph, 14 March 1708 in *Feldzüge*, 10: supplement, pp. 57-59.

29. Eugene to Tiell, 6 June 1709 in ibid., 11: supplement, p. 117.

30. For a copy of the treaty see Fedor F. Martens, ed., *Recueil des traités et conventions conclus par la Russe avec les puissances étrangères*, 13 vols. (St. Petersburg, 1874-1902), 1: 20-27. Russia, Denmark, and Poland signed as associate members.

31. Erich Hassinger, *Brandenburg-Preussen, Russland, und Schweden, 1700-1713* (Munich, 1953), p. 244.

32. Hofkriegsrat to Talman, 5 April 1710 in *Feldzüge*, 12: 53. At the same time Eugene instructed his commander in Transylvania to observe the Swedish king's supporters carefully and "to resist with force" any violation of the Austrian frontier by his people. Hofkriegsrat to Count Montecuccoli, 25 April 1710 in ibid., p. 54.

33. Eugene to Joseph, 23 August 1710 in ibid., supplement, pp. 291-92.

34. Eugene to Locher von Lindenheim, 7 September 1710; Eugene to Leopold Herberstein, 17 September 1710; and Eugene to Hofkriegsrat, 24 September 1710 in ibid., pp. 324-25, 349, 366.

35. Prince Eugene to Hofkriegsrat, 23 August 1710 in ibid., p. 294.

36. Ingrao, *In Quest and Crisis*, pp. 54-59.

37. Gabor Kiss, "Franz Rákóczi II, Peter der Grosse, und der polnische Thron," *Jahrbücher für Geschichte Osteuropas* 13 (1965): 344-60.

38. Conference Protocol, 23 February 1711, "Vorträge," 16, HHSA.

39. Conference Protocol, 15 February 1710, ibid., 15. Eugene to Joseph, 23 August 1710 in *Feldzüge*, 12: supplement, pp. 284-93.

40. Eugene to Locher von Lindenheim, 1 October 1710 in ibid., pp. 378-79.

41. Eugene to Heems, 29 September 1710 in ibid., p. 78.

42. Talman to Hofkriegsrat, 27 November 1710 in Hurmuzaki, *Documente*, 6: 628.

43. The best description of the fanfare accompanying the meetings between Eugene and Seifullah Aga can be found in Arneth, *Prinz Eugen*, 2: 158-59.

44. Ingrao, *In Quest and Crisis*, pp. 148-60.

45. Sutton to Dartmouth, 7/18 January 1710/11 in Sir Robert Sut-

ton, *The Despatches of Sir Robert Sutton, Ambassador in Constantinople (1710-1714)* (London, 1953), pp. 21-22.

46. Charles to Talman, 27 April 1711 in Hurmuzaki, *Documente*, 6: 126-27. Rákóczi fled to the Ottoman Empire after the collapse of his revolt and remained there until his death in 1735. Although he fomented little upheaval from his exile, Vienna constantly feared that he would do so.

47. Braubach, *Prinz Eugen*, 3: 53. See also Eugene to Charles, 21 August 1711 and to Eleanore Magdalena, 24 August 1711 in *Feldzüge*, 13: supplement, pp. 97, 101.

48. The Treaty of Prut has long been cited as an example of the failure of a power to take advantage of a crushing defeat it has inflicted upon an adversary. In his study of the campaign and the peace, A. Nimet Kurat writes that the grand vizier was not influenced as much by Russian gold as by his fear that Austria was on the verge of mobilizing against the Ottoman Empire. A. Nimet Kurat, "Der Prutfeldzug und der Prutfrieden von 1711," *Jahrbücher für Geschichte Osteuropas* 10 (1962): 22.

49. Eugene to Eleanore Magdalena, 15 September 1711 in *Feldzüge*, 13: supplement, p. 109.

50. Otto Haintz, *König Karl XII von Schweden*, 3 vols. (Berlin, 1958), 2: 116.

51. Talman to Hofkriegsrat, 19 September 1711 in Hurmuzaki, *Documente*, 6: 122.

52. Braubach, *Prinz Eugen*, 3: 156. The ministerial deputation concerned with Turkish business at this time included the prince, Leopold Trautson, Johann Friedrich Seilern, Gundaker Starhemberg, Leopold Herberstein, and Leopold Schlick.

53. Eugene to Charles, 18 December 1712 in *Feldzüge*, 14: supplement, pp. 330-32.

54. Eugene to Talman, 20 December 1712 in ibid., pp. 332-35.

55. Braubach, *Prinz Eugen*, 3: 156.

56. Sutton to Dartmouth, 7/18 January 1710/11 in Sutton, *Despatches*, p. 33.

VICTORY, 1716-1718

1. For a discussion of what the Morea meant to Venice see Ekkehard Eickhoff, *Venedig, Wien, und die Osmanen: Umbruch in Südosteuropa* (Munich, 1970), pp. 432-33.

2. Francesco Pometti, "Studi sul pontificato di Clemento XI, 1700-21," *Archivio della R. Società Romana di Storia Patria* 22 (1899): 122.

3. Fleischmann to Hofkriegsrat, 17 October 1714, "Türkei," I, 180, HHSA.

4. See the letters of Johann Baptiste Colloredo and Malanoth de Caldes to Charles, "Venedig," 19, HHSA.

5. Charles to Colloredo, 28 November 1714, ibid., 7.

6. "Kriegsakten," 268, HHSA.

7. Beer, *Orientalische Politik*, p. 5.

8. For Charles's opinion of the importance of East and West at this time, see Walter Leitsch, "Die Ostpolitik Kaiser Karls VI," *Veröffentlichen des Verbandes österreichischer Geschichtsvereine* 11 (1957): 151-52. One observer at the Habsburg court remarked that Charles just seemed reluctant to fight any war after so many years of struggle. Jean-Baptiste Rousseau to Brousette, 15 October 1715 in Paul Bonnefon, ed., *Correspondance de Jean-Baptiste Rousseau et de Brousette*. 2 vols. (Paris, 1910-1911), 1: 24.

9. Adolf Beer, "Zur Geschichte der Politik Karl's VI," *Historische Zeitschrift* 55 (1886): 14. See also Hamel Bruyninx to the Readpensionaris, 25 July 1715 in G. van Antal and J.C.H. de Pater, eds., *Weensche Gezantschapsberichten van 1670 tot 1720*, 2 vols. (The Hague, 1929-1934), 2: 633-35; and Conference Protocol, 24 June 1715, "Vorträge," 20, HHSA.

10. Conference Protocol, 5 May 1715, "Vorträge," 20, HHSA.

11. Fleischmann to Hofkriegsrat, 5 January 1715, "Türkei," I, 180, HHSA. For the official Turkish release justifying the assault on Venice and the wish to maintain peace with Austria see Lamberty, *Mémoires*, 9: 587-91.

12. The minutes of the meeting and the ceremony that accompanied it can be found in "Türkei," I, 180, HHSA.

13. Josef Odenthal, *Oesterreichs Türkenkrieg, 1716-1718* (Düsseldorf, 1938), p. 12.

14. Arneth, *Prinz Eugen*, 2: 391. The author of volume 16 of the *Feldzüge* ascribed the crusading impulse not only to Prince Eugene: "Just as the crusaders again and again saw the liberation of Jerusalem as their goal, the commanders of the imperial armies all agreed that the overriding strategic goal was the conquest of Belgrade. The interest of all Christendom seemed

to concentrate on the expulsion of the half moon from the fortress on the Danube and replacing it with the imperial banner." *Feldzüge*, 16: 116.

15. Rudolph Neck, "Österreich und die Osmanen," *Mitteilungen des österreichischen Staatsarchivs* 10 (1957): 462; Derek McKay, *Prince Eugene of Savoy* (London, 1977), p. 159. Odenthal called this war specifically a preventive one. Odenthal, *Oesterreichs Türkenkrieg*, p. 12. Eugene was suspicious of Ottoman sincerity for good reason. Since late 1714 Fleischmann had been reporting that, if successful in the Morea, the Turks would turn on Hungary. Fleischmann to Hofkriegsrat, 10 December 1714, "Türkei," I, 180, HHSA. See also Fleischmann to Hofkriegsrat, 8 March 1715 in *Feldzüge*, 16: 20-21.

16. Oswald Redlich, *Das Werden einer Grossmacht* (Baden bei Wien, 1938), p. 158; Beer, "Geschichte," pp. 13-14.

17. John Stoye, "Emperor Charles VI: The Early Years of his Reign," *Transactions of the Royal Historical Society*, 5th series, 12 (1962): 71.

18. Braubach, *Prinz Eugen*, 3: 304-311. "Ratio status" was the term used by the prince to persuade Charles of the need to go to war. See especially the formal document entitled "Why the Emperor has the legitimate cause to declare war on Turkey when it has declared war only against Venice," 16 June 1715, 1715, Hofkriegsrat Expedit 474, Kriegsarchiv, Vienna.

19. Fleischmann to Hofkriegsrat, 12 February 1715 in *Feldzüge*, 16: 158-59. See also Fleischmann to Hofkriegsrat, 8 March 1715, "Türkei," I, 180, HHSA.

20. Fleischmann to Hofkriegsrat, 25 October 1715, "Türkei," I, 180, HHSA. Odenthal believes Fleischmann's assessment of Turkish military prowess incorrect and attributes it to his unfamiliarity with the lack of drill and variety of dress among the Ottoman units. However, the Austrian's assessment agrees with that of Benjamin Brue, who accompanied the Turkish army into the Morea. Benjamin Brue, *Journal de la campagne que le grand vesir Ali Pacha a faite en 1715 pour la conquête de la Morée* (Paris, 1870). Brue attributed the Turkish success not to the quality of the Ottoman army but to the bungling of the Venetians.

21. Leitsch, "Ostpolitik," p. 151.

22. Eugene to Charles, 23 January 1715 in *Feldzüge*, 16: supplement, pp. 14-15.

23. Memorandum to Charles, 18 May 1715, 1715, Hofkriegsrat Expedit 408, Kriegsarchiv.

24. Norbert Huber, "Österreich und der heilige Stuhl vom Ende des spanischen Erbfolgekrieges bis zum Tode Papst Klemens' XI, 1714-1721," *Archiv für österreichische Geschichte* 126 (1967): 109.

25. Ludwig von Pastor, *Geschichte der Päpste im Zeitalter des fürstlichen Absolutismus von der Wahl Klemens' XI bis zum Tode Klemens' XII (1700-1740)* (Freiburg im Breisgau, 1930), p. 122.

26. The Privy Conference agreed that it was impractical to rely on the British because they give "only words for work." Conference Protocol, 20 July 1715, "Vorträge," 20, HHSA. For a scathing contemporary criticism of the Dutch, see Johann Franz Dumont to Sinzendorf, 27 May 1715 in Johann Franz Dumont, "Bittschriften und politische Denkschriften 1715-1726 über die Generalstaaten, Ostindische Compagnie," "Handschriften," W941, HHSA.

27. When speaking of Philip, the Habsburg ministers had to be extremely cautious not to annoy their sovereign. On one occasion they recommended that the emperor work out a settlement with Philip although the Spanish monarch was "unworthy to speak to him." "Vorträge," 20, HHSA.

28. For an excellent eyewitness account of the campaign from the Ottoman side, see Brue, *Journal*.

29. In the spring and summer, Versailles expressed confidence that Vienna planned war against the Turks and informed Vienna that it did not really care. Instructions to M. Mandat, 17 March 1715 in *Recueil des instructions données aux ambassadeurs et ministres de France depuis les traités de Westphalie jusqu'à la revolution française*, 25 vols. (Paris, 1884-1929), 1 (Autriche): 188-89. Nonetheless, Austria's fear of Louis XIV was so deep that it distrusted Versailles's expressions of good will. Max Braubach, *Versailles und Wien von Ludwig XIV bis Kaunitz* (Bonn, 1952), p. 87.

30. Dumont to Sinzendorf, 8 September 1715, "Bittschriften," pp. 81-92.

31. Theo Gehling, *Ein europäischer Diplomat am Kaiserhof zu Wien:*

François Louis de Pesme, Seigneur de Saint-Saphorin, als englischer Resident am Wiener Hof, 1718-1727 (Bonn, 1964), p. 121.

32. Huber, "Österreich," p. 112. Clement's concession to Philip for this promise was a cardinal's hat for Giulio Alberoni, his wife's favorite.

33. Pastor, *Geschichte*, p. 127. To the chagrin of the Austrian minister in Rome, Philip sent a small naval force anyway.

34. Eugene to Charles, 21 April 1715 in *Feldzüge*, 16: supplement, p. 17.

35. Conference Protocol, 6 October 1716, "Vorträge," 21, HHSA.

36. Charles to Eugene, 25 July 1717 in *Feldzüge*, 17: 406. See also Conference Protocol, 11 July 1717, "Vorträge," 22, HHSA.

37. Eugene to Clement XI, 29 July 1718, "Grosse Korrespondenz," 40, HHSA.

38. Johann Matthias Schulenburg, *Leben und Denkwürdigkeiten*, 2 vols. (Leipzig, 1834), 2: 5.

39. Anonymous, "Impartial considerations on the current state of the military, 1715," "Kriegsakten," 268, HHSA. This view was apparently widely held, for instructions to the French ambassador in Vienna in 1715 read: "If the emperor wishes aggrandizement and does not want his troops to lie idle, he must occupy them with a war against the Turks; it is from the Turks that it is necessary to achieve conquests, to provide for the expenses of the officers and men who want this war very much; and finally to lighten the burden on the hereditary lands by making the imperial troops live off the provinces of the Ottoman Empire." Instructions to Du Luc, 2 March 1715 in *Recueil*, 1: 163-64.

40. For the financing of the war, see Gertrude Pruckner, "Der Türkenkrieg von 1716-1718. Seine Finanzierung und militärische Vorbereitung" (Ph.D. diss., University of Vienna, 1946).

41. Eugene to Grand Vizier Damad Ali, 2 April 1715 in *Feldzüge*, 16: supplement, p. 18.

42. Fleischmann to Hofkriegsrat, 7 May 1716, "Türkei," I, 180, HHSA.

43. Eugene to Charles, 20 May 1716 in *Feldzüge*, 16: supplement, p. 25.

44. Helmut Oehler, *Prinz Eugen in Volkslied und Flugschrift* (Giessen, 1941), pp. 94-96.

45. The strategic and tactical aspects of the battle are discussed in *Feldzüge*, 16: 170-216.
46. Ibid., 17: 2.
47. Eugene to Charles, 15 June 1717 in ibid., supplement, p. 338.
48. Charles to Eugene, 20 June 1717 in ibid., p. 397.
49. Hamel-Bruyninx to the secretary of the Estates-General, 31 March 1717 in Antal, *Weensche Gezantschapsberichten*, 2: 665-66.
50. For a discussion of the siege and battle, see *Feldzüge*, 17: 137-73. For the siege, battle, and famous song, see Braubach, *Prinz Eugen*, 3: 349-62.
51. His chief critic at the time was Count Mérode-Westerloo. See his *Mémoires*, 2 vols. (Brussels, 1840), 2: 180-81. His chief critic among historians has been Odenthal.
52. Eugene to Marlborough, 17 August 1717 in Ernst Joseph Görlich and Felix Romanik, *Geschichte Österreichs* (Innsbruck, 1970), p. 258.
53. Conference Protocol, 22 September 1717, "Türkei," I, 181, HHSA.
54. Charles to Eugene, 25 September 1717 in *Feldzüge*, 17: 438.
55. Ibid., p. 280.
56. Eugene to Charles, 20 June 1716 in ibid., 16: supplement, pp. 25-26.
57. "I put little trust in these distant and various proposals, but I also reject no apparent opportunity to make a diversion behind the enemy." He suggested that the Hofkriegsrat send them arms. Eugene to Hofkriegsrat, 16 July 1716 in ibid., pp. 47-51.
58. Despite the treaties, Vienna never really believed that Philip would remain at peace. Conference Protocol, 26 October 1716 and 10 August 1717, "Vorträge," 21, 22, HHSA; and Eugene to Count Daun, 23 January 1717 in *Feldzüge*, 17: supplement, p. 5.
59. Braubach, *Prinz Eugen*, 4: 23.
60. Eugene to Charles, 3 September 1717 in *Feldzüge*, 17: supplement, pp. 152-53.
61. For a study of this offer, see H. W. Duda, "Die ersten Friedensfühler der Pforte nach der Eroberung von Belgrad im Jahre 1717," in *Documenta Islamica Inedita*, ed. Johann Fück (Berlin,

1952), pp. 262-73. Duda argues that Mustapha Pasha was acting on his own.

62. Eugene to Charles, 12 September 1717 in *Feldzüge*, 17: supplement, pp. 167-68. *Vortrag* to Charles, 22 September 1717, "Türkei," V, "Acta Pacis Pasarovicensis de Anno 1718," I, 58-97, HHSA.

63. Eugene to Charles, 6 October 1717 in *Feldzüge*, 17: supplement, p. 202.

64. The Turks sent a list of towns as possible meeting places and asked the Austrians to choose one. Talman, who served as a delegate, selected Passarowitz. For his reasons, see Talman to Hofkriegsrat, 21 March 1718, "Türkei," V, "Acta Pacis . . . ," I, 637-46, HHSA.

65. In his report summing up the negotiations, Count Virmond selected the arrival of the news of Ibrahim's appointment as the crucial event for it "facilitated matters in all ways." Virmond to Charles, 20 December 1718, "Türkei," I, 183, HHSA.

66. Until then the Turks had refused to talk to the Venetians.

67. Grand Vizier Ibrahim to Eugene, 11 June 1718 in Johann Graf Browne, "Geschichte des von der kaiserlichen Armee geführten Krieges wieder die Türken in denen Jahren 1716 und 1717 und bis zu dem Jahr 1718 bei Passarowitz geschlossene Frieden," 4 vols., 1718, fol. 6, in Kriegsarchiv.

68. Ibid. Shortly after the meeting the prince notified the emperor of the change in terms. Eugene to Charles, 20 June 1718 in *Feldzüge*, 17: supplement, pp. 236-41.

69. Virmond to Charles, 14 July 1718, "Türkei," I, 181, HHSA. Austria insisted that Venice be included in the talks and in the signing of the treaty.

70. Charles to Eugene, 28 July 1718 in *Feldzüge*, 17: 385.

71. Eugene to Charles, 20 June 1718 in ibid., supplement, p. 238.

PEACE WITH TURKEY, ALLIANCE WITH RUSSIA, 1718-1736

1. In December 1718 Prince Eugene remarked that, because of continuing border violations on both sides, the frontiers should be "put in order the sooner the better." Eugene to Charles, 22 December 1718, "Türkei," I, 183, HHSA.

2. Hammer, *Geschichte*, 7: 248, 567-69.

3. Charles Lewis Pollnitz, *Memoirs,* 4 vols. (London, 1739-1740), 4: 64-65.

4. Mérode-Westerloo, *Mémoires*, 2: 227-28.

5. Kraelitz-Greifenhorst describes the Turkish ambassador in Vienna as occupying his time with visits to the home of Prince Eugene, sightseeing tours, hunts, and "other entertainments." Friedrich von Kraelitz-Greifenhorst, "Bericht über den Zug des Gross-Botschafters Ibrahim Pasha nach Wien im Jahre 1719," *Sitzungsberichte der philosophisch-historischen Klasse der Kaiserlichen Akademie der Wissenschaften* 158 (1908): pt. 3, p. 3.

6. When the dey learned that the return of the ship that he had captured was part of the proposed treaty, he rejected it. Franz Hartmann, "Österreichs Beziehungen zu den Barbaresken und Marokko, 1725-1830" (Ph.D. diss., University of Vienna, 1970), p. 14.

7. Hammer, *Geschichte*, 7: 313-15. Eugene, not the emperor, was the signatory for Austria since the bey of Tunis was not a sovereign.

8. The text can be found in Lamberty, *Mémoires*, 10: 176-77. In 1724 the dey of Tripoli sent a delegate to Vienna to arrange the ransom of slaves and goods taken from Neapolitan and Sicilian vessels. Since this was the first time that an envoy from the African coast had formally visited the city, Eugene appointed Leopold von Talman, son of Michael von Talman, to entertain the guest and to keep a register of all that happened—receptions, balls, visits to the theater, conferences—as a model for receiving such visitors in the future. Klesl, "Leopold von Talman," p. 19. Records of his and other visits can be found in the Haus- Hof- und Staatsarchiv in Vienna under "Relationes und Protocol Extract über die in Jahren 1704, 1715, 1724, 1726, 1727, 1731, und 1733 an k. k. Hofe zu Wienn anwesend geweste türckischen und africanischen Gesandschafften."

9. Hartmann, "Österreichs Beziehungen," p. 15. Hartmann notes that there was some confusion at the time as to whether the treaty with Algiers was ever ratified.

10. Eugene to Charles, 28 October 1720 in *Feldzüge*, 18: supplement, p. 185.

11. Arneth, *Prinz Eugen*, 3: 149.

12. Heinrich Benedikt, *Der Pascha-Graf Alexander von Bonneval, 1675-1747* (Graz and Cologne, 1959), p. 66.

13. Ibid., pp. 82-83.

14. Ibid., p. 88.

15. Albert Vandal, *Une ambassade française en orient sous Louis XV: la mission du Marquis de Villeneuve, 1728-1741*, 2nd ed. (Paris, 1887), pp. 138-39. Poisoning was apparently an accepted method of eliminating unwanted characters among the Europeans in the Ottoman Empire. Uebersberger writes that in 1710 the Russian representative, anxious to dissuade the Porte from taking up arms against his country, tried to poison his "most dangerous" antagonists, two Poles who were agents of Charles XII. Hans Uebersberger, *Russlands Orientpolitik in den letzten zwei Jahrhunderten* (Stuttgart, 1913), p. 92. Gorceix suggests but does not prove that the Austrians poisoned Joseph Rákóczi, the son of Francis, who came to the Ottoman capital in 1738. Septime Gorceix, "Bonneval-Pacha et le jeune Rákóczi," *Mélanges offerts à M. Nicolas Iorga* (Paris, 1933), p. 359.

16. Max Braubach, *Geschichte und Abenteuer: Gestalten um den Prinzen Eugen* (Munich, 1950), p. 340. Benedikt writes that even at Sarajevo Bonneval maintained a bodyguard of thirty stray dogs who served as watchdogs and food-tasters. On one occasion four of them died after drinking milk from a pan. Benedikt, *Bonneval*, pp. 97-98.

17. Memorandum to Charles, n.d., 1724, "Vorträge," 25, HHSA.

18. Sinzendorf to Charles, 10 November 1724, ibid. Braubach, *Prinz Eugen*, 4: 279.

19. Conference Protocol, 5 April 1726, "Vorträge," 26, HHSA. A fuller story can be found in Grete Mecenseffy, *Karls VI spanische Bündnispolitik, 1725-1729* (Innsbruck, 1934). See also the letters of Charles to Count Königsegg in "Grosse Korrespondenz," 46, HHSA.

20. The Dutch Republic was not one of the original signatories of the Alliance of Herrenhausen but in late 1725 was strongly recruited by the British. At that time the Austrian ambassador at The Hague wrote that an alliance with Russia might be just the thing to keep the Dutch neutral. Königsegg to Charles, 6 November 1725, "Grosse Korrespondenz," 58, HHSA.

21. A masterful study of the negotiations leading to the treaty is Walter Leitsch, "Der Wandel der österreichischen Russland-

politik in den Jahren 1724-1726," *Jahrbücher für Geschichte Ost-europas* 6 (1958): 33-91. For a published text of the treaty, see Martens, *Recueil*, 1: 32-44.

22. *Vortrag* to Charles, 8 March 1726, "Vorträge," 26, HHSA.
23. Dirling to Hofkriegsrat, 26 November 1726 in Eudoxiu de Hurmuzaki, *Fragmente zur Geschichte der Rumänen*, 5 vols. (Bucharest, 1878-1886), 5: 8-9. The Porte's role in improving Austria's diplomatic position at the time was appreciated in Vienna. "What renders our situation even better is the news from Constantinople where the grand vizier has given assurances so positive that the Porte wants to continue the peace with the Emperor. One can ask for nothing more." Sinzendorf to Fonseca, 4 February 1727, "Grosse Korrespondenz," 51.
24. The Venetian ambassador wrote, "Not since Charles V has a prince of the House of Austria enjoyed such an imposing position of power as the current Emperor." Arneth, "Relationen," p. 27.
25. Eugene to Grand Vizier Ali Pasha, September 1733 in *Feldzüge*, 19: supplement, pp. 17-23.
26. Ibid., 19: 29.
27. Report of the Russian ambassador, 3 September 1733, *Russland*, 1: 224.
28. Charles to the Russian ambassador, 18 September 1733, ibid.
29. Ostein to Charles, 12 February 1736, ibid., 2: 13.

DEFEAT, 1737-1739

1. See Talman's dispatches to Eugene, 1735-1736, "Türkei," I, 211-13, HHSA.
2. Count Luigi Ferdinando Marsigli, *Stato militare dell'imperio ottomano*, 2 vols. (The Hague, 1732), 2: 199.
3. Talman to Hofkriegsrat, 14 June 1736, "Türkei," I, 213, HHSA.
4. Eugene to Charles, 9 February 1736, ibid., 217.
5. For a painstakingly detailed study of the talks ending the Polish war, see Braubach, *Versailles*, pp. 186-239.
6. Talman to Hofkriegsrat, April 1737 in Johann Georg Browne, "Türkenkrieg, welcher im Jahr 1737 angefangen und im Jahr 1739 mit dem Belgrader Frieden sich geendiget hat," 5 vols., 1: fol. 73-74, in Kriegsarchiv.

7. Instructions to Ostein, 19 July 1736, "Russland," II, 131, HHSA.

8. Instructions to Ostein, 23 May 1736, ibid.

9. Ostein to Charles, 23 May 1736, ibid., 14.

10. Bartenstein declared that the emperor expected Bosnia, Albania to the Drin River, and the Danube Valley as far as Braila as his reward and would agree to the Russian annexation of the Crimea and Azov and restoration of the Russo-Turkish borders of 1700. Project for a plan of operations in Charles to Ostein, 19 July 1736, ibid., 131.

11. Ostein to Charles, 21 August 1736, ibid., 14.

12. Bartenstein to Charles, 12 September 1736, "Vorträge," 44, HHSA.

13. For the text see Martens, *Recueil*, 1: 69-80.

14. Franz von Mensi, *Die Finanzen Oesterreichs von 1701 bis 1740* (Vienna, 1890), p. 682.

15. Karl A. Roider, Jr., *The Reluctant Ally: Austria's Policy in the Austro-Turkish War, 1737-1739* (Baton Rouge, La., 1972), p. 100.

16. Browne, "Türkenkrieg," 1737, appendix CC.

17. Lavender Cassels, *The Struggle for the Ottoman Empire, 1717-1740* (London, 1966), p. 122.

18. Arneth, *Prinz Eugen*, 3: 440.

19. Moriz von Angeli, "Der Krieg mit der Pforte, 1736 bis 1739," *Mitteilungen des k. k. Kriegs-Archivs* (1881): 287.

20. The commander of the fortress and the man who had supervised the rebuilding of the fortifications at Belgrade between 1723 and 1736, Nicolaus Doxat de Morez, was placed on trial for cowardice, found guilty, sentenced to death, and executed in March 1738. A., "Marginalien zu dem Aufsätze 'Nikolaus Doxat, ein Officer des Prinzen Eugenius und ein Opfer des damaligen Hofkriegsrathes,' " *Mitteilungen des k. k. Kriegs-Archivs* (1881): 239-46.

21. Russia's other demands included the annexation of the Crimea and Kuban and free trade for Russian merchants on the Black Sea. Privat Protokolle of Nemirov, "Kriegsakten," 324, HHSA.

22. For further information on Austria's role at the congress, see Elfriede Heinrich, "Die diplomatischen Beziehungen Österreichs zur Türkei, 1733-1737" (Ph.D. diss., University of Vienna, 1944), pp. 193-221; and Karl A. Roider, Jr., "Futile

Peacemaking: Austria and the Congress of Nemirov," *Austrian History Yearbook* 12-13 (1976-1977): 95-115.

23. Bartenstein to Charles, 24 November 1737, "Vorträge," 47, HHSA.

24. Charles to Hohenholz and Ostein, 8 November 1737, "Russland," II, 134, HHSA.

25. Honorary commander of the army in 1738 was Charles's son-in-law, Francis Stephen of Lorraine, whose primary function was to observe the senior officers and to report any personality clashes among them. Browne, "Türkenkrieg," 1737, appendices KK, LL.

26. M. de Keralio, *Histoire de la guerre des russes et des imperiaux contre les turcs*, 2 vols. (Paris, 1780), 2: 93-94.

27. Conference Protocol, 19 January 1739, "Vorträge," 48, HHSA.

28. Sinzendorf to Villeneuve, 11 March 1739, "Türkei," I, 220, HHSA.

29. Browne, "Türkenkrieg," 1739, 91-93.

30. Ibid., 111-25.

31. Angeli, "Krieg," pp. 454-56.

32. Conference Protocol, 31 July 1739, "Vorträge," 49, HHSA.

33. Charles to Neipperg, 11 August 1739, "Türkei," I, 220, HHSA.

34. For accounts of some of the curious details surrounding Neipperg's actions, see Karl A. Roider, Jr., "Perils of Eighteenth-Century Peacemaking: Austria and the Treaty of Belgrade," *Central European History* 5 (1972): 195-207; and Oskar Regele, "Die Schuld des Grafen Reinhard Wilhelm von Neippergs am Belgrader Frieden, 1739, und an der Niederlage bei Mollwitz, 1741," *Mitteilungen des österreichischen Staatsarchivs* 7 (1954): 373-98.

35. Alfred von Arneth, "Johann Christoph Bartenstein und seine Zeit," *Archiv für österreichische Geschichte* 46 (1871): 170.

36. Alfred von Arneth, ed., "Zwei Denkschriften der Kaiserin Maria Theresia," *Archiv für österreichische Geschichte* 47 (1871): 303.

37. Bartenstein to Charles, 6 May 1740, "Vorträge," 50, HHSA.

38. For Seckendorf's case, see Browne, "Türkenkrieg," 1737, appendices ZZZ-NNNN.

39. Frederick II, *Mémoires pour servir à l'histoire de la maison de Brandenbourg* (Berlin, 1846), p. 172.

40. Charles to all ministers, 9 September 1739, "Russland," II, 140, HHSA.

41. The evidence in the cases of Wallis, Neipperg, Seckendorf, and Doxat can be found in Johann Georg Browne, "Untersuchungs-akten über General Doxat, Feldmarschall Graf von Seckendorf, Feldmarschall Graf Wallis, und Feldzeugmeister Graf Neipperg," 4 vols. in Kriegsarchiv.

PEACE, 1740-1769

1. Arneth, *Geschichte*, 4: 262-83; Kaunitz to Maria Theresa, 28 August 1755 in Adolf Beer, ed., "Denkschriften des Fürsten Wenzel Kaunitz-Rittberg," *Archiv für österreichische Geschichte* 48 (1872): 39-56.
2. William Coxe, *History of the House of Austria*, 4 vols., 4th ed. (London, 1862-1864), 3: 364.
3. Alfred von Arneth, "Biographie des Fürsten Kaunitz," *Archiv für österreichische Geschichte*, 88 (1900): 159.
4. Ibid., 169-70.
5. Schönwetter, *Ausführliche Beschreibung*, pp. 3-4.
6. Fritsch, *Paschas und Pest*, p. 100.
7. Penkler to Maria Theresa, 11 January and 6 February 1747, "Türkei," II, 11, HHSA. At one meeting the *reis effendi* joked about Penkler's dislike of the French in the presence of the grand vizier.
8. Penkler to Hofkriegsrat, 20 January 1746, ibid., 10.
9. Benedikt, *Bonneval*, pp. 156 ff. Heinrich Benedikt, "Die europäische Politik der Pforte vor Beginn und während des österreichischen Erbfolgekrieges," *Mitteilungen des österreichischen Staatsarchivs* 1 (1948): 163-68.
10. Penkler to Maria Theresa, 11 September 1745, "Türkei," II, 9, HHSA.
11. Penkler to Hofkriegsrat, 30 April 1745, ibid., 8.
12. Penkler to Hofkriegsrat, 14 January 1745, ibid.
13. The memoranda of the Privy Conference in 1741 reflect as much bitterness toward France as toward Prussia and considerable concern that France would enlist Turkey to fight in the war. "Vorträge," 52, HHSA.
14. Constantine Dapontès, *Éphémérides Daces ou chronique de la guerre de quatre ans (1736-1739)*, 3 vols. (Paris, 1881), 2: 358.
15. Saint-Priest, *Mémoires*, pp. 248-68; Paul Masson, *Histoire de*

commerce française dans le Levant au XVIIIe siècle (Paris, 1911), pp. 261-62.

16. In early 1746 Bonneval complained about Castellane to the French foreign minister. He wrote that France must have an ambassador with all the qualities Castellane lacked: "a superior genius, especially a man of war, clever, politic, a skillful negotiator, responsive to needs, and generous." Hammer, *Geschichte*, 8: 487.

17. Johann Wilhelm Zinkeisen, *Geschichte des osmanischen Reiches in Europa*, 7 vols. (Gotha, 1840-1863), 5: 826.

18. Arneth, *Geschichte*, 2: 262. As early as 5 July 1741 Penkler reported that the Turks were preparing for war with Persia. Hurmuzaki, *Fragmente*, 5: 101.

19. "Memorandum concerning the Porte's offer to mediate," 1745, "Vorträge," 55, HHSA.

20. Memorandum, 7 February 1745 and Penkler to Hofkriegsrat, 2 March 1745, "Türkei," II, 8, HHSA.

21. Maria Theresa to Penkler, 24 April 1745, ibid., 9.

22. Dutch reply to the grand vizier's offer of mediation, 3 June 1745, "Holland," 47, HHSA.

23. Harrach to the grand vizier, 6 September 1745, "Türkei," II, 9, HHSA.

24. Penkler to Maria Theresa, 6 October 1745, ibid. In the meantime, Penkler had learned that the *reis effendi* was the instigator of the Porte's offer, but, while he passed on various rumors and speculations, he was unable to discover the fellow's motive. Penkler was disturbed that Austria and the other powers would reject the offer—and he knew that they would—because the "*reis effendi* and his adherents will have especially great convulsions which only money will easily still." Penkler to Hofkriegsrat, 3 June 1745, ibid., II, 8.

25. Penkler to Hofkriegsrat, 21 November 1745 in Hurmuzaki, *Fragmente*, p. 122.

26. Penkler to Hofkriegsrat, 10 March 1745, "Türkei," II, 8, HHSA.

27. Penkler to Hofkriegsrat, 30 April 1745, ibid.

28. Harrach to Penkler, 9 June 1745, ibid.

29. Maria Theresa to Penkler, 11 August 1745, ibid., 9.

30. Arneth, *Geschichte*, 4: 52-60.

31. Penkler to Maria Theresa, 8 November 1745, "Türkei," II, 9, HHSA.
32. Hammer, *Geschichte*, 8: 88-90. The correspondence dealing with these arrangements can be found in "Türkei," II, 10-11, HHSA.
33. Penkler to Maria Theresa, 13 November 1746, "Türkei," II, 10, HHSA.
34. Benedikt, "Europäische Politik," pp. 186-87.
35. Penkler to Maria Theresa, 30 December 1746, "Türkei," II, 10, HHSA.
36. For the text of the treaty, see Martens, *Recueil*, 1: 147-48. For the negotiations and motives leading to it, see Paul Karge, *Die russisch-österreichische Allianz von 1746 und ihre Vorgeschichte* (Göttingen, 1886), pp. 51-65.
37. Penkler to Maria Theresa, 30 December 1746, "Türkei," II, 10, HHSA.
38. Des Alleurs also told the Porte of the alliance and asked what action the sultan would take if he learned that 30,000 Russian troops were marching through Austria on their way to Flanders. The *reis effendi* responded that his master would be delighted "that the Russians were marching elsewhere instead of toward the Turkish border." Hammer, *Geschichte*, 8: 103-104.
39. Penkler to Maria Theresa, 11 January 1747, "Türkei," II, 11, HHSA.
40. Marianne von Herzfeld, "Zur Orienthandelspolitik Oesterreichs unter Maria Theresia in der Zeit von 1740-1771," *Archiv für österreichische Geschichte* 108 (1919-1920): 223.
41. Zinkeisen, *Geschichte*, 5: 861. Bonneval died on 23 March 1747.
42. Vienna frequently asked Penkler to investigate rumored direct contacts between Berlin and Constantinople, and Penkler frequently replied that he found none.
43. Rexin, as Haude, had enjoyed an adventurous life, serving as a trooper in an Austrian cavalry regiment, as a lieutenant in the Prussian army, and, most importantly, as an agent for a commercial house of Breslau in the Levant. Since he had a passing acquaintance with the Ottoman language and still had associates in the Ottoman capital, Frederick chose him to serve the Prussian cause there. Before leaving for his new post he changed his name; apparently he or some other Haude had become involved in trouble there earlier. The nature of that trouble seems unclear, one scholar remarking only that "danger

lurked for the name Haude." Rudolf Porsch, *Die Beziehungen Friedrichs des Grossen zur Türkei* (Marburg, 1897), p. 24.

44. W. Nottebohm, "Die preussisch-türkische Defensivallianz (1763-1765)," in *Festschrift zu der zweiten Saculärfeier des Friedrichs-Werderschen Gymnasiums zu Berlin* (Berlin, 1881), p. 127.

45. Benedikt, "Europäische Politik," p. 161.

46. Uebersberger, *Russlands Orientpolitik*, pp. 256-57.

47. Gaston Zeller, *Les temps modernes. De Louis XIV à 1789* (Paris, 1955), p. 228.

48. Hammer, *Geschichte*, 8: 187.

49. Stanford Shaw, *History of the Ottoman Empire and Modern Turkey*, 2 vols. (Cambridge, 1976-1977), 1: 246-47.

50. Ernst Kühnel, "Erinnerungen an eine Episode in der Türken-politik Friedrichs des Grossen," *Oriens* 5 (1952): 71.

51. Porsch, *Beziehungen*, pp. 45-47.

52. Helmut Scheel, *Preussens Diplomatie in der Türkei* (Berlin and Leipzig, 1931), pp. 42-47.

53. Kühnel, "Erinnerungen," p. 72.

54. Kaunitz to Schwachheim, 20 July 1761, "Türkei," II, 38, HHSA.

55. Porsch, *Beziehungen*, pp. 69-76.

56. Kühnel, "Erinnerungen," p. 72.

57. Kaunitz to Schwachheim, 6 April 1762, "Türkei," II, 40, HHSA.

58. Schwachheim to Kaunitz, 1 May 1762, ibid., 38.

59. Mercy to Kaunitz, 6 and 22 August 1762 in *Sbornik Russkago istoricheskago Obshchestva*, 148 vols. (St. Petersburg, 1867-1916), vol. 46 (1870): 33, 37.

60. Kaunitz to Penkler, 19 August 1762, "Türkei," II, 41, HHSA.

61. Penkler to Kaunitz, 15 September 1762, ibid., 39.

62. Penkler to Kaunitz, 21 October 1762, ibid., 40.

63. Penkler to Kaunitz, 3 November 1762, ibid.

64. Porsch, *Beziehungen*, p. 16.

ALLIES? 1769-1771

1. Colonel J. Nosinich and Major Wiener, "Kaiser Joseph II als Staatsmann und Feldherr: Oesterreichs Politik und Kriege in den Jahren 1763-1790," *Mitteilungen des k. k. Kriegs-Archivs* (1882): 228.

2. Kaunitz to Brognard, 6 October 1767 in Hurmuzaki, *Documente*, 7: 41-47.

3. Herbert Kaplan, *The First Partition of Poland* (New York, 1962), 100-105.

4. Saul K. Padover, "Prince Kaunitz and the First Partition of Poland" (Ph.D. diss., University of Chicago, 1932), pp. 30-31.

5. Arneth, *Geschichte*, 8: 157-58.

6. Ibid., p. 146.

7. Adolf Beer, *Die erste Theilung Polens*, 3 vols. (Vienna, 1873), 1: 297-98.

8. Hammer, *Geschichte*, 8: 559-60.

9. Ibid., pp. 414-15. See also Arneth, *Maria Theresia und Joseph*, 1: 302-307.

10. Kaunitz to Thugut, 5 January 1770, "Türkei," II, 56, HHSA. Not everyone interpreted the Russian victories as did Kaunitz. The French foreign minister, Etienne François Choiseul, thought them worth little. "John Sobieski, Peter I, and General Münnich were masters of that province [Moldavia] when the resources of the Ottoman Empire were not as complete as they are at present; and moreover that very conquest proved fatal to all those generals." Choiseul to Sabatier, 30 November 1769 in *Sbornik*, vol. 143 (1913): 64-65.

11. Josef Franz to Maria Theresa, 22 October 1753, "Interiora," 55, HHSA.

12. Kaunitz to Herich, 4 August 1769, "Türkei," II, 55, HHSA.

13. Thugut to Kaunitz, 18 November 1769, ibid.

14. Kaunitz to Thugut, 19 December 1769, ibid.

15. Kaunitz to Thugut, 3 January 1770, ibid., 56.

16. Lobkowitz to Kaunitz, 28 November 1769 in *Sbornik*, vol. 109 (1901): 413.

17. Kaunitz to Maria Theresa, undated but probably December 1770, "Vorträge," 106, HHSA.

18. Kaunitz and Frederick met at Neustadt in Moravia in September 1770, and there the chancellor emphasized strongly to the Prussian king that Austria could not allow Russian hegemony in the Principalities.

19. Joseph to Maria Theresa, 23 November 1770, "Vorträge," 106, HHSA.

20. Joseph to Maria Theresa, 14 January 1771 in Nosinich and Wiener, "Joseph" (1882): 263-70.

21. Maria Theresa's note on Joseph to Maria Theresa, 19 January 1771 in Arneth, *Maria Theresia und Joseph*, 1: 325.

22. Albert Sorel, *The Eastern Question in the Eighteenth Century* (1898; reprint, New York, 1969), p. 138.

23. A French historian called the accord "an event without precedent, a true rejoinder to the reversal of alliances of 1756, or, more exactly, the logical outcome of the reversal of alliances." Zeller, *Temps modernes*, p. 259.

24. Thugut to Kaunitz, 24 March 1770, "Türkei," II, 55, HHSA.

25. Kaunitz to Maria Theresa, 16 April 1770, "Vorträge," 105, HHSA.

26. Joseph to Maria Theresa, 23 November 1770, ibid., 106; Joseph to Maria Theresa, 29 January 1771 and Field Marshal Lacy to Maria Theresa, 2 February 1771, ibid., 107.

27. Kaunitz to Maria Theresa, 23 January 1771, ibid., 107.

28. Kaunitz to Thugut, 27 January 1771, "Türkei," II, 58, HHSA.

29. Ibid.

30. Kaunitz to Thugut, 19 April 1771, ibid.

31. Kaunitz even forbade correspondence between the Austrian army commanders in Transylvania and their Turkish counterparts in the Principalities for fear that someone might discover it and surmise that an Austro-Ottoman agreement existed.

32. Meetings at night apparently did not achieve the secrecy desired. Thugut complained after this one that in Pera "everyone seems to know everyone else's comings and goings." Thugut to Kaunitz, 21 March 1771, ibid., 57.

33. Ibid.

34. Thugut to Kaunitz, 21 March 1771, ibid.

35. Maria Theresa was already having doubts about this policy, but since she had given her support to it earlier, she did not stop it, at least for now. To her ambassador in France she wrote, "I have no opinion of these costly and ruinous ostentations, but I will have more difficulties resolving myself to make war. . . . Two wars, against the Russians and likely against the Prussians we cannot sustain at the same time. . . ." Maria Theresa to Mercy, 1 April 1771 in Alfred von Arneth and M. A. Geffroy, eds., *Correspondance secrète entre Marie-Thérèse et le comte de Mercy-Argenteau*, 3 vols. (Paris, 1875), 1: 146.

36. Kaunitz was referring to the proposals of Chevalier Massin, which will be discussed in Chapter Eight.
37. Kaunitz to Thugut, 19 April 1771, "Türkei," II, 58, HHSA.
38. Thugut to Kaunitz, 20 May 1771, ibid., 57.
39. Thugut to Kaunitz, 17 June 1771, ibid.
40. A published copy of the agreement can be found in Hammer, *Geschichte*, 8: 567-70; but a more revealing document is Thugut's explanation of the provisions in Thugut to Kaunitz, 12 July 1771, "Türkei," II, 57, HHSA.
41. Beer, *Theilung*, 2: 98.
42. Thugut remarked that he tried to persuade the Turks to send 6,000,000 as the first payment, but the Porte refused, explaining that so much money leaving the capital might prompt a revolution. Thugut to Kaunitz, 12 July 1771, "Türkei," II, 57, HHSA.
43. Thugut reported that some officials who did not know of the treaty complained that the cost of supplies was truly exorbitant. Thugut to Kaunitz, 28 July 1771, ibid.
44. Thugut to Kaunitz, 3 September 1771, ibid.
45. Kaunitz to Thugut, 4 October 1771, ibid., 58. Kaunitz knew that an unratified treaty was easier to cancel than a ratified one, so he recommended that Austria ratify it "only when use is made of it, if the Porte strongly insists upon it, or other conditions demand it." Kaunitz to Thugut, 6 August 1771, ibid. Kaunitz did send a personal letter to the *kaim-makam* of the grand vizier assuring him that Vienna considered the treaty binding. Beer, *Theilung*, 2: 245.
46. In April the Austrian ambassador in St. Petersburg notified the chancellor that Catherine might be willing to concede Moldavia and Walachia but that she did not want the Principalities returned to Turkey. Therefore, the Russians suggested that they be given to "Prince Albert of Saxony [Maria Theresa's favorite son-in-law] or another one of the [Austrian] archdukes as his personal possession." Lobkowitz to Kaunitz, 12 April 1771, "Russland," II, 50, HHSA.
47. Lobkowitz to Kaunitz, 20 December 1771, ibid. When the news of St. Petersburg's concession reached Vienna, Kaunitz advised Maria Theresa that " 'there is . . . nothing left . . . for us to do but to join . . . in the partition agreement, on

the principle of . . . equality between . . . the three powers.' "
Kaplan, *First Partition*, pp. 159-60.

48. Thugut to Kaunitz, 26 January 1772, "Türkei," II, 58, HHSA.
49. Kaunitz to Thugut, 8 April 1772, ibid., 60.
50. Thugut to Kaunitz, 4 May 1772, ibid., 59.
51. Thugut to Kaunitz, 21 May 1772, ibid.
52. Thugut to Kaunitz, 8 June 1772, ibid.
53. Kaunitz to Thugut, 4 August 1772, ibid., 60.

PARTITIONS GREAT AND SMALL, 1772-1775

1. Padover, "Prince Kaunitz," p. 75.
2. Leopold to Joseph, 17 February 1771 in G. B. Volz, "Die Massinschen Vorschläge: Ein Beitrag zur Vorgeschichte zur ersten Teilung Polens," *Historische Vierteljahrschrift*, 10 (1907): 358.
3. Leopold to Joseph, 21 January 1771 in ibid., p. 374. See also Th. E. Modelski, "Ein Vorschlag zur Theilung der Türkei aus dem Jahr 1771," *Österreich* (1918-1919): 126-39.
4. Volz, "Vorschläge," p. 376.
5. Kaunitz to Thugut, 19 April 1771, "Türkei," II, 58, HHSA.
6. Kaunitz to Joseph and Maria Theresa, 25 September 1771, ibid.
7. Joseph to Kaunitz and Maria Theresa, 26 September 1771, ibid. Joseph noticed that it was somewhat unusual to talk of taking Ottoman lands while an Austro-Turkish convention remained in force, but he added that the wording of the agreement gave Vienna considerable latitude.
8. Sorel, *Eastern Question*, p. 166.
9. This proposal first appeared in the spring of 1770. Kaunitz had notified Thugut of it and remarked that he really had no thoughts about it. Kaunitz to Thugut, 4 May 1770, "Türkei," II, 56, HHSA.
10. Kaunitz to Maria Theresa, 17 January 1772 in Volz, "Vorschläge," p. 368. The entire document, including all seven plans, can be found in this article, pp. 367-73.
11. The revelation to the Austrian minister in Warsaw is studied in Horst Glassl, "Pläne zur Lösung der orientalischen Frage nach dem Siebenjährigen Krieg," *Saeculum* 20 (1969): 71-74.

12. Proposed partition of the Ottoman Empire by Baron Binder, n.d., "Türkei," III, 15, HHSA.

13. Maria Theresa to Joseph, January 1772 in Arneth, *Maria Theresia und Joseph*, 1: 263.

14. She refused, of course, on the grounds that such an act would violate Austria's trust with the Turks. She did, however, mention what value she placed on the Ottoman provinces that might someday be within Vienna's reach. " ' . . . there can be absolutely no talk of Serbia and Bosnia, the only provinces that would be appropriate for us. There remains nothing else but Walachia and Moldavia, unhealthy, ruined lands, which stand open to the Turks, Tartars, and Russians without any means of defense, lands finally in which we would have to invest many millions and many lives in order to govern.' " Maria Theresa to Kaunitz, 12 February 1772 in Arneth, *Geschichte*, 8: 359.

15. Despite the empress's refusals, Kaunitz persistently tried to change her mind, but, just as she seemed to concede, word came of the Prusso-Russian agreement to dismember Poland. Kaunitz then decided to drop the Ottoman matter altogether. Padover, "Kaunitz," pp. 104-105.

16. Kaunitz to Maria Theresa, 15 September 1772 in ibid.

17. Arneth, *Geschichte*, 8: 454.

18. Kaunitz to Maria Theresa, 19 February 1773, "Vorträge," 111, HHSA.

19. Maria Theresa's marginal note on ibid.

20. Joseph to Maria Theresa, 21 February 1773, ibid.

21. Joseph to Maria Theresa, c. June 1773 in Arneth, *Maria Theresia und Joseph*, 2: 8. Concerning the Olt (Aluta) River, both of whose banks Kaunitz suggested annexing, Joseph wrote, "The Olt is . . . in no way advantageous for shipping and, even if it were, what would one ship on it?"

22. Memorandum of Joseph regarding the Bukovina and Orsova, 31 December 1773 in ibid., p. 113.

23. Joseph to Maria Theresa, 19 June 1773 in Arneth, *Geschichte*, 8: 613.

24. Kaunitz to Thugut, 23 February, 23 June, and 6 July 1773, "Türkei," II, 62, HHSA.

25. Thugut to Kaunitz, 17 July 1773, ibid., 61.

26. Thugut to Kaunitz, 3 August 1773, ibid.

27. Thugut to Kaunitz, 17 March 1773, ibid.

28. Thugut to Kaunitz, 3 April 1773, ibid.
29. Thugut to Kaunitz, 3 September 1773, ibid., 63.
30. Kaunitz to Thugut, 6 October 1773, ibid.
31. Kaunitz to Mercy, 4 April 1773 in Arneth and Geffroy, *Correspondance*, 2: 416.
32. Thugut to Kaunitz, 3 February 1774, "Türkei," II, 62, HHSA.
33. Hurmuzaki, *Fragmente*, 5: 380.
34. Kaunitz to Thugut, 7 December 1773, "Türkei," II, 62, HHSA.
35. Kaunitz to Maria Theresa, 1 May 1774, "Vorträge," 114, HHSA. The Austrians formally claimed the Bukovina on the grounds that it had originally belonged to the Polish province of Potukia, which was a part of Austria's share of the partition. Despite their researches in Warsaw and in the Bukovina, Habsburg investigators could find no good claim. Daniel Werenka, "Bukowinas Entstehen und Aufblühen. Maria Theresias Zeit," *Archiv für österreichische Geschichte* 78 (1892): 111-15; Raimond Friedrich Kaindl, "Die Bukowina unter der Herrschaft des österreichischen Kaiserhauses," in his *Geschichte der Bukowina* (Czernowitz, 1898), p. 10.
36. Kaunitz to Maria Theresa, 4 August 1774, "Vorträge," 115, HHSA.
37. Instructions to Field Marshal Barco, 8 August 1774, ibid.
38. Kaunitz to Thugut, 5 November 1774, "Türkei," II, 64, HHSA.
39. Thugut to Kaunitz, 3 October 1774, ibid., 63.
40. Thugut to Kaunitz, 3 February 1774, ibid., 62.
41. Thugut to Kaunitz, 17 October 1774, ibid., 63.
42. Ibid.
43. Kaunitz to Thugut, 6 December 1774, ibid., 64. Ghika was assassinated by the sultan's men in 1777.
44. Thugut to Kaunitz, 4 January 1775, ibid., 64.
45. Kaunitz to Thugut, 6 January 1775 in Hurmuzaki, *Documente*, 6: 118-20.
46. Thugut to Kaunitz, 17 February 1775, "Türkei," II, 64, HHSA.
47. Thugut to Kaunitz, 3 April 1775, ibid.
48. The text can be found in Werenka, "Bukowinas Entstehen," pp. 278-84.
49. The boundary commission's work can be found in "Türkei," III, 5, HHSA.
50. Thugut to Kaunitz, 3 April 1775, ibid., II, 64.

51. Hanns Leo Mikoletzky, *Österreich: Das grosse 18. Jahrhundert* (Vienna, 1967), p. 306. Hurmuzaki, *Fragmente*, 5: 379.
52. Robert Kann, *A History of the Habsburg Empire, 1526-1918* (Berkeley, 1974), p. 164.
53. Maria Theresa to Marie Antoinette, 30 November 1774 in Alfred von Arneth, ed., *Maria Theresia und Marie Antoinette* (Vienna and Paris, 1865), p. 128.
54. Thugut to unknown correspondent, 15 December 1775, "Grosse Korrespondenz," 447, HHSA.

TAMING THE BEAR, 1774-1786

1. See particularly M. S. Anderson, *The Eastern Question, 1774-1923* (New York, 1966), and Sorel, *Eastern Question.*
2. For an edited copy of the treaty in English, see J. C. Hurewitz, ed., *Diplomacy in the Near and Middle East: A Documentary Record*, 2 vols. (Princeton, 1956), 1: 54-61.
3. Kaunitz to Thugut, 19 August 1774, "Türkei," II, 64, HHSA.
4. Zinkeisen, *Geschichte*, 6: 85.
5. Thugut to Kaunitz, 3 September 1774 in Hammer, *Geschichte*, 8: 577-82. Two weeks earlier, before the final provisions of the treaty became known, Thugut remarked that the agreement would be a terrible one for Turkey, but what would really destroy the Ottoman state was the "unbelievable foolishness" that pervaded the administration. "Never was a nation at its demise less worthy of condolences." Thugut to Kaunitz, 17 August 1774, "Türkei," II, 63, HHSA.
6. Kaunitz was notoriously inconsistent about evaluating the Balkan lands Austria might win. At times he talked about them as hopeless wastelands and at times as full of potential wealth. His assessments changed with needs, and he probably knew little about them anyway.
7. Kaunitz to Joseph, n.d., 1776 in Beer, "Denkschriften," pp. 82-85.
8. Ibid., p. 85.
9. Alan Fisher, *The Russian Annexation of the Crimea, 1772-1783* (Cambridge, 1970), pp. 73-81.
10. Joseph to Maria Theresa, 31 March 1772 in Ernst Benedikt, *Kaiser Joseph II* (Vienna, 1936), pp. 279-80.

11. Memorandum of Field Marshal Lacy, 2 May 1777, "Vorträge," 122, HHSA.

12. Maria Theresa to Mercy, 31 July 1777 in Arneth and Geffroy, *Correspondance*, 3: 99-100.

13. Fisher, *Russian Annexation*, p. 108.

14. See Paul P. Bernard, *Joseph II and Bavaria* (The Hague, 1965), pp. 35-133.

15. Beer, *Orientalische Politik*, pp. 42-43.

16. Erwin Peters, "Die Orientpolitik Friedrichs des Grossen nach dem Frieden von Teschen (1779-1786)," in *Historische Studien*, ed. Richard Fester (Halle, 1914), 41: 14-15. Paul Bailleu, "Der Ursprung des deutschen Fürstenbundes," *Historische Zeitschrift*, 41 (1879): 413.

17. Arneth, *Geschichte*, 10: 667-70. Scholars who have examined this event agree with Arneth that it was Joseph's initiative.

18. Benedikt, *Joseph II*, p. 216.

19. See Kaunitz to Joseph, 23 April 1780 and L. Cobenzl to Joseph, 5 May 1780 in Adolf Beer and Joseph von Fiedler, eds., *Joseph II und Graf Ludwig von Cobenzl: Ihr Briefwechsel*, 2 vols. (Vienna, 1901), 1: ix, 11.

20. Joseph to Maria Theresa, 4 July 1780 in Arneth, *Maria Theresia und Joseph*, 3: 268.

21. Joseph to Maria Theresa, 18 July 1780 in ibid., pp. 285-86.

22. Frederick tried to counter the good impression that Joseph made upon the Russian court by sending first his brother and then his heir for a visit. Both were snubbed by Catherine and compelled to leave. Meanwhile, Joseph described Catherine in lustrous terms: "Her spirit, the height of her soul, her courage, and with that the pleasantness of her conversation must be known and experienced for one to be able to appreciate their extent." Joseph to Mercy, 31 August 1780 in Alfred von Arneth and Jules Flammermont, eds., *Correspondance secrète du Comte de Mercy-Argenteau avec l'empereur Joseph II et le prince de Kaunitz*, 2 vols. (Paris, 1889), 2: 560.

23. Leopold von Ranke maintains that the empress's death really made no difference in the final form of the Austro-Russian accord, while Robert Salomon argues that it made possible a far bolder policy on Vienna's part. Leopold von Ranke, *Die deutschen Mächte und der Fürstenbund*, 2 vols. (Leipzig, 1872), 1: 142; Robert Salomon, *La politique orientale de Vergennes 1780-*

1784 (Paris, 1935), pp. 55-56. Isabel de Madariaga agrees with Salomon. Isabel de Madariaga, "The Secret Austro-Russian Treaty of 1781," *Slavonic and East European Review* 38 (1959-1960): 116.

24. Joseph to Maria Theresa, 12 July 1780 in Arneth, *Maria Theresia und Joseph*, 3: 278-81.
25. Beer, *Orientalische Politik*, p. 49.
26. Ibid., p. 50.
27. Joseph to Catherine, 21 May 1781 in Alfred von Arneth, ed., *Joseph II und Katharina von Russland: Ihr Briefwechsel* (Vienna, 1869), pp. 72-81. De Madariaga presents the marvelous tale of the "alternative" and states that Arneth errs in dating Joseph's letter 21 May; it should be 18 May. Isabel de Madariaga, *Britain, Russia and the Armed Neutrality of 1780* (New Haven, 1962), p. 315.
28. Kaunitz to Joseph, 2 March 1781 in Adolf Beer, ed., *Joseph II, Leopold II, und Kaunitz: Ihr Briefwechsel* (Vienna, 1873), p. 39.
29. De Madariaga, "Secret," p. 124.
30. Ibid., pp. 129, 131.
31. Joseph did all that he could to like the future Russian tsar and his wife and to get them to like him; he failed on both counts.
32. Joseph expressed disgust at joining the League because Prussia had joined a short while earlier, and it appeared that he was simply following in Frederick's wake. "This accession to the Armed Neutrality is truly unuseful and ridiculous, but whatever such a woman wants, God wants, as the saying goes, and once in their hands one is always going further than one wants to." Joseph to L. Cobenzl, 19 August 1781 in Beer and Fiedler, *Joseph und Cobenzl*, 1: 196-97.
33. Catherine to Joseph, 15/26 June 1782 in Arneth, *Joseph und Katharina*, p. 134.
34. Joseph to Catherine, 12 July 1782, in ibid., p. 136.
35. Catherine to Joseph, 10/21 September 1782 in ibid., pp. 143-57. For an analysis of the plan, see Edgar Hösch, "Das sogenannte 'griechische Projekt' Katharinas II," *Jahrbücher für Geschichte Osteuropas* 12 (1964): 168-206.
36. Catherine to Joseph, 10/21 September 1782 in Arneth, *Joseph und Katharina*, p. 146.
37. Anonymous Memorandum (but surely Kaunitz's), 26 October

1782, "Vorträge," 136, HHSA. Kaunitz added one note of interest concerning the partition of Turkey by suggesting that France receive the Asiatic side of the Straits so it could act as "a very useful barrier against the expansion of Russian indirect or direct control of Asia."

38. Philip Cobenzl to Joseph, 26 October 1782 in Sébastien Brunner, ed., *Correspondances intimes de l'empereur Joseph II avec son ami le comte de* [Philip] *Cobenzl et son premier ministre le prince de Kaunitz* (Mainz, Paris, Brussels, 1871), pp. 29-30.

39. Joseph to Catherine, 13 November 1782 in Arneth, *Joseph und Katharina*, 169-75. Kaunitz to L. Cobenzl, 22 November 1782, "Russland," II, 172, HHSA.

40. Joseph to L. Cobenzl, 22 November 1782 in Beer and Fiedler, *Joseph und Cobenzl*, 1: 345.

41. Zinkeisen, *Geschichte*, 6: 349. Two other demands included Turkish promises not to disturb Russian trade in the Black Sea and to follow Kuchuk Kainarji in all matters relating to the Russian consuls in Moldavia and Walachia.

42. Kaunitz to L. Cobenzl, 29 January 1783, "Russland," II, 173, HHSA.

43. Kaunitz to L. Cobenzl, 24 February 1783, ibid. Joseph to Catherine, 25 February 1783 in Arneth, *Joseph und Katharina*, pp. 188-91.

44. Kaunitz to Joseph, 12 May 1783 in Beer and Fiedler, *Joseph und Cobenzl*, 1: 435-51.

45. Ibid.

46. Joseph to Kaunitz, 19 May 1783, "Vorträge," 137, HHSA; Joseph to Catherine, 19 May 1783 in Arneth, *Joseph und Katharina*, pp. 202-204.

47. Kaunitz suggested both banks of the Sava River to the Unna River, the left bank of the Unna, and Little Walachia. Kaunitz to Joseph, 11 July 1783, "Vorträge," 138, HHSA.

48. Joseph to Leopold, 10 August 1783 in Alfred von Arneth, ed., *Joseph II und Leopold von Toscana: Ihr Briefwechsel von 1781 bis 1790*, 2 vols. (Vienna, 1872), 1: 165.

49. Joseph to Mercy, 31 July 1783 in Arneth and Flammermont, *Correspondance*, 1: 195. See also M. S. Anderson, "The Great Powers and the Russian Annexation of the Crimea, 1783-1784," *Slavonic and East European Review* 37 (1958-1959): 17-41.

50. Although the Hofkriegsrat first requested that area because its

remaining in Ottoman possession exposed Croatia to the depredations of Turkish bandits, Joseph believed it would considerably aid Austrian commerce from the Carlstadt military border to the Dalmatian coast. Kaunitz to Joseph, 13 August 1782 and Joseph's marginal notes on Kaunitz to Joseph, 30 January 1784, "Vorträge," 136, 138, HHSA.

51. Joseph's marginal notes on Kaunitz to Joseph, 30 January 1784, ibid., 138. Kaunitz to Herbert, 4 February 1784, "Türkei," II, 86, HHSA.

52. Herbert to Kaunitz, 10 December 1783, "Türkei," II, 82, HHSA.

53. Herbert to P. Cobenzl, 10 July 1783 in Hans Halm, *Oesterreich und Neurussland* (Breslau, 1943), pp. 142-43.

AUSTRIA'S LAST TURKISH WAR, 1787-1790

1. Joseph to L. Cobenzl, 5 April 1784 in Beer and Fiedler, *Joseph und Cobenzl*, 1: 460.

2. For the Bavarian-Belgian exchange project, see Bernard, *Joseph II and Bavaria*, pp. 134-216. For the League of German Princes, see John G. Gagliardo, *Reich and Nation: The Holy Roman Empire as Idea and Reality, 1763-1806* (Bloomington, Ind., 1980), pp. 66-98.

3. Oscar Browning, "The Triple Alliance of 1788," *Transactions of the Royal Historical Society*, n.s. 2 (1885): 86. See also J. Holland Rose, *William Pitt and the National Revival* (London, 1911), p. 316.

4. Kaunitz to Joseph, 12 February 1787, "Vorträge," 143, HHSA.

5. Joseph to Kaunitz, 6 December 1786 in Ranke, *Deutschen Mächte*, 2: 298.

6. Hanns Schlitter, ed., *Kaunitz, Philipp Cobenzl und Spielmann: Briefwechsel (1779-1792)* (Vienna, 1899), p. ix.

7. P. Cobenzl to Joseph, 23 February 1787 in Brunner, *Correspondances*, pp. 60-61. Spielmann advocated what would come to pass in a modified form in the nineteenth century: a Russo-Prusso-Austrian alliance guaranteed by exchanges of territory. Austria and Russia would partition the Ottoman Empire while Prussia would acquire the Austrian Netherlands as a barrier against France. Spielmann, "Memoir relating to the Partition of Turkey," n.d., "Türkei," III, 15, HHSA. The date on this

document is 1782, but it was obviously added later in pencil. The internal evidence suggests that the document was composed in early 1787.

8. See Karl A. Roider, Jr., "Kaunitz, Joseph II and the Turkish War," *Slavonic and East European Review* 54 (1976): 538-56.
9. See Kaunitz's instructions to Seddeler, January-June 1786, "Russland," II, 174, HHSA.
10. Kaunitz to Joseph, 21 November 1786 in Beer, *Joseph, Leopold, und Kaunitz,* p. 244.
11. Joseph first received the invitation in 1782.
12. Joseph made a particularly good impression on the French ambassador, who contrasted his appearance with that of the king of Poland. "I had seen at Kanieff a king [of Poland] without power and without authority, surrounded by the magnificence and éclat of the greatest monarchs; by remarkable contrast I saw at Cherson a powerful emperor, simple in appearance, modest in manner, familiar in his greeting, opponent of all etiquette, permitting and provoking conversation on all subjects and wanting no conspicuous display other than that which gave him particular information, solid judgment, or an improved spirit." Louis Philippe Ségur, *Mémoires: ou souvenirs et anecdotes,* 3 vols. (Paris, 1824-1827), 3: 126.
13. L. Cobenzl to Kaunitz, 3 June 1787 in Beer and Fiedler, *Joseph und Cobenzl,* 2: 151.
14. Ibid., 150-55.
15. Herbert to Kaunitz, 25 January 1787, "Türkei," II, 91, HHSA.
16. For the best summary of the problems as interpreted by Vienna, see Kaunitz to Mercy, 30 June 1787, "Frankreich," 174, HHSA.
17. Herbert to Kaunitz, 23 December 1786, "Türkei," II, 90, HHSA; Herbert to Kaunitz, 23 February 1787, "Türkei," II, 91, HHSA.
18. Herbert to Kaunitz, 25 June 1787, ibid., 92.
19. Herbert to Kaunitz, 10 July 1787, ibid., 93.
20. Herbert to Kaunitz, 4 and 16 August 1787, ibid. The grand vizier, Koca Yusuf, was the leader of the war party but was opposed by the grand admiral, who had been his patron. When the admiral left for Egypt to put down a Mamluk uprising, the way was clear for Yusuf to control the divan. Shaw, *History,* 1: 258.

21. Herbert to Kaunitz, 2 September 1787, "Türkei," II, 93, HHSA.
22. Joseph to Leopold, 30 August 1787 in Arneth, *Joseph und Leopold,* 2: 115.
23. Kaunitz to L. Cobenzl, 30 August 1787, "Russland," II, 174, HHSA.
24. Herbert to Kaunitz, 1 May 1785, "Türkei," II, 87, HHSA.
25. L. Cobenzl to Kaunitz, 9 August 1787, "Russland," II, 65, HHSA.
26. Ibid. For a detailed Austrian assessment of Russia's strength, see L. Cobenzl to Kaunitz, 27 December 1787, ibid.
27. Max von Theilen, "Geschichte des Krieges der ottomanischen Pforte und dem verbündeten Österreich und Russland," in Kriegsarchiv, vol. 1 (of the six volumes in this study, only volume 4 has folio page numbers). Oskar Christe, *Kriege unter Kaiser Josef II* (Vienna, 1904), pp. 155, 270-71.
28. Rainer Leignitz, *Des Kaisers Partisanen: Türkenkriege und der Freiheitskampf auf dem Balkan* (Vienna, 1972), p. 117.
29. Brognard's 150-folio-page report can be found in "Türkei," V, 24, HHSA.
30. For a bibliography on the *freikorps*, see Leignitz, *Partisanen.*
31. Memorandum on the reports of Petrov and Metzbourg from Moldavia, 6 January 1788, "Vorträge," 145, HHSA.
32. Joseph's marginal notes on Kaunitz to Joseph, 17 March 1788, ibid. Vienna even tried to foment rebellion in Egypt and at least considered a plan to incite the Arabian tribes to revolt. Kaunitz to Joseph, 20 July 1788 and 17 February 1789, ibid., 145, 146.
33. The correspondence between Vienna and its Balkan agents can be found in "Türkei," V, 20, HHSA.
34. Kaunitz to Joseph, 6 July 1788, "Vorträge," 145, HHSA.
35. L. Cobenzl to Kaunitz, 23 October 1787, "Russland," II, 65, HHSA.
36. Kaunitz to L. Cobenzl, 12 October 1787, ibid., 174.
37. Kaunitz to Mercy, 6 October 1787 in Arneth and Flammermont, *Correspondance,* 2: 127.
38. Kaunitz to L. Cobenzl, 7 December 1787, "Russland," II, 174, HHSA.
39. Joseph to L. Cobenzl, 7 January 1788, ibid., 213.

40. L. Cobenzl to Joseph, 3 February 1788 in Beer and Fiedler, *Joseph und Cobenzl*, 2: 237.
41. Theilen, "Geschichte," vol. 1.
42. Of Potemkin's effort at Ochakov, the French ambassador wrote, "In order not to fail, he made such extensive preparations against this weak village that one would have thought that he was invading Luxembourg." Ségur, *Mémoires*, 3: 290.
43. Joseph's marginal notes on Kaunitz to Joseph, 9 May 1788, and Joseph to Kaunitz, 27 May 1788, "Vorträge," 145, HHSA. Joseph to Leopold, 13 May 1788 in Arneth, *Joseph und Leopold*, 2: 178.
44. Theilen, "Geschichte," vol. 1. One scholar estimates that 33,000 Austrian soldiers died of illness during the campaign of 1788. Leignitz, *Partisanen*, p. 118.
45. Rose, *William Pitt*, pp. 389-90.
46. L. Cobenzl to Kaunitz, 21 July 1788, "Russland," II, 67, HHSA.
47. Joseph to Kaunitz, 28 August 1788 in Beer, *Joseph, Leopold, und Kaunitz*, pp. 305-310.
48. Kaunitz to Joseph, 9 August 1788, "Vorträge," 145, HHSA.
49. Joseph to Kaunitz, 15 September 1788, ibid.
50. Joseph to Kaunitz, 7 November 1788, ibid.
51. L. Cobenzl to Joseph, 7 January 1789 in Beer and Fiedler, *Joseph und Cobenzl*, 2: 317-24.
52. Noailles to Kaunitz, 2 February 1789, "Friedensakten," 71, HHSA; Kaunitz to L. Cobenzl, 8 March 1789, "Russland," II, 175, HHSA.
53. Mercy to Kaunitz, 2 April 1789, "Frankreich," 177, HHSA.
54. Kaunitz to Mercy, 17 May 1789, ibid.
55. Robert Golda, "Der Friede von Sistov" (Ph.D. diss., University of Vienna, 1941), p. 23.
56. Kaunitz to Joseph, 25 June 1789, "Vorträge," 146, HHSA.
57. Beer, *Orientalische Politik*, p. 125.
58. Theilen, "Geschichte," 4: 14.
59. Joseph to Laudon, 23 August 1789, "Vorträge," 146, HHSA.
60. Theodor von Stefanović-Volovsky, "Belgrad während des Krieges Österreichs und Russland gegen die Pforte, 1787-1792," *Beiträge zur neueren Geschichte Österreichs* 4 (1909): 150.
61. Joseph's marginal note on Kaunitz to Joseph, 5 October 1788, "Vorträge," 146, HHSA.

62. See Walter W. Davis, *Joseph II: An Imperial Reformer for the Austrian Netherlands* (The Hague, 1974), pp. 236-64.
63. In November Kaunitz notified Mercy that France had become so unstable that he was dropping French mediation in favor of direct negotiations with the Turks. Kaunitz to Mercy, 3 November 1789 in Arneth and Flammermont, *Correspondance*, 2: 280.
64. Joseph to Leopold, 3 December 1789 in Arneth, *Joseph und Leopold*, 2: 293.
65. L. Cobenzl to Kaunitz, 11 January 1790, "Russland," II, 71, HHSA; Choiseul to Kaunitz, 1 February 1790, "Friedensakten," 71, HHSA.
66. Kaunitz to L. Cobenzl, 6 March 1790, "Russland," II, 176, HHSA.
67. See especially Leopold to Joseph, 17 September and 17 December 1787 in Arneth, *Joseph und Leopold*, 2: 120, 150-54.
68. Adam Wandruszka, *Leopold II*, 2 vols. (Vienna and Munich, 1965), 2: 265.
69. Attending were Leopold, Kaunitz, Leopold's son and heir Archduke Francis, Count Georg Adam von Starhemberg, Count Franz Xavier Rosenberg, Philip Cobenzl, Anton Spielmann, Field Marshal Lacy, Field Marshal Laudon, and Protocol Chief Baron Kollenbach.
70. Conference Protocol, 26 April 1790, "Vorträge," 147, HHSA.
71. See Robert Howard Lord, *The Second Partition of Poland* (Cambridge, Mass., 1915), pp. 128-52; and Max Duncker, "Friedrich Wilhelm II und Graf Herzberg," *Historische Zeitschrift* 37 (1877): 1-43.

EPILOGUE

1. Keith to his sisters, 1 November 1780 in Sir Robert Murray Keith, *Memoirs and Correspondence* (London, 1849), 300. Harold Gardos, "Österreich und die Türkei nach Sistowa. Das Jahr 1792," *Mitteilungen des österreichischen Staatsarchivs* 24 (1971): 352.
2. Kaunitz's instructions to Herbert at Sistova can be found in "Friedensakten," 72, HHSA. Kaunitz could still not bear the thought of having fought the hapless Turk and won nothing.
3. Golda, "Friede," pp. 238ff.

4. Gardos, "Österreich," p. 347.
5. L. Cobenzl to Kaunitz, 16 August 1790, "Russland," II, 73, HHSA.
6. Leopold Heinrich Goltz to Frederick William II, 10 September 1790 in Bronislaw Dembinski, ed., *Documents relatifs à l'histoire du deuxième et troisième partage de la Pologne* (Léopol, 1902), pp. 319-21.
7. Leopold to Kaunitz, 17 February 1791, "Vorträge," 148, HHSA.
8. Ibid.
9. Kaunitz to L. Cobenzl, 28 March 1791, "Russland," II, 176, HHSA.

Bibliography

PRIMARY SOURCES

MANUSCRIPT COLLECTIONS

Vienna. Haus- Hof- und Staatsarchiv. Staatskanzlei
Collection diplomatique, carton 24.
Frankreich, cartons 174-75, 177.
Friedensakten, cartons 71-72.
Grosse Korrespondenz, cartons 40, 46, 51, 58.
Handschriften, carton W941.
Holland, carton 47.
Interiora, cartons 55-56, "Orientalische Akademie."
Kabinettsarchiv, Kaunitz-Voten zu Staatsratakten, carton 6.
Kriegsakten, cartons 268, 324, 444.
"Relationes und Protocol Extract über die in Jahren 1704, 1715,
   1724, 1726, 1727, 1731, und 1733 an k. k. Hofe zu Wienn
   anwesend geweste türkischen und africanischen Gesandschaff-
   ten."
Russland, old acts I, carton 224; modern acts II, cartons 13, 50,
   65, 67, 71, 73, 134, 140, 172-76, 213.
Türkei, cartons I, 180-83, 211-13, 220; II, 8-11, 14, 38-41, 55-
   65, 79, 82, 86-87, 90-94, 131; III, 5, 15; V, 19-20, "Acta
   Pacis Pasarovicensis de Anno 1718," I-III.
Venedig, cartons 7, 19.
Vorträge, Konferenz-Protokolle, Referate, cartons 15-16, 20-26, 44,
   47-50, 52, 55, 105-107, 111, 114-15, 122, 143, 145-48,
   236-38.

Vienna. Kriegsarchiv.
Browne, Johann Graf. "Geschichte des von der kaiserlichen Armee
   geführten Krieges wieder die Türken in denen Jahren 1716
   und 1717 und bis zu dem Jahr 1718 bei Passarowitz geschlossene Frieden." 4 vols.
———. "Türkenkrieg, welcher im Jahr 1737 angefangen und im
   Jahr 1739 mit dem Belgrader Frieden sich geendiget hat." 5
   vols.
———. "Untersuchungsakten über General Doxat, Feldmarschall

Graf von Seckendorf, Feldmarschall Graf Wallis, und Feldzeugmeister Graf Neipperg." 4 vols.

1715, Hofkriegsrat Expediten, 408, 474.

Theilen, Max von. "Geschichte des Krieges der ottomanischen Pforte
und dem verbündeten Österreich und Russland." 6 vols.

PRINTED MATERIALS

Antal, G. van and Pater, J.C.H. de, eds. *Weensche Gezantschapsberichten van 1670 tot 1720.* 2 vols. The Hague, 1929-1934.

Arneth, Alfred von, ed. "Eigenhändige Correspondenz des Königs
von Spanien (nachmals Kaiser Karl VI) mit dem Obersten Kanz-
ler des Königreiches Böhmen, Grafen Johann Wenzel Wratis-
law." *Archiv für österreichische Geschichte* 16 (1856): 1-224.

————. "Johann Christoph Bartenstein und seine Zeit." *Archiv für
österreichische Geschichte* 46 (1871): 3-214.

————. *Joseph II und Katharina von Russland: Ihr Briefwechsel.* Vienna, 1869.

————. *Joseph II und Leopold von Toscana: Ihr Briefwechsel von 1781
bis 1790.* 2 vols. Vienna, 1872.

————. *Maria Theresia und Joseph II: Ihre Correspondenz.* 3 vols.
Vienna, 1867-1868.

————. *Maria Theresia und Marie Antoinette.* Vienna and Paris, 1865.

————. "Die Relationen der Botschafter Venedigs über Österreich
im 18. Jahrhundert." *Fontes Rerum Austriacarum*, series 2, vol.
22 (1863): 1-351.

————, ed. "Zwei Denkschriften der Kaiserin Maria Theresia."
Archiv für österreichische Geschichte 47 (1871): 269-354.

———— and Flammermont, Jules, eds. *Correspondance secrète du Comte
de Mercy-Argenteau avec l'empereur Joseph II et le prince de Kaunitz.*
2 vols. Paris, 1889.

———— and Geffroy, M. A., eds. *Correspondance secrète entre Marie-
Thérèse et le comte de Mercy-Argenteau.* 3 vols. Paris, 1875.

Beaujour, Felix de. *Tableau du commerce de la Grèce.* 2 vols. Paris,
1800.

Beer, Adolf, ed. "Denkschriften des Fürsten Wenzel Kaunitz-Rittberg." *Archiv für österreichische Geschichte* 48 (1872): 1-162.

————. *Die erste Theilung Polens.* 3 vols. Vienna, 1873.

————. *Joseph II, Leopold II, und Kaunitz: Ihr Briefwechsel.* Vienna,
1873.

———— and Fiedler, Joseph von, eds. *Joseph II und Graf Ludwig von*

Cobenzl: Ihr Briefwechsel. 2 vols. *Fontes Rerum Austriacarum,* series 2, vols. 53 and 54 (1901).

Bonnefon, Paul, ed. *Correspondance de Jean-Baptiste Rousseau et de Brossette.* 2 vols. Paris, 1910-1911.

Brue, Benjamin. *Journal de la campagne que le grand vesir Ali Pacha a faite en 1715 pour la conquête de la Morée.* Paris, 1870.

Brunner, Sébastien, ed. *Correspondances intimes de l'empereur Joseph II avec son ami le comte de* [Philip] *Cobenzl et son premier ministre le prince de Kaunitz.* Mainz, Paris, Brussels, 1871.

Dembinski, Bronislaw, ed. *Documents relatifs à l'histoire du deuxième et troisième partage de la Pologne.* Léopol, 1902.

Driesch, Gerard Cornelius von. *Historische Nachricht von der Röm. Kaiserl. Grossbotschaft nach Constantinopel welche auf allergnädigsten Befehl Sr. Röm. Kaiserlichen und Catholischen Majestät Carl des Sechsten Der hoch- und wohlgebohrne des H. R. Reichsgraf Damian Hugo von Virmondt rühmlichst verrichtet.* Nuremberg, 1723.

Feldzüge des Prinzen Eugen von Savoyen. 20 vols. Vienna, 1876-1892.

Frederick II. *Mémoires pour servir à l'histoire de la maison de Brandenbourg.* Berlin, 1846.

Fritsch, Gerhard. *Paschas und Pest.* Graz and Vienna, 1962.

Hammer-Purgstall, Joseph von. *Constantinopolis und der Bosporos.* 2 vols. 1822. Reprint. ed. Osnabrück, 1967.

Hurewitz, J. C., ed. *Diplomacy in the Near and Middle East: A Documentary Record.* 2 vols. Princeton, 1956.

Hurmuzaki, Eudoxiu de, ed. *Documente privitóre la Istoria Românilor.* 19 vols. Bucharest, 1876-1922.

Jahn, Karl. *Türkische Freilassungserklärungen des 18. Jahrhunderts (1702-1776).* Naples, 1963.

Kallbrunner, Joseph and Winkler, Melitta, eds. *Die österreichische Staatsverwaltung von der Vereinigung der österreichischen und böhmischen Hofkanzlei bis zur Einrichtung der Ministerialverfassung (1749-1849).* Part II, vol. 2. Vienna, 1925.

Karamuk, Gümec, ed. *Ahmed Azmi Efendis Gesandtschaftsbericht als Zeugnis des osmanischen Machtverfalls und der beginnenden Reformära unter Selim III.* Bern, 1975.

Keith, Sir Robert Murray. *Memoirs and Correspondence.* London, 1849.

Kraelitz-Greifenhorst, Friedrich von. "Bericht über den Zug des Gross-Botschafters Ibrahim Pascha nach Wien im Jahre 1719." *Sitzungsberichte der philosophisch-historischen Klasse der Kaiserlichen Akademie der Wissenschaften* 158 (1908): pt. 3, pp. 1-62.

Lamberty, Guillaume de. *Mémoires pour servir à l'histoire du XVIIIe siècle.* 14 vols. The Hague, 1724-1740.

Marsigli, Count Luigi Ferdinando. *Stato militare dell'imperio ottomano.* 2 vols. The Hague, 1732.

Martens, Fedor F., ed. *Recueil des traités et conventions conclus par la Russe avec les puissances étrangères.* 13 vols. St. Petersburg, 1874-1902.

Mérode-Westerloo, M. le comte de. *Mémoires.* 2 vols. Brussels, 1840.

Montague, Lady Mary Wortley. *Letters from the Levant during the Embassy to Constantinople, 1716-1718.* 1838. Reprint. New York, 1971.

Noradounghian, Gabriel, ed. *Recueil d'actes internationaux de l'empire ottoman, 1300-1789.* 4 vols. Paris, 1897-1903.

Numan, Ebu Sehil. *Molla und Diplomat. Der Bericht des Ebu Sehil Numan Effendi über die österreichisch-osmanische Grenzziehung nach dem Belgrader Frieden, 1740-41.* Graz, 1972.

Osman Aga (Utman Aga Ibn-Ahmad). *Zwischen Paschas und Generälen: Bericht des Osman Aga aus Temeschwar Banat über die Höhepunkt seines Wirkens als Diwansdolmetscher und Diplomat.* Graz, 1966.

Pollnitz, Charles Lewis. *Memoirs.* 4 vols. London, 1739-1740.

Recueil des instructions données aux ambassadeurs et ministres de France depuis les traités de Westphalie jusqu'à la revolution française. 25 vols. Paris, 1884-1929.

Saint-Priest, Comte de. *Mémoires sur l'ambassade de France en Turquie, 1525-1770.* 1877. Reprint. Amsterdam, 1974.

Sbornik Russkago istoricheskago Obshchestva [Collections of the Russian Historical Society]. 148 vols. St. Petersburg, 1867-1916.

Schlitter, Hanns, ed. *Correspondance secrète entre le comte A. W. Kaunitz-Rietberg, ambassadeur impérial à Paris et le Baron Ignaz de Koch, secrétaire de l'impératrice Marie-Thérèse, 1750-52.* Paris, 1899.

————. *Kaunitz, Phillip Cobenzl und Spielmann: Briefwechsel (1779-1792).* Vienna, 1899.

Schönwetter, Johann Baptist. *Ausführliche Beschreibung des prächtigst und herzlichen Empfangs und Einbegleitung wie auch Einzugs welchen der türkische Gross-Botschafter Vizier Mückerera, Rumeli Valesi Bajesile Taja-Sade, Ibrahim Pasha, etc. dahier in die kaiserliche Residenz-Stadt Wien den 14. August 1719 gehalten.* Vienna, n.d.

Schulenburg, Johann Matthias. *Leben und Denkwürdigkeiten.* 2 vols. Leipzig, 1834.

Ségur, Louis Philippe. *Mémoires: ou souvenirs et anecdotes.* 3 vols. Paris, 1824-1827.

Simonyi, Ernö, ed. *Angol diplomatiai iratok. II. Rákóczi Ferencz Korára.* 3 vols. Pest, 1871-1877.

Sutton, Sir Robert. *The Despatches of Sir Robert Sutton, Ambassador in Constantinople (1710-1714).* London, 1953.

SECONDARY SOURCES

BOOKS

Anderson, M. S. *The Eastern Question, 1774-1923.* New York, 1966.

Aretin, Karl Otmar von. *Heiliges Römisches Reich, 1776-1806.* 2 vols. Wiesbaden, 1967.

Arneth, Alfred von. *Geschichte Maria Theresias.* 10 vols. Vienna, 1863-1879.

————. *Das Leben des kaiserlichen Feldmarschalls Grafen Guido Starhemberg, 1657-1737.* Vienna, 1853.

————. *Prinz Eugen von Savoyen.* 3 vols. 2nd ed. Gera, 1888.

Barker, Thomas M. *Double Eagle and Crescent: Vienna's Second Turkish Siege in its Historical Setting.* Albany, 1967.

Beer, Adolf. *Die orientalische Politik Österreichs seit 1774.* Prague, 1883.

Benedikt, Ernst. *Kaiser Joseph II.* Vienna, 1936.

Benedikt, Heinrich. *Das Königreich Neapel unter Kaiser Karl VI.* Vienna and Leipzig, 1927.

————. *Der Pascha-Graf Alexander von Bonneval, 1675-1747.* Graz and Cologne, 1959.

Bernard, Paul P. *Joseph II and Bavaria.* The Hague, 1965.

Braubach, Max. *Geschichte und Abenteuer: Gestalten um den Prinzen Eugen.* Munich, 1950.

————. *Prinz Eugen von Savoyen.* 5 vols. Vienna, 1963-1965.

————. *Versailles und Wien von Ludwig XIV bis Kaunitz.* Bonn, 1952.

Cassels, Lavender. *The Struggle for the Ottoman Empire, 1717-1740.* London, 1966.

Christe, Oskar. *Kriege unter Kaiser Josef II.* Vienna, 1904.

Coxe, William. *History of the House of Austria.* 4 vols. 4th ed. London, 1862-1864.

Dapontès, Constantine. *Éphémérides Daces ou chronique de la guerre de quatre ans (1736-1739).* 3 vols. Paris, 1881.

Davis, Walter W. *Joseph II: An Imperial Reformer for the Austrian Netherlands.* The Hague, 1974.

Eickhoff, Ekkehard. *Venedig, Wien, und die Osmanen: Umbruch in Südosteuropa, 1645-1700.* Munich, 1970.

Fisher, Alan. *The Russian Annexation of the Crimea, 1772-1783.* Cambridge, 1970.

Gagliardo, John G. *Reich and Nation: The Holy Roman Empire as Idea and Reality, 1763-1806.* Bloomington, Ind., 1980.

Gehling, Theo. *Ein europäischer Diplomat am Kaiserhof zu Wien: François Louis de Pesme, Seigneur de Saint-Saphorin, als englischer Resident am Wiener Hof, 1718-1727.* Bonn, 1964.

Görlich, Ernst Joseph and Romanik, Felix. *Geschichte Österreichs.* Innsbruck, 1970.

Haintz, Otto. *König Karl XII von Schweden.* 3 vols. Berlin, 1958.

Halm, Hans. *Oesterreich und Neurussland.* Breslau, 1943.

Hammer-Purgstall, Joseph von. *Geschichte des osmanischen Reiches.* 10 vols. Pest, 1827-1835.

Hassinger, Erich. *Brandenburg-Preussen, Russland, und Schweden, 1700-1713.* Munich, 1953.

Hurmuzaki, Eudoxiu de. *Fragmente zur Geschichte der Rumänen.* 5 vols. Bucharest, 1878-1886.

Ingrao, Charles. *In Quest and Crisis: Emperor Joseph I and the Habsburg Monarchy.* West Lafayette, Ind., 1979.

Kann, Robert. *A History of the Habsburg Empire, 1526-1918.* Berkeley, 1974.

Kaplan, Herbert. *The First Partition of Poland.* New York, 1962.

Karge, Paul. *Die russisch-österreichische Allianz von 1746 und ihre Vorgeschichte.* Göttingen, 1886.

Keralio, M. de. *Histoire de la guerre des russes et des imperiaux contre les turcs.* 2 vols. Paris, 1780.

Leignitz, Rainer. *Des Kaisers Partisanen: Türkenkriege und der Freiheitskampf auf dem Balkan.* Vienna, 1972.

Lord, Robert Howard. *The Second Partition of Poland.* Cambridge, Mass., 1915.

Madariaga, Isabel de. *Britain, Russia, and the Armed Neutrality of 1780.* New Haven, 1962.

Masson, Paul. *Histoire du commerce française dans le Levant au XVIIIe siècle.* Paris, 1911.

McKay, Derek. *Prince Eugene of Savoy.* London, 1977.

Mecenseffy, Grete. *Karls VI spanische Bündnispolitik, 1725-1729.* Innsbruck, 1934.

Meienberger, Peter. *Johann Rudolf Schmid zum Schwarzenhorn als kaiserlicher Resident in Konstantinopel, 1629-1643.* Bern, 1973.

Mensi, Franz von. *Die Finanzen Oesterreichs von 1701 bis 1740.* Vienna, 1890.

Mikoletzky, Hanns Leo. *Österreich: Das grosse 18. Jahrhundert.* Vienna, 1967.

Mosel, Edlen von. *Geschichte der kaiserlich-königlichen Hofbibliothek zu Wien.* Vienna, 1835.

Neumann, Wilhelm Anton. *Ueber die orientalischen Sprachstudien seit dem XIII. Jahrhunderte mit besonderer Rücksicht auf Wien.* Vienna, 1899.

Odenthal, Josef. *Oesterreichs Türkenkrieg, 1716-1718.* Düsseldorf, 1938.

Oehler, Helmut. *Prinz Eugen in Volkslied und Flugschrift.* Giessen, 1941.

Pastor, Ludwig von. *Geschichte der Päpste im Zeitalter des fürstlichen Absolutismus von der Wahl Klemens' XI bis zum Tode Klemens' XII (1700-1740).* Freiburg im Breisgau, 1930.

Porsch, Rudolf. *Die Beziehungen Friedrichs des Grossen zur Türkei.* Marburg, 1897.

Ranke, Leopold von. *Die deutschen Mächte und der Fürstenbund.* 2 vols. Leipzig, 1872.

Redlich, Oswald. *Das Werden einer Grossmacht.* Baden bei Wien, 1938.

Roider, Karl A., Jr. *The Reluctant Ally: Austria's Policy in the Austro-Turkish War, 1737-1739.* Baton Rouge, La., 1972.

Rose, J. Holland. *William Pitt and the National Revival.* London, 1911.

Salomon, Robert. *La politique orientale de Vergennes (1780-1784).* Paris, 1935.

Scheel, Helmuth. *Preussens Diplomatie in der Türkei.* Berlin and Leipzig, 1931.

Shaw, Stanford J. *Between Old and New: The Ottoman Empire under Sultan Selim III, 1789-1807.* Cambridge, Mass., 1971.

―――. *History of the Ottoman Empire and Modern Turkey.* 2 vols. Cambridge, 1976-1977.

Sorel, Albert. *The Eastern Question in the Eighteenth Century.* 1898. Reprint ed. New York, 1969.

Spielman, John P. *Leopold I of Austria*. New Brunswick, N.J., 1977.
Stefanović-Volovsky, Theodore von. *Belgrad unter der Regierung Kaiser Karls VI, 1717-1739*. Vienna, 1908.
Stoye, John. *The Siege of Vienna*. New York, 1964.
Sturminger, W. *Bibliographie und Ikonographie der Türkenbelagerungen Wiens 1529 und 1683*. Graz, 1955.
Tapié, Victor-L. *L'Europe centrale et orientale de 1689-1796*. Paris, 1969.
Uebersberger, Hans. *Russlands Orientpolitik in den letzten zwei Jahrhunderten*. Stuttgart, 1913.
Vandal, Albert. *Une ambassade française en orient sous Louis XV: la mission du Marquis de Villeneuve, 1728-1741*. 2nd ed. Paris, 1887.
Wandruszka, Adam. *Leopold II*. 2 vols. Vienna and Munich, 1965.
Weiss von Starkenfels, Viktor. *Die k. k. orientalische Akademie zu Wien*. Vienna, 1839.
Zeller, Gaston. *Les temps modernes. De Louis XIV à 1789*. Paris, 1955.
Zinkeisen, Johann Wilhelm. *Geschichte des osmanischen Reiches in Europa*. 7 vols. Gotha, 1840-1863.

ARTICLES

A. "Marginalien zu dem Aufsätze 'Nikolaus Doxat, ein Officer des Prinzen Eugenius und ein Opfer des damaligen Hofkriegsrathes.' " *Mitteilungen des k. k. Kriegs-Archivs* (1881): 239-46.
Anderson, M. S. "The Great Powers and the Russian Annexation of the Crimea, 1783-1784." *Slavonic and East European Review* 37 (1958-1959): 17-41.
Angeli, Moriz von. "Der Krieg mit der Pforte, 1736 bis 1739." *Mitteilungen des k. k. Kriegs-Archivs* (1881): 247-338, 409-479.
Arneth, Alfred von. "Biographie des Fürsten Kaunitz." *Archiv für österreichische Geschichte* 88 (1900): 1-201.
Bailleu, Paul. "Der Ursprung des deutschen Fürstenbundes." *Historische Zeitschrift* 41 (1879): 410-33.
Beer, Adolf. "Zur Geschichte der Politik Karl's VI." *Historische Zeitschrift* 55 (1886): 1-70.
Benedikt, Heinrich. "Die europäische Politik der Pforte vor Beginn und während des österreichischen Erbfolgekrieges." *Mitteilungen des österreichischen Staatsarchivs* 1 (1948): 137-92.

Browning, Oscar. "The Triple Alliance of 1788." *Transactions of the Royal Historical Society*, n.s. 2 (1885): 77-96.

Duda, H. W. "Die ersten Friedensfühler der Pforte nach der Eroberung von Belgrad im Jahre 1717." In *Documenta Islamica Inedita*, ed. Johann Fück, pp. 262-73. Berlin, 1952.

Duncker, Max. "Friedrich Wilhelm II und Graf Herzberg." *Historische Zeitschrift* 37 (1877): 1-43.

Gall, Franz. "Türkisch-österreichische Beziehungen in der Geschichte der Wissenschaft." In *Internationales Kulturhistorisches Symposion Mogersdorf 1969: Österreich und die Türken*, pp. 85-94. Eisenstadt, 1972.

Gardos, Harold. "Österreich und die Türkei nach Sistowa. Das Jahr 1792." *Mitteilungen des österreichischen Staatsarchivs* 24 (1971): 347-70.

Glassl, Horst. "Pläne zur Lösung der orientalischen Frage nach dem Siebenjährigen Krieg." *Saeculum* 20 (1969): 69-81.

Gorceix, Septime. "Bonneval-Pacha et le jeune Rákóczi." In *Mélanges offerts à M. Nicolas Iorga*, pp. 341-63. Paris, 1933.

Herzfeld, Marianne von. "Zur Orienthandelspolitik Österreichs unter Maria Theresia in der Zeit von 1740-1771." *Archiv für österreichische Geschichte* 108 (1919-1920): 215-344.

Hösch, Edgar. "Das sogenannte 'griechische Projekt' Katharinas II." *Jahrbücher für Geschichte Osteuropas* 12 (1964): 168-206.

Huber, Norbert. "Österreich und der heilige Stuhl vom Ende des spanischen Erbfolgekrieges bis zum Tode Papst Klemens' XI, 1714-1721." *Archiv für österreichische Geschichte* 126 (1967): 6-216.

Kaindl, Raimond Friedrich. "Die Bukowina unter der Herrschaft des österreichischen Kaiserhauses." In his *Geschichte der Bukovina*. Czernowitz, 1898.

Kiss, Gabor. "Franz Rákóczi II, Peter der Grosse, und der polnische Thron." *Jahrbücher für Geschichte Osteuropas* 13 (1965): 344-60.

Kühnel, Ernst. "Erinnerungen an eine Episode in der Türkenpolitik Friedrichs des Grossen." *Oriens* 5 (1952): 70-81.

Kurat, A. Nimet. "Der Prutfeldzug und der Prutfrieden von 1711." *Jahrbücher für Geschichte Osteuropas* 10 (1962): 13-66.

Leitsch, Walter. "Die Ostpolitik Kaiser Karls VI." *Veröffentlichen des Verbandes österreichischer Geschichtsvereine* 11 (1957): 150-55.

———. "Der Wandel der österreichischen Russlandpolitik in den

Jahren 1724-1726." *Jahrbücher für Geschichte Osteuropas* 6 (1958): 33-91.

Madariaga, Isabel de. "The Secret Austro-Russian Treaty of 1781." *Slavonic and East European Review* 38 (1959-1960): 114-45.

Modelski, Th. E. "Ein Vorschlag zur Theilung der Türkei aus dem Jahr 1771." *Österreich* (1918-1919): 126-39.

Neck, Rudolph. "Österreich und die Osmanen." *Mitteilungen des österreichischen Staatsarchivs* 10 (1957): 434-68.

Nosinich, Colonel J. and Wiener, Major. "Kaiser Joseph II als Staatsmann und Feldherr: Österreichs Politik und Kriege in den Jahren 1763-1790." *Mitteilungen des k. k. Kriegs-Archivs* (1882): 219-88, 349-416; (1883): 1-109, 131-79; (1885): 74-145.

Nottebohm, W. "Die preussisch-türkische Defensivallianz (1763-1765)." In *Festschrift zu der zweiten Säcularfeier des Friedrichs-Werderschen Gymnasiums zu Berlin*, pp. 123-57. Berlin, 1881.

Peters, Erwin. "Die Orientpolitik Friedrichs des Grossen nach dem Frieden von Teschen (1779-1786)." In *Historische Studien*, edited by Richard Fester, 41: 1-55. Halle, 1914.

Pometti, Francesco. "Studi sul pontificato di Clemento XI, 1700-21." *Archivio della R. Società Romana di Storia Patria* 22 (1899): 106-137.

Regele, Oskar. "Die Schuld des Grafen Reinhard Wilhelm von Neippergs am Belgrader Frieden, 1739, und an der Niederlage bei Mollwitz, 1741." *Mitteilungen des österreichischen Staatsarchivs* 7 (1954): 373-98.

Roider, Karl A., Jr. "Futile Peacemaking: Austria and the Congress of Nemirov." *Austrian History Yearbook* 12-13 (1976-1977): 95-116.

————. "Kaunitz, Joseph II and the Turkish War." *Slavonic and East European Review* 54 (1976): 538-56.

————. "The Perils of Eighteenth-Century Peacemaking: Austria and the Treaty of Belgrade." *Central European History* 5 (1972): 195-207.

Spuler, Bertold. "Die europäische Diplomatie in Konstantinopel bis zum Frieden von Belgrad." *Jahrbücher für Kultur und Geschichte der Slaven* 11 (1935): 53-115, 171-222.

Stefanović-Volovsky, Theodor von. "Belgrad während des Krieges Österreichs und Russland gegen die Pforte, 1787-1792." *Beiträge zur neueren Geschichte Österreichs* 4 (1909): 129-96.

Stoye, John. "Emperor Charles VI: The Early Years of his Reign." *Transactions of the Royal Historical Society*, 5th ser. 12 (1962): 63-84.

Sturmberger, Hans. "Türkengefahr und österreichische Staatlichkeit." *Südostdeutsches Archiv* 10 (1967): 132-45.

Volz, G. B. "Die Massinschen Vorschläge: Ein Beitrag zur Vorgeschichte der ersten Teilung Polens." *Historische Vierteljahrschrift* 10 (1907): 355-81.

Werenka, Daniel. "Bukowinas Entstehen und Aufblühen. Maria Theresias Zeit." *Archiv für österreichische Geschichte* 78 (1892): 100-296.

Wittek, Paul and Kraelitz-Greifenhorst, Friedrich. "Introduction" to *Mitteilungen zur osmanischen Geschichte* 1 (1922): 1-11.

DISSERTATIONS

Golda, Robert. "Der Friede von Sistov." Ph.D. dissertation, University of Vienna, 1941.

Hartmann, Franz. "Österreichs Beziehungen zu den Barbaresken und Marokko, 1725-1830." Ph.D. dissertation, University of Vienna, 1970.

Heinrich, Elfriede. "Die diplomatischen Beziehungen Österreichs zur Türkei, 1733-1737." Ph.D. dissertation, University of Vienna, 1944.

Klesl, Wolfgang. "Leopold von Talman." Ph.D. dissertation, University of Vienna, 1966.

Padover, Saul K. "Prince Kaunitz and the First Partition of Poland." Ph.D. dissertation, University of Chicago, 1932.

Pruckner, Gertrude. "Der Türkenkrieg von 1716-1718. Seine Finanzierung und militärische Vorbereitung." Ph.D. dissertation, University of Vienna, 1946.

Slottman, William. "Austro-Turkish Relations: Carlowitz and the Rákóczi Rebellion." Ph.D. dissertation, Harvard University, 1958.

Index

247

Karl A. Roider, Jr. is Associate Professor of History at Louisiana State University. He is the author of *The Reluctant Ally: Austria's Policy in the Austro-Turkish War of 1737-1739* (LSU Press) and editor of *Maria Theresa* (Prentice-Hall).

LIBRARY OF CONGRESS CATALOGING IN PUBLICATION DATA

Roider, Karl A.
Austria's eastern question, 1700-1790.

Bibliography: p.
Includes index.
1. Austria—Foreign relations—18th century.
2. Austria—Foreign relations—Turkey.   3. Turkey—
Foreign relations—Austria.   4. Austria—Foreign rela-
tions—Soviet Union.   5. Soviet Union—Foreign relations—
Austria.   I. Title.
DB66.5.R64   327.436   81-48141
ISBN 0-691-05355-3   AACR2